One More Croissant for the Road

Felicity Cloake

MUDLARK

Mudlark
An imprint of HarperCollins*Publishers*
1 London Bridge Street
London SE1 9GF

www.harpercollins.co.uk

First published by Mudlark 2019
This paperback edition published 2020

5 7 9 10 8 6 4

Text © Felicity Cloake 2019
Illustrations © Sara Mulvanny 2019

A catalogue record of this book is
available from the British Library

ISBN 978-0-00-837726-7

Printed and bound in Great Britain by
CPI Group (UK) Ltd, Croydon

MIX
Paper from
responsible sources
FSC™ C007454

Felicity Cloake is the author of the *Guardian*'s long-running weekly food column, How to Cook the Perfect ..., and has been the *New Statesman*'s food columnist since 2011. She was named Cookery Journalist of the Year at the 2016 Fortnum & Mason Food & Drink Awards, and won the Cookery Journalist of the Year and New Media trophies at the 2011 Guild of Food Writers Awards. *One More Croissant for the Road* is Felicity's fifth book, and her first piece of food and travel writing.

'This is the kind of food book I thought people had stopped writing. A journey with stops for lunch (and coffee and dinner) which ultimately provide the recipes. And *in France*! I loved it.'

Diana Henry

'Such a brilliant book, funny, captivating and wonderfully written. I feel like I was packed up in Felicity's pannier for the ride (with a croissant to snack on obviously).'

Anna Jones

'From start to finish, this book is a joy: the perfect antidote to a world of diets and bad news.'

Bee Wilson

'Felicity Cloake is the new Wainwright, only much funnier and in France with a bicycle and an appetite. This is a joyful hunger-stoking and eye-opening journey across France.'

Meera Sodha

'An appetite-piquing paean to bikes, boulangeries and all things edibly Gallic, this is a Tour de France to truly relish.'

Tom Parker Bowles

'A highly entertaining, tough-minded and enchanting book where the spirit of freewheeling travel writing is grounded perfectly with Felicity's sure-fire recipes. I had great trouble putting it down.'

Caroline Eden

'Felicity Cloake combines the authority and lyricism of a young Elizabeth David with the determined eccentricity to eat her way through France on a bike. Brilliant and bonkers.'

Tim Hayward

For my sausage-scoffing, plonk-sinking peloton –
with whom the glass was *always* half full

CONTENTS

PROLOGUE

A green bike drunkenly weaves its way up a cratered hill in the late-morning sun, the gears grinding painfully, like a pepper mill running on empty. The rider crouched on top in a rictus of pain has slowed to a gravity-defying crawl when, from somewhere nearby, the whine of a nasal engine breaks through her ragged breathing.

A battered van appears behind her, the customary cigarette dangling from its driver's-side window, and shakily she rears out of the saddle, grubby legs pumping in a surprising turn of speed. As he passes, she casually reaches down for some water, smiling broadly in the manner of someone having almost too much fun. 'No sweat,' she says jauntily to his retreating exhaust pipe. '*Pas de problème, monsieur.*'

The van disappears round the next hairpin. Abruptly our heroine dismounts, allowing the heavily laden bike to crash into a pile of brambles, describing an arc of chain grease across her bruised shins en route. Grumpily slapping away a thirsty horsefly, she reaches into the handlebar bag and pulls out a half-eaten croissant.

After peeling off a baby slug and flicking it expertly onto her own shoes, she sinks her teeth into the desiccated pastry, and squints at the map on her phone. Only another 40km to go before lunch.

In the distance, there's a rumble of thunder.

It's not like I wasn't warned. I'd witnessed the danger of turning a hobby into a job first-hand at a magazine publisher I'd once worked for, who regularly offered a bonus for anyone willing to give up their weekend to help with photoshoots for some of their more niche titles. No one ever did it twice.

As the new IT manager wearily switched my computer off and then on again one Monday morning, I asked him how his first gig for *Mega Boobs* had gone – he'd been so excited about it on Friday. He shook his head: 'Believe me, Felicity,' he said in a small, sad voice, 'you really can have too much of a good thing.'

Poor Hamid. Almost a decade later, I can still see the betrayal in his eyes – but those who don't learn from history are doomed to repeat it, and, hard as I tried, I just couldn't shake the urge to eat my way around France. (I'll be honest, I didn't try that hard.)

The absurd notion of doing it on two wheels came later, in the summer of 2017, when I rode from the Channel coast to the Mediterranean with a friend who'd recently quit her job in London to move to Provence. In the interests of wringing maximum drama from her departure, Caroline decided to make the journey by bike. I went along on a whim and realised, somewhere around La Rochelle, that I'd never had so much fun in my life.

France, I found, is a place built for cycling and, happily, for eating, too – a country large enough to give any journey an epic quality, but with a bakery on every corner. Here, it seemed to me as I rode through shady forests and sun-baked vineyards, you could go from beach to mountain, Atlantic to Mediterranean, polder to Pyrenees, and taste the difference every time you stopped for lunch.

Three weeks away from a computer gives you a lot of time to think, and as our little peloton pedalled south, a book began to take shape, a Grand Tour of French gastronomy, visiting dishes in their terroir, picking up tips, putting on wisdom as well as weight. The idea marinated for the next 697km, becoming increasingly less ludicrous with every pichet of local wine we swallowed.

When I got home, I told everyone I was going to do a Tour de France.

The indefinite article is important. I'm no Geraint Thomas, but I've always ridden a bike, pootling round town on a beautiful but big-boned Pashley, often with a similarly built dog ensconced in its capacious wicker basket. To my own surprise, in recent years I've fallen in love with cycling for its own sake too, mostly, but certainly not only, because of the amount you can get away with eating under the flimsy pretext of refuelling.

It all started when I joined a group of friends on a trip from Calais to Brussels in 2014, simply because I'd just been dumped, and it seemed like a good time to do stupid things. Until then, with the exception of the odd flash of elation while careering down Highgate Hill after a glass of wine, I had never really realised that cycling could be fun. Efficient, yes; cheap, certainly! – but enjoyable? In London, a city of mad bus drivers and careless cabbies, where every second pedestrian is FaceTiming their mum in Melbourne rather than looking at the road, and the Boris Bikers are the worst of the lot? No.

That trip, however, was quite different. No one had told me of the quiet satisfaction of pumping your way up a hill, weaving over the saddle like Lance Armstrong on a blood bender, knowing you have just enough left in the tank to make it over the brow, or the eye-watering thrill of the open road on a fast bike with the wind behind you. No one mentioned how sometimes it feels like the bike is part of you, an extension of your limbs, and sometimes, when the sodding chain pops off for the fourth time it feels like you're locked in noble mortal combat. And most of all, no one told me about the giddy camaraderie of the peloton … even when your only goal is getting somewhere in time for lunch.

From the frankly dreadful fry-up on the ferry, feeling like bold adventurers among the dull hordes of motorists, to the commemorative cream cakes we ate on the steps of a bakery after our first, modest ascent (who knew they had hills in Flanders?), it was a joy from start to greedy finish, and not just because of the ready supply of hot crispy frites.

Two-wheeled travel offered other pleasures, too. Coming up close and personal with big-eyed cows, and stopping to gaze at hot-air balloons as they drifted across the vast Belgian skies. Rounding a corner to find an immaculately tended Great War graveyard, the endless rows of neat white gravestones causing us to fall silent for the next few kilometres and feel glad to discover, mooching around a market the next morning, that life in Ypres hadn't stopped in 1918. Scoffing cider and cake in an orchard outside Bruges, and making friends with an enormous slavering Bernese mountain dog as the owner lectured us on the folly of the British attitude to Europe (yes, even in 2014, that pot was already coming to the boil). Racing each other through the flat, gravelled trails of the Ardennes forest, and wandering, slightly bow-legged, through a misty Ghent at dusk, high on life after getting my tyres trapped in some tram tracks. Posing for photos by the sign to Asse, pointing saucily at our padded bottoms like Benny Hill's backing band, as a couple of bemused locals clicked the shutter. And falling asleep in full gear on the Eurostar home with a tiny bottle of wine and a lingering sadness that it was over – and suddenly, I was a Cyclist.

Like all new cyclists, I celebrated by buying loads of kit – stupid clicky shoes that made me walk like a duck, and technical fleece-lined leggings entirely de trop for expeditions around Home Counties pubs, or the trip to Brighton where I made the mistake of eating fish and chips just before tackling Ditchling Beacon. I did a couple of 100-mile sportives, fuelled almost entirely by malt loaf, a glorious four days eating crêpes and drinking cider from teapots in Brittany – and then, summer 2017, came that ride down to the Mediterranean, the biggest and greediest yet, when I finally realised my destiny lay in pedalling round France, eating stuff.

Of course, cycling is a pleasure in itself – as an adult, there's little as thrilling as freewheeling downhill, wind deafening in your ears, eyes streaming, mouth open in a silent scream of pure joy – but for me at least, there's as much pleasure in a pint and a pie afterwards, to say nothing of the snacks en route. I firmly maintain that any ride over an hour and a half requires emergency rations; what are you supposed to put in all those pockets if not chocolate and a hip flask? Someone else will always have tyre levers, but not everyone, sad to say, knows the restorative powers of Cadbury's Wholenut.

Yet, spindly though the pros may be, cycling has always been a peculiarly epicurean pursuit. In the early days of the Tour de France, one wealthy competitor had his butler lay out lavish picnics by the side of the road, while Henri Cornet, winner of the second race in 1904, apparently achieved victory on daily rations that included a staggering 11 litres of hot chocolate, 4 litres of tea and 1.5 kilos of rice pudding. Bernard Hinault, who triumphed five times in the late Seventies and Eighties, glugged champagne on the last climb of the day, while the equally great Eddy Merckx refuelled with patisserie, on the basis that 'It's not the pastries that hurt, it's the climbs' (it is this quote that later moves me to name my beloved new bike after the great man).

Even in the 1990s, Dutch pro Tristan Hoffman recalls a fellow rider starting the day with that breakfast of champions, two Mars Bars and a litre of Coke. Now, of course, nutrition is taken much more seriously, which is why you no longer get brilliant stories like that of Abdel-Kader Zaaf, who is claimed (slightly dubiously) to have got so inadvertently drunk on wine offered by generous spectators on the blisteringly hot 1951 Tour that he passed out underneath a tree.

Modern pro teams travel with their own chef, whose job it is to keep the supply of low-salt, high-protein, easily digestible food and drink coming: as Sean Fowler of Cannondale-Drapac delicately put it in a 2017 interview, 'intestinal stress' is less than ideal in a tour situation. That means rice rather than glutinous pasta, lots of fish and white meat, and definitely no salty ingredients that might lead to water retention. Understandably, no one wants to carry a single extra ounce up an Alp.

Sickly energy gels and bars are handed out to riders en route, along with rice cakes, fizzy drinks ('for a bit of pleasure') and the odd ham sandwich, if they're lucky. On particularly tough stages, however, competitors struggle to find the time to swallow all the calories they need and still keep up with the race – 'You kind of have to force it down,' according to current pro Joe Dombrowski. I literally cannot imagine burning 7,000kcal in a day, and not stopping for a bar of Milka. In fact, so much wasted opportunity for sugar makes me feel a little bit weepy.

As a result, I never watch the Tour on TV without a large box of chocolates; though I'm no sports fan, it has a nostalgic pull for me. The occasionally excitable, generally soporific commentary was the soundtrack to the summer holidays of my childhood, turned up loud in the campsite bar to compete with the thwack of plastic on rubber and the squealing ruckus around the babyfoot table. Those endless afternoons eating Mr Freeze lollies and waiting for a turn at ping-pong have left me with a lifelong weakness for men in Lycra and cycling's most famous race.

The glorious backdrops are a part of it, of course: no one who spent every childhood summer somewhere in *l'hexagone* can be entirely immune to the attractions of a neat Norman village flashing by at speed, or indeed one of those endless straight *routes départementales* flanked with poplars and enormous billboards for thrillingly large *hypermarchés 'à gauche au feu'*. I see France zip past behind the riders, and my heart aches for it – for the landscapes and people, the Orangina and bad pop music, and most of all, for its glorious, glorious food.

My tour will be in less of a hurry than the actual race – bad for the digestion, and if I'm going to do this properly, there will be a lot of digesting on the menu. When I sit down and try to make a list of my 21 favourite French foods (to match the number of stages in the real Tour), not only is it hard to whittle them down, but those that make the cut come from almost every corner of the country, with the exception of the far Nord, which, despite an admirable facility with the deep-fat fryer, did not particularly wow me with its cuisine on my previous visit.

And whereas a list of my most treasured British dishes would skew heavily towards stodge, this lot, though a little low on salad, is pleasingly varied: (almost*) anything we can do, France does better. They've even beaten us on our specialist subject, the spud – I like a baked potato as much as the next noted gourmand, but I think we can all agree that Alpine tartiflette takes it to the next level. (Mostly by adding more cheese.)

The dog and I make a trip to Stanfords in Covent Garden, home of every map under the sun, and pick up a massive road atlas that seems to list every hamlet and track I might possibly wish to traverse, as well as a map of national bike routes, which, it quickly becomes clear, will be of almost no use to me whatsoever. These purchases give me the pleasing sense, as I spread the map out on the floor at home and try to stop Wilf trampling muddy paws across the Bay of Biscay, of embarking on an expedition. They also make terrifyingly clear how large France is.

Taking a deep breath, I open the atlas. Dodging Calais and its horse-fat frites, it makes sense to start off with moules in Normandy, then curve round the coast to Brittany, which does such good crêpes and butter and, even better, crêpes with butter. From the wind-swept Atlantic coast I'll start to head south, first to the Loire Valley, home of the tarte Tatin, as well as all those famous chateaux everyone goes on about, then down to Limousin to coo over some of its famous cattle, before zipping through Bordeaux towards the Spanish border and Bayonne, the French capital of chocolate.

---

* With the exception of breakfast, picnic food and cakes, all of which I reckon the UK has the edge on.

Having run out of France to the south, and skirting a furry tail currently draped over the Pyrenees, my route turns east for poule au pot, and the cassoulet country of the Languedoc, before hitting the Côte d'Azur, with its rust-red fish soups and deliciously oily ratatouille. Tempting as it is to head for Provence proper at this point, that herb-scented heaven-on-earth where I spent every rosé-soaked summer of my twenties, I fear I'd never tear myself away in mid-June and I cannot ignore the siren call of tartiflette from my second-favourite place in France, the Haute Savoie. I wish I could say that it's the thrill of the physical challenge that attracts me to the mountains, but it isn't, it's the cheese.

From there, the map suggests I'm quite close (i.e. a-whole-day-on-a-train close, due to aforementioned size of country) to Lyon, often touted as the culinary capital of France. Though I've only driven past it, my reading suggests it specialises in an extraordinary array of animal parts, and oddly, one of France's best salads, the lyonnaise, with its bitter leaves dressed with salty bacon fat and rich, runny egg yolk.

The logical next stop on my way north is Burgundy, for all sorts of things cooked in its perfect wine, but particularly beef, sticky, soft and intensely savoury, and then, looking at the route I've traced thus far, which flirts with the Spanish, Italian and Swiss borders, it feels like a dereliction of duty not to go and make eyes at the Germans in Strasbourg, too.

It's a long way to go for some fermented cabbage and faggots, and yet I have a lot of time for fermented things and sausages, especially washed down with cold beer. Also, I note with satisfaction that this puts me in the ideal place to knock off a wobbly quiche Lorraine in Lorraine, and the fluffy little madeleines that occupy such a central place in the national psyche, before making a triumphant entry into Paris via Champagne, which may or may not have invented French onion soup (and God, who doesn't love French onion soup, all cheesy and oozy and glorious?), but which does, happily, have an awful lot of fizzy wine going for it.

Paris, of course, like any cosmopolitan capital city, is a place where you can eat yourself around the globe, but my ambitions are more modest. I'm hoping, as a crescendo of my trip, to achieve croissant nirvana in the city of light. Certainly, I'll have eaten enough of the things by then to judge what's good and what's not – I'm intending to put away at least one a day, barring any more interesting offers.

PAUSE-CAFÉ – The Croissant Rating System

Pay attention, because you're going to be seeing a lot more of this. I started rating croissants on the coast-to-coast trip of 2017, for no better reason than they're reliably found throughout France, I enjoy over-thinking food and most importantly I like them. The perfect croissant is, of course, entirely a matter of taste – professional pâtissières put a lot of store by the lamination of the dough, or how skilfully the pastry and butter have been folded together to create hundreds of distinct layers: according to one equation I find online, the average croissant has 649. Me, I'm less concerned with looks; some of the most disappointing pastries I've eaten in London are the ones flaunting their perfect strata of dough all over social media, but which turn out to have very little in the way of flavour. What I look for in a good croissant is:

1   butteriness (no margarine-based croissants for me)
2   a good balance of caramelised sweetness and bready savoury notes
3   a crisp base
4   a slightly damp middle – squidgy but not doughy

In the text that follows, all scores are out of 10: 1–4 denotes a poor croissant not even worth finishing (a croissant contains about 260kcal); 5–7 as a mediocre-to-decent example not worth complaining about and 8+ as a good croissant worth repeating immediately if time permits.

―――――――――――――――――――――――――――

It's a satisfyingly neat loop around the country, but one, I note, that covers an awful lot of ground. A cursory google turns up the terrifying fact that France is the largest country in Western Europe, a whopping 27 times the size of Wales. Distances are vast – it looks like it might take me at least three days to cycle across Brittany alone.

Unfortunately, I have a day job as a weekly columnist, and a mortgage to pay, to say nothing of a terrier with a truly prodigious appetite; I can't afford to dawdle around this place like a tourist – I need to be a Tourist. So like the boys in Lycra,* I'll need the odd lift. Until quite recently I'd assumed the Tour de France actually rode around France, but they don't; they get on team coaches and doze their way to the next starting line. Me, I'm going to let the train take the strain.

To add to the fun, I've hit a summer of rail strikes: two days out of every seven are to be given over to industrial

* Don't get me started on the iniquities of the Women's Tour.

action in a dispute over President Macron's attempts to open the passenger network up to competition. On the plus side, the dates have been announced in advance. On the minus side, the actual services affected won't be decided until the night before, which makes the whole thing a bit of a Russian roulette.

PAUSE-CAFÉ – Cycle Touring: A Bluffer's Guide

If the reactions of my friends and family are anything to go by, anyone who hasn't ridden a bike since childhood finds the idea of weeks doing nothing but this a bit daunting. In fact, as I always breezily explain, cycling is much easier than running, especially when your feet are actually stuck to the bike. Once you've got going, momentum will keep your legs spinning round with surprisingly little effort on your part, and on good roads with a forgiving gradient, you can cover a decent distance without much expertise: it's not for nothing that 100 miles is said to be the cycling equivalent of running a marathon, though having done both (preens), I can confirm a marathon is a lot more unpleasant.

Cyclists tend to measure distances in kilometres rather than miles, just like they tend to drink espressos rather than tea, and call their silly hats casquettes rather than caps. It's Rule 24 in the Velominati handbook (the Velominati being a half-jokey online cult to the two-wheeled god) and one of the few that I obey, mostly because 50km sounds a lot more impressive than 31 miles (though they're also right that all shorts should be black

– 'wet, dirty white Lycra is basically transparent; enough said on that matter').

I've found that, when riding all day, it's reasonable to cover between 70 and 150km depending on the terrain, weather and how much of interest is along the way, with an average speed of about 15km/h. That said, not everyone falls easily into sitting in the saddle for six hours on the trot, so 50–70km feels like a more manageable distance with company desirous of a nice holiday rather than a wholesale reconfiguration of their nether regions.

My recommendation for anyone thinking of embarking on anything similar for the first time is to make sure you have a bike that's both light and sturdy: dedicated touring bikes will never be as featherlight as racers, but you can stick a rack on most things, and if you're staying on tarmac, a robust road bike has always been my choice.

Other things you'll need, apart from all the obvious stuff you'd take on holiday if you had to carry it round with you:

Panniers and rack. A bar or frame bag is also useful for your
   wallet, etc., though I like to keep my phone attached to my
   handlebars to help with navigation/show those
   all-important Instagram alerts on the go.
Basic toolkit: inner tube, patches, pump, multitool, tyre levers,
   chain lube. France in particular is well supplied with bike
   shops; if you're going somewhere that isn't, you might
   want to consider spare brake pads, etc.
Padded shorts and gloves: trust me, you won't regret these if
   you're doing more than a day in the saddle.
Decent lights – naive urban cyclists (me) may be startled at
   how dark it is on country roads.
Water bottles – I took two and ran out several times. Get
   big ones.

Chunky but not too heavy bike lock.

Portable phone charger – or actual maps, given that's mostly
   what you'll be using it for.

Tent, sleeping bag, rollmat (only if planning to camp, obviously).

Wet wipes. They hide a multitude of bike-oil-based sins.

Trains or not, it's still a daunting prospect as I gaze at the little
map, stuck with flags like a ham studded with cloves. Yet just the
names involved make my heart leap, bringing back happy
memories of summers past and journeys taken, squashed sandwiches scoffed on ski lifts and arguments in the hot, sticky back
seat of a Vauxhall Cavalier.

These places might sound familiar, but I know they'll look
different from a bike. A cyclist's pace is swift enough to make
satisfying progress, yet slow enough to enjoy it, to notice the
landscape changing before and, of course, under the tyres – it's
hard to get a sense of the terrain when it's flashing past you in
the car, or on the train, but when you're forced to really feel it
in your legs, it's hard to ignore. Places seem to stamp themselves on your consciousness with startling firmness, as Graham
Robb writes in his book *The Discovery of France*, which is to be
my only constant companion, despite his admission that it's 'too
large to justify its inclusion in the panniers' (yep, thanks,
Graham, I noticed): 'A bicycle unrolls a 360-degree panorama of
the land, allows the rider to register its gradual changes in gear
ratios and muscle tension, and makes it hard to miss a single
inch of it, from the tyre-lacerating suburbs of Paris to the
Mistral-blasted plains of Provence.'

A cyclist can embrace the leisurely passage of time on the
smaller roads, weaving as they do through hamlets on the way

to nowhere, past tumbledown chateaux and fields of somnam-
bulant cattle, and then stop for refreshments in a prosperous
little town, watching the world go by at some bustling café in
the soothing company of small dogs.

A bike also, of course, offers a unique opportunity to plod
miserably through *Zones Industrielles* in the rain, and dodge
lorries on a road that turns out to be bigger and scarier than
Google Maps is prepared to admit, to say nothing of the
ever-present and exciting possibility of eating lunch outside a
Total garage because nowhere else will let you in dressed like
that. They're pretty good at both highs and lows, bikes, and
that's what makes them fun. I can't wait.

Robb describes the actual Tour de France as 'a joyful beating
of the bounds that millions of people with no interest in sport
still enjoy every summer'. Mine feels rather like that, too: a way
to see how the country fits together, how the Wild West of
craggy Atlantic granite and wide ocean beaches becomes the
south-west of duck fat and complicated Basque consonants, to
get a feeling for the state of regional French cooking, so long
lauded around the world, yet as vulnerable to the very 21st-
century pressures of time and convenience as anywhere else.

Is it still possible, I wonder, to find roadside places full of
what the redoubtable Fanny Cradock described as 'heavily
tattooed, burly camion drivers ... where the soap is attached to
a string in the communal loo and the tablecloths may be of
paper, but where an excellent five-course meal can be found for
well under a pound'? Will I eat better in France than I would at
home, and come back two stone heavier, with incipient scurvy?

My tour will have several, not insignificant diversions from its more famous namesake. For a start, as described above in luxuriant detail, my route is going to be based solely around the greatest hits of French cuisine, rather than its landscapes and local politics. Secondly, though there will be a rag-tag peloton for the most scenic bits, I'll be mostly on my own, as it seems most of my friends, very inconsiderately, have proper jobs that preclude going away for five weeks. Thirdly, I'm going to have to lug everything with me, including a tent and sleeping bag, to leave me more to spend on food (pro teams sleep in hotels where they don't even carry their bags upstairs themselves). And lastly … I'm a 35-year-old food writer who spends most of her working week testing recipes – and when I say testing, I mean eating them all up and licking the plate while the dog looks on with jealous eyes. Tour riders start off with about 4–5 per cent body fat. I suspect mine, though mercifully unmeasured, is more akin to a pot of clotted cream.

The problem with this last point, of course, is that it means my power-to-weight ratio – that most vital of statistics in modern sport – is sub-optimal. I'm going to be hauling a lot of unnecessary baggage round France, which is unfortunate when, according to British Cycling, 'one of the best ways to get quicker on the bike, especially on hills, is to drop a few pounds'. I have a go, I really do, but there's the small matter of six weeks' worth of recipes to write and perfect before I go, and eventually I concede defeat, which is unfortunate, because the rather chi-chi cycling outfitters Café du Cycliste, based in Nice but with a smart little shop in East London, are kind enough to step in at the last minute with the offer of some gear. I'm not quite sure that I'm exactly the clothes horse they had in mind to sport the two elegant outfits they've picked out. 'Does … does this come in large?' I ask tentatively, stepping from the changing room in something so skintight you'd be able to count my ribs if they hadn't disappeared some time in the late 1980s.

More pressingly, I don't have a proper bike. My last true love was trashed by couriers on the way back from Marseille last summer and my first reserve, the Pashley, which weighs over 20kg even without a dog on board, is clearly not up to the task. I seek expert advice from friends like Rich, who's into long, long rides and recommends various bikes that are eminently practical and reasonably priced, Jon, who's into spending money on really sexy-looking bikes, and Max, who's into cycling up mountains with the minimum of kit, and then I ignore it all in favour of one that makes my heart flutter when I look at it, and my accountant weep, despite my parents' generous contribution in lieu of all future Christmas and birthday gifts.

Eddy (named for the pastry-loving Merckx) is a steel-framed (more flexible than aluminium on bumpy terrain, less risky than the pricy but delicate carbon frames used by the pros) Condor touring bike in Paris Green, a colour which feels auspicious. I spend an expensive afternoon in a basement on the Grays Inn Road being measured up ('your arms are … really long') and then a nervous month praying he will be ready in time for the off after discovering belatedly that delivery is scheduled for around the time I should be in the Loire Valley.

Fortunately, after I look ready to burst into tears in front of other customers, they manage to hurry things along and he arrives a week before the off, a thing of rare and lustrous beauty, though unfortunately I'm so hungover after a work party the night before that I fail to listen when they explain technical points about how to trim the chain, on the basis I have no idea what this means and am in no state to learn. Instead, I have a vivid flashback to telling a completely sober Nigel Slater that I

loved him, over and over, and clench my fists around the handlebars in hot shame.

So I've got the bike and the kit and the rudimentary vocab,
having enrolled in a panic cramming course at the French
Institute in South Kensington and ploughed my way through
various Inspector Maigret mysteries instead of packing. This at
least means I'll be able to discuss murder weapons with confi-
dence on my journey, if required.

Yet such is the rush before I go that I don't quite make time
to check if all my gear will fit in my new bright yellow panniers.
Sitting in the corner of the bedroom gathering dust, they look
vast in comparison with the one I've used previously, yet I have
a sneaking suspicion that once I've included important
morale-boosting items like Marmite and sloe gin, there might
not be an awful lot of room for luxuries like spare inner tubes
and plasters.

Naturally, instead of dealing with the problem, I insist on
throwing a Royal Wedding Party for the nuptials of Harry and
Meghan, to the evident dismay of my friends, who nevertheless
come and support me, because that's what friends do.
Gemma even brings me a tiny bottle of Echo Falls rosé to stick
in my panniers.

'I'm really looking forward to it,' says Matt, who is accompanying me for the first few days and claims he's 'all sorted', as the
three of us – the last survivors of the Happy Event – sit outside
the pub at dusk, drinking snakebite and black (it seemed funny
when I ordered them).

I giddily watch the dog begging for crisps on the other side
of the bar, and vaguely wonder who he belongs to. 'Yeah, me
too,' I say. 'Do you think I should go home and pack?'

STAGE 1

THE GRAND DÉPART, LONDON TO CHERBOURG

Douillons aux Poires – or Pears in Pyjamas

The Norman equivalent of an apple turnover but with a much
cooler name. Considered rather homely fare, you won't see them
on many restaurant menus, but you may well find them in
boulangeries. They're best eaten warm from the oven,
with a big dollop of crème fraîche.

It's 3 a.m., and things are not going according to plan. Instead of the sound night's sleep I'd been planning, perhaps after a couple (definitely just a couple) of farewell drinks with friends, I'm sitting glumly on a pile of new Lycra, chilled fizz unopened in the fridge, the bin overflowing with packaging, struggling to keep my eyes open and wondering if I should just open the Echo Falls and be done with it. An old friend who offers to pop in on her way home from a night out to say goodbye 'if you're still awake!' gets a couple of paces through the door, regards the chaos before her with visible alarm and declines my kind offer to stay and chat – 'you look like you're a bit busy'.

Frankly, I don't know how I do it, let alone find the time to post a jaunty photo of my almost-empty fridge on Instagram ('I hope those ferments don't explode,' someone comments, once it's far too late to be helpful) and send friends a mad-eyed selfie wearing my ridiculous new sardine-patterned cap ... but somehow I get a couple of hours' kip before getting up to check yet again that I have the essentials, like a salami knife and a pot of pink nail varnish, and enjoy a final, vast cup of tea.

It's a solemn moment. I start every day with a mug of English Breakfast, the colour of damp – but not wet, not even *soggy* – sand, made with boiling water and fresh milk, which definitely rules out anything from the train catering trolley, let alone any prettily tinted tisanes the French might serve under the name of *thé*. This will be my last cuppa until July, and let me tell you, it's emotional. Though to be honest, that could also be the exhaustion setting in.

Pushing past Eddy waiting patiently in the hall, I go to meet a friend and her baby who've come to wave me off – and, listening to the gory details of the birth, feel relieved to be able to spend a few minutes revelling in someone else's suffering instead of my own. I'd planned to have a symbolic full English, but in the end, thinking of what's to come, I wimp out and go for avocado on toast with a feral-tasting kombucha on the side as a final taste of Islington.

Back home, while Hen changes Gabriel on the sitting-room floor (there's about as much dignity in being a baby as a long-distance cyclist, it seems), I change my own clothes from those appropriate for breakfast with a friend to those needed to ride a Grand Tour – or at least the 4.73km I'll be covering on the way to Waterloo. To their credit, neither of them laugh when I emerge.

Sweetly, Hen obligingly takes several photos of me standing proudly with my unwieldy steed outside the house as passers-by gawp, trying her hardest to find a good angle for a food writer clad entirely in Lycra, and then I can delay no longer – it's time to leave. Eddy and I wobble unsteadily out of the gate and down the kerb, I manage a half-wave and smile for the camera, and ride straight into the back of a stationary double-decker bus – thankfully at very low speed, denting nothing but what little is left of my pride.

After peeling myself off an advert for an evangelical concert in Leytonstone, I discover, within two turns of the pedals, that my shiny new yellow panniers are on wrong. As I said, I didn't have much time to prepare, what with asking the dog if he was going to miss me 63 times and spending 13 minutes staring vacantly at socks in the wee small hours. Luggage situation sorted and finally over-taking Hen and the pram, I race across town – a familiar journey fraught with new significance. I become obsessed by the idea that I'm going to have an accident of some sort before I even leave London (it's not beyond the realms of possibility dressed like this; at least two vans make an attempt on my life on the Farringdon Road), so it's with some relief that I finally unclip my feet in SE1 and click-click my way into the scrum within to pick up the train tickets.

Here I encounter a new problem. I haven't had the chance or indeed inclination to ride Eddy fully laden before, and the vastly uneven distribution of weight means I'm destined to spend the next five weeks battling his desperate desire to plunge to the floor at every given opportunity. Waterloo station on a Friday afternoon is not, I discover, the ideal location to kick off this particular fight.

Tickets safely stuck in my back pouch, I locate Matt, a university friend and a veteran of that fateful first Brussels trip. He's recently been working so hard doing something mysterious for the Civil Service that he hasn't had much of a chance to get on a bike full stop, though I have in my possession a text claiming he's been to a spinning class that 'nearly killed me'. In the circumstances, it's kind of him to offer to accompany me on the *Grand Départ*, and cheering to find someone who looks more nervous than me. I perk up immediately.

We'd both talked the talk about bringing a proper British picnic for the train, but clearly this hasn't happened thanks to a mutual lack of organisation, so, once the bikes are installed by the inevitable foul-smelling lavatory, and we've found seats a safe distance away, we make do with wistful chat about Fortnum's Scotch eggs and how to make a perfect cheese and pickle sandwich instead (mature Cheddar, sliced rather than grated, Branston, no salad). Once I've exhausted him on chutneys, Matt is keen to know my plans and I'm equally keen to divert attention away from the glaring lack of them, so the journey proves a polite clash of wills, broken only by the first sight of the sea.

Pushing through the Bank Holiday crowds at Portsmouth Harbour, we climb gingerly onto our bikes for the last leg on home soil, pedalling past the defeated-looking Victory Shopping Centre on a classic British cycle lane that terminates abruptly in the middle of a junction. How I'll miss these soon, I think nostalgically as an ancient Toyota Yaris lurches across my path without indicating.

I soon get my revenge as we sail past it at the ferry terminal, and straight into the usual lines of idling cars, the occupants sitting on the tarmac in their folding chairs, gawping at each new arrival like paparazzi at the world's worst film premiere. We attract particular attention; I'd like to think it's because we look so dashing, but they might well just be rubbernecking at my Lycra (Matt, meanwhile, is dressed like a normal person).

Having breezed through the ticket gates with the kind of cheer that a pair of rogue cyclists in a queue of cars often seem to be met with, my heart sinks as we approach the customs post. I have never managed to make it past one of these on two wheels without being pulled in for checking, less (I think) because of my shifty demeanour and more because it's considerably quicker and easier to search a pushbike than a four-by-four with an Alsatian in the back. As the finger of suspicion inevitably beckons us over, I remember the trusty salami slicer stashed somewhere behind me – though it's a modest blade of the sort you'll find in the window of newsagents all over France, often along with child-sized versions labelled 'my first knife', I have a nasty feeling these chaps won't appreciate how essential it is to a decent picnic.

'I'll take the gentleman's right pannier, and your left one,' the officer says, once we've finally managed to prop the ungainly bikes upright against their corrugated lair. I frantically try to remember which pannier contains the offending item, but they both look identical until I hoist the left one onto the conveyor belt for scanning and hear the clink of tent poles within. Of *course* it's in this one – I try to look nonchalant, but it's with a sinking sense of inevitability that I obediently pull out the catering bag containing Marmite, Tabasco and my lovely Opinel for inspection.

The man in charge goes from bored to outraged in under 10 seconds, even as I point out – quite calmly, I think – that it's a steak knife. 'There's no way that's for cutting meat,' he counters, staring at the tiny blade as if examining it for incriminating marks. Before I can testily reply that in that case it's probably quite safe, I'm saved from myself by Matt, a man never known to lose his temper, who gently points out the name of an Alpine restaurant carved onto the wooden handle. The guard, perhaps a vegetarian, is unimpressed (though, as I decide not to point out, it's in the *Michelin Guide* and everything). Just as my bottom lip begins to tremble embarrassingly, he calls his supervisor. 'Oi, mate, over here a second.'

The boss appraises the situation with a cursory glance.

'Look behind you,' he tells me. 'What's in there?'

I turn to see a Perspex box a little over half full of vicious-looking flick knives and something that appears to be a large cutlass.

'Offensive weapons?' I suggest tentatively.

'THEY'RE THE SAME,' he says firmly. (They're totally not.)

It seems because my little knife has a locking function (useful with a crag of Alpine cheese, or a well-matured saucisson), it's illegal under UK law – but possibly because I'm at serious risk of Making a Scene, and seem unlikely to stab anyone but customs officials, I'm eventually allowed to keep it on the strict basis that I never attempt to travel with it again. As the homeward leg seems laughably far off, I make the promise in good faith and we're allowed to pedal off with picnic kit intact. Matt swears blind he hears one of them mutter that it was more trouble than it was worth to fill in the confiscation paperwork, but I prefer to believe that I just don't look like the kind of girl to go on the rampage with a steak knife. (In Paris, five weeks later, this same knife is waved through by security guards at the Musée d'Orsay, who presumably realise any civilised person likes picnics too much to want to slash Manet's *Le Déjeuner sur l'herbe*.)

After this drama, I accept the official prohibition on cycling onto the ferry itself without a murmur, so my final, anticlimactic contact with British soil comes while battling to keep Eddy upright as I wheel him onto the ramp, his generous rear end trying desperately to remain in Hampshire as I steer him onwards to adventure. Lashed to a large pipe on the back of the ship, perfectly positioned to catch the salty swell over the stern, I quietly forget Condor's advice about never letting him get wet in favour of skipping up the stairs to find the restaurant.

In the absence of any pork pies, I've been distracting Matt with titbits about Brittany Ferries catering, lovingly detailing the glorious buffet of hors d'oeuvres awaiting us on board, plates groaning with prawns and smoked trout, Russian salad and devilled eggs, and as much baguette and Breton butter as you can fill your boots with. After ranging the length of the *Normandie Express*, dodging excited children and clicking up and down stairs in shoes already beginning to annoy me, I'm forced to concede that this particular vessel boasts little more than a bar – so as the engine finally grinds to life, and Portsmouth's Spinnaker Tower recedes into the distance, we head out on deck to raise a bottle of 'Gourmandie' cider (see what they did there? I didn't, until Matt pointed out) to the success of the expedition instead.

Once on the open sea, having realised Matt knows an awful lot about the Royal Navy and its various aircraft carriers for a man who allegedly works in another department entirely (definite spy), the cider and the excitement soon catch up with me, and I spend much of the rest of the voyage passed out in a reclining chair, waking up only once when my companion brings a microwaved boeuf bourguignon back from the café, and then, apparently only seconds later, finding myself staring at the foggy harbour walls of Cherbourg in puzzled stupefaction.

'Why does it say *port militaire* in English?' I ask Matt, discreetly wiping the dribble from my cheek.

'I think you may need a coffee,' comes the polite reply.

If cycling onto a ferry is a joy, disembarking is the reverse: there's nothing like a boatful of Brits eager to get to their chateaux in the Dordogne to put the wind up you when you're not quite sure which side of the road to choose. Special as we may have felt among the cars in Portsmouth, turns out we aren't the only cyclists to have made the crossing, just the tardiest, and as we wait in line for passport control we discreetly size each other up. Only one woman has more luggage than me, and, sensing the chance for some friendly one-upmanship, I try to get close enough to ask her what she's up to, but on seeing her American papers, the gendarme whisks her to one side to fill in various forms and we stream past, casually flapping our maroon passports. 'Wonder what it'll be like next summer,' I hear a man behind me say.

The rumbles of continental geopolitics come a distant second to those of our stomachs, however; having not eaten more than a few peanuts since that avo toast back in King's Cross, I'm ravenously hungry – which is, of course, the very best way to arrive in France. After only a few angry honks, we lose the stream of ferry traffic to the autoroute and find ourselves in a prosperous-looking little port, the quayside thronged with people strolling in the evening sunshine, boats bobbing in the breeze. I check Eddy into the luxury of the hotel's laundry room, where I suspect he's gearing up to leak chain grease onto the stacks of clean sheets, hang up my Lycra ready for tomorrow (spoiler: this is the last time it will be thus honoured until my mum gets hold of it in the Alps), and go downstairs to find Matt already halfway through a bottle of La Cotentine Blanche, named after the Norman peninsula we'll be tackling over the next few days.

First beer polished off at appropriately British speed, we repair next door to the Café de Paris, recommended as 'a true seafood brasserie – invigorating!' by the *Michelin Guide*. The dining room is full to bursting with tables of merry French eating seafood.

'Well, this looks good!' said Matt cheerfully as we're led to the back of the dining room ... and then up some curved stairs to an empty room decorated in the height of 1980s ferry chic, all pale pine and frosted lights and napkin fans on the tables.

'Do you think this is where they put the British people?' he whispers, his voice echoing around the space.

We laugh and order kirs (because one celebratory drink is never enough), and are halfway down them when another party is ushered in, men and women alike clad in faded chino shorts, pressed polo shirts and expensive waterproof sailing jackets. Before they even begin to speak, Matt winks. We are indeed in the Anglo-Saxon ghetto.

The food, happily, is pure French, and proves a distraction from their disappointingly dull boat-related conversation. Star of the show is a magnificent platter of fruits de mer bedecked with fat oysters and tiny crunchy little prawns barely bigger than Morecambe Bay shrimps, and just small enough to pop in whole in all their whiskery glory. Below sit bigger prawns, firm and salty-sweet, the best winkles I've ever had (too much information?) and a selection of curiously round clams I later discover are known as dog cockles in English, and more poetically in French as almonds of the sea. On the side, half a baguette and a bowl of piquant yellow mayonnaise.

The punchy Calvados sorbet that follows, melting into granular fruity sweetness on the tongue, is pure delight – the first in a long line of shots of local firewater masquerading as desserts that make me wonder why we don't make more of the digestif tradition in the UK. I, for one, would certainly order a sloe gin slushy if I saw it on the menu.

Strong liquor it may be, but excited to be off at last, I spring eagerly from bed the next morning as the chilly light of morning brightens the eaves (happily ignorant of the fact that this will be the last such springing for several weeks) and pull at the curtains to reveal … a misty grey world of damp slate rooftops.

Oh well, I think cheerfully, yanking on the Lycra, at least this will give me the chance to make a pretentious joke about the *Parapluies de Cherbourg* when I see Matt. Every cloud and all that.

Clearly, it's important to start as I mean to go on, so, joke dispensed to only moderate acclaim, the second item on the day's itinerary is to find a croissant. After politely rejecting the hotel breakfast, I don't feel brave enough to solicit a recommendation from Madame, so we wander the backstreets in search of something, anything open. Cherbourg looks rather more down-at-heel than in the honeymoon glow of last night, though among the boarded-up businesses we do stumble upon a rather spectacular basilica: as one TripAdvisor review notes, 'inside is calm and smells of history – so does the entrance that reeks of urine'.

Following an old lady with a large wicker shopping bag, we finally hit what passes for a jackpot in my world: a Saturday market full of spider crabs imprisoned in lobster pots, trays of cockles and mussels, wheels of cheese and a big terracotta dish of something with a burnt orange, wrinkly skin that I book-mark for further investigation once we've fulfilled a more immediate need.

Having located a boulangerie with an impressive display of patisserie, which often augers well for the general standard of baking, I secure the first croissant of the trip, along with a douillons aux poires – unseasonal in May, perhaps, but we are in Normandy, apple and pear country, famous for its cider-based sauces, often gilded with lashings of cream, and fruity patisserie. It's also the home of the aforementioned apple brandy, christened for the region of the same name, which is so punchy the local apple crop was apparently requisitioned during the Great War to make explosives for armaments. (As I said, it's good stuff.)

Once money has changed hands, I can finally draw breath and explain the art of the *petit déjeuner* to a slightly twitchy Matt. I will also share this wisdom – accrued through much trial and error, disappointment and pastry-based joy – with you, gentle reader, in case you find it helpful.

PAUSE-CAFÉ – Breakfast in France: A Beginner's Guide

In general, the best breakfasts in France are bread based – yes, you might well enjoy a bowl of sun-warmed figs and sheep yoghurt at your villa in Provence, but just so you know, most people around you would regard this as an eccentric way to start the day. God gave us the boulangerie for a reason, and that reason is breakfast. (The sensible French householder also keeps a stock of *pain grillé*, or toast crackers, which can be purchased in the biscuit aisle of supermarkets, to guard against the terrible eventuality of ever running out of bread.)

Baguette with butter and jam is a lovely thing, but on the move, it's handier to go for something with the butter already baked in. I never deviate from the plain croissant, the apotheosis of the baker's art, but you could also go with the child-friendly pain au chocolat, the sugary almond croissant (which, according to my friend Caroline, who worked for a spell in a Parisian bakery, is yesterday's leftovers drenched in syrup and rebaked) or any number of regional specialities. Indeed, the benefit of cycling long distances is you can usually justify several items: I even have a Paris–Brest for breakfast one day, though I'm not sure I'd recommend it unless you want to feel slightly queasy for the first few kilometres.

If you're in a hurry, or simply wish to take your bounty for a scenic picnic, then you may get lucky and find the boulangerie has a coffee machine as well. The coffee is usually mediocre (see page 290, *Pause-Café – Coffee Break*), but certainly no worse than the average British stuff, and this does cut out the next step, which is trying to find somewhere to provide the liquid element of proceedings. Note that in my experience, boulangeries in the south and east seem more clued into the coffee wheeze – I didn't find many in Normandy or Brittany – and not all have milk.

If you want to sit down and enjoy your breakfast like a civilised person, then head straight to the nearest bar, which isn't just a place to booze – though you are likely to see a surprising number of respectable-looking people sipping beers or glasses of pastis first thing – but a place to drink coffee, read the paper and catch up with friends. Kind of like a pub, if the British were made differently. (Because of this you won't see many dedicated coffee shops in France, or at least I didn't, though there's the odd Starbucks in Paris.)

As long as they don't serve breakfast themselves, it's perfectly acceptable to sit down, order a coffee, and bring out the stuff you bought round the corner to enjoy with it: no need for snatching furtive bites under the table while the waiter's back is turned, though you might want to take the empty bags with you, especially if you hope to repeat the experience tomorrow.

A suitable café is located, overlooking the market, and business concluded fairly satisfactorily, though the croissant itself proves a mere 7/10 – rather soft and bland by French standards. Still, brushing the crumbs from my lips and tucking the petite galette that accompanied my *café crème* in my pocket for later, it feels like a good start.

Douillons aux Poires, or Pears in Pyjamas

This buttery, lightly spiced Norman classic, which can be made with apples or pears, is usually served warm, rather than scoffed straight from the boulangerie bag as we did, and is lovely with a glass of sweet cider or perry.

Makes 6
6 small, hard pears
500ml cider or perry
100g sugar
1 egg, beaten
Crème fraîche, to serve

For the pastry (or use 500g bought puff)
250g plain flour, plus a little extra to roll out
¼ tsp fine salt
85g caster sugar
150g well-chilled butter

1 Put the flour, salt and sugar into a mixing bowl and grate the butter into it. Stir with a table knife to coat the butter, then drizzle over 2 tablespoons of cold water and keep stirring, gradually adding more (probably about 3 tablespoons more)

until it starts to come together. At this point you can use your hands. Wrap and chill for at least 30 minutes.

2 Meanwhile, peel the pears and core from the bottom, leaving the stalks on. Bring 500ml of water, the cider or perry and sugar to the boil in a pan just large enough to hold all the pears, then add the fruit. Poach until just tender, but not soft; how long will depend on the ripeness of your pears. Drain and dry well with kitchen paper.

3 Preheat the oven to 200°C/180°C fan/gas 6. Roll the pastry out on a lightly floured surface to about 3mm thick. Cut into thick strips, long enough to wrap round the base of each pear, then roll up to encase it, leaving the stalk sticking out at the top. Pinch together with damp fingers to seal. Brush with beaten egg.

4 Bake for about 35–40 minutes, until deep golden. Serve warm, with crème fraîche.

Km: 7.3

Croissants: 1 (7/10)

High: Actually making it onto the train

Low: Crying over a steak knife

STAGE 2

CHERBOURG TO AVRANCHES

Moules Marinières

*Moules marinières is not an exclusively Norman dish – you'll find
it all over northern France and Belgium – but Normandy has been
exporting mussels to the discerning diners of Paris since at least the
16th century, so they probably know what they're doing by now.*

Aptly, the first 30 minutes of my epic journey are in the
wrong direction. A route that looked simple on the map
proves easily lost once the signs, so assiduous for the first couple
of kilometres through central Cherbourg, stop abruptly, as if
the person responsible knocked off for lunch and never came
back. All options are thrillingly open as we circumnavigate a
busy roundabout searching in vain for clues, eventually ending
up in a grim retail park inadvertently following signs for Oncle
Scott's '1er restaurant franco-américain aux ambiances country de la
longue liste des restaurants en France' rather than Bricquebec, the
town I've earmarked for lunch.

My falsely breezy claim that getting out of cities is always the
worst part of any ride doesn't make either of us feel any better,

especially after a promising-looking cycle path down the side of a fast dual carriageway is belatedly revealed to be a works entrance when several pieces of heavy machinery overtake us at speed, horns blaring. Thank God, then, for the kind fellow cyclist who, seeing my face contorted with rage over my phone, stops and points us in the right direction: through a housing estate and a dark, dank tunnel under the road, from which we emerge, blinking, into the countryside.

And what countryside! Normandy has turned on a full charm offensive, as if in a belated attempt to erase this morning's carwashes and tile showrooms from our minds – we pedal past sleepy cottages with chickens pecking away placidly in their shadow, through banks of tall rhododendrons in full flower and, very soon, behind iron railings and a placid lake, hit the bullseye: a real-life chateau, all pointy turrets and grim stone. I insist on stopping to get a picture, and promptly fall off my bike, as I yet again fail to remember that I have 25kg strapped onto the back wheel.

It's all bucolic as hell: Normandy is a soft, lush landscape of culinary riches – salt-marsh lamb, seafood, dairy, and dry cider. In fact, in terms of raw ingredients, it's not a million miles away from the milder regions of our own South-West. More than one source I consult mentions the 'gargantuan appetites' of the heartily sized locals, which may be attributing too long a reach to Vikings who settled here in the 10th century, but if I lived in this land of Camembert and Calvados, I'd probably blame my corpulence on genetics, too.

The sun finally comes out as we bowl along hedge-fringed country lanes, attracting barking dogs to their gates like Pied Pipers with pockets full of sausages. I'm particularly taken with one tiny Yorkshire terrier whose warning sign declares it to be '*en psychoanalyse*'. At one o'clock precisely, we hit Bricquebec, a prosperous town with a 12th-century castle that feels like it ought to be full of restaurants, but oddly enough isn't, with the exception of a forbidding medieval cellar with definite pretensions to grandeur that don't quite feel appropriate to our clothing or general odour. Mindful of the five weeks of dining out ahead of me, I push for a picnic, but Matt is a man who likes to eat properly, and he tells me so, albeit in such incredibly diplomatic language that it takes me a while to get the hint.

Needless to say, he wins and we end up at a bar that sells pizzas and smells promisingly of toasting Emmental. Thin and crisp, they come laden with unapologetically French toppings. I choose one with Camembert, potatoes, smoked ham and cream, which arrives with a glossy egg yolk goggling at me from the centre. Throw in a cold Orangina and a big bottle of Badoit, and the disastrous start is all but forgotten.

To Matt's considerable relief, given the strength of the sun and the fact that he's packed so light he hasn't even brought suncream, the route climbs on to an old railway line after lunch – 'They're always flat!' – and shepherds us in shaded comfort almost all the way to the coast, with just a brief break for a drink in Saint-Saveur-le-Vicomte. I say a drink – Matt appears from the bakery with the requested Perrier, plus a surprise box of cakes: lemon for him, rhubarb for me, both crammed into our mouths standing up as if we'd just climbed Mont Ventoux rather than slow-pedalled 25km across a pancake.

We're staying in a *chambre d'hôte* this evening; the French equivalent of a bed and breakfast, in the tiny marshy village of Saint-Germain-sur-Ay. Unfortunately, neither of us has even a whisper of signal out here, and though I insist it's likely to be signed, it really isn't, forcing me to duck into the only shop in sight to ask for help. The place is totally empty apart from a startled child stacking shelves who points mutely through a doorway to the village pub. At the bar, nursing drinks, sit the international standard measure of grumpy old men.

They perk up as I explain our situation, arguing among themselves as to where this place could be, until one of them has the bright idea that I can come and stay with him instead, a suggestion that makes the rest of them laugh so hard they can't speak. The landlord takes advantage of the brief wheezy silence to tell me it's the second right, out over the salt marshes, down a road which we later discover spends much of its time underwater. I make a hasty exit, thanking them all for their kindness over my shoulder.

It feels a bit like we're riding into a dream as we cross the lonely marshes, grasses whipping in the breeze, the only sound the mournful call of birds settling down to roost, and I'm relieved to finally see a sturdy-looking building on the horizon, though owner Nathalie tells us it's taken a lot of work to get the old barn that way. 'The first year was all mud,' she says, showing us a series of traumatic photos straight out of the *Grand Designs* living-in-a-caravan-on-a-building-site-with-a-small-child playbook, 'but I like … how do you say …? The wildness here.'

It is indeed a lovely spot if you haven't read *The Woman in Black*, and fortunately not so lonely that there isn't a fancy hotel restaurant a 15-minute pitch-black walk away, neatly saving us from a cosy night in the village with my helpful knights in shining armour. On a fine Saturday in May, it seems we're lucky to score a table at La Ferme des Mares with its immaculately gravelled courtyard and spotlit wisteria: thank God we've decided not to cycle, or we might have been forced to hide the bikes behind the row of shiny Range Rovers to avoid embarrassing ourselves.

The series of low-beamed dining rooms, with windows set in massive stone walls, are politely full, the tables spaced discreetly across a thick carpet, which contributes to the general hush. It all feels expensive (it is), and I'm firmly of the irresponsible mindset that if you're going to blow your budget, you may as well do so in style, which is why I immediately order the house aperitif, an amber flute of apple syrup, apple cider, apple brandy and a shot of apple and green walnut liqueur for good measure. As a statement of decadent intent, it's perfect: simultaneously sweet and tannic, fruity and a little bit nutty, and so very delicious with a bowl of papery-skinned roasted almonds that I almost forget about the menu, despite the fact that this hardback tome takes up half the table.

It kicks off with a list of suppliers and their distance from the restaurant, culminating in the jaunty humblebrag: 'not forgetting the slightly weird-looking vegetables from our vegetable garden – 0km!'

These, and others from further afield, are, I'm pleased to see, unusually abundant in the dishes that follow: my rabbit comes with two different preparations of the (locally) famous *carottes des sables*, grown in sand and fertilised with seaweed, which, along with a scattering of tiny green leaves, almost qualifies it as a salad in this part of the world. It's light, elegant and very tasty indeed: modern French cooking at its finest.

Light is all very well, of course, but being in Normandy, we can't bypass the cheese trolley – and what a feast of softly stinking delights glides over the plush in our direction, crowned by … it isn't, could it be …? '*Oui, c'est* CheDDAR!' our waiter announces proudly. I express surprise at finding this black-waxed interloper in one of France's great cheese-producing regions. '*Ah, mais monsieur le chef, il est anglais!*' he explains.

Certainly, the Cheddar has been hacked away at energetically for other diners this evening, but nevertheless, I stick to local boys Livarot, a sticky, spicy washed-rind cheese, creamy salty

Neufchâtel and an exceptionally powerful Camembert (my general tactic with a cheese trolley is to keep going until the curator starts to look anxious), all of which come in squidgy slabs, rather than slices. Not that I'm complaining.

A lesser person would have regretted also ordering dessert in advance, but not me: and I see away the *presqu'îles flottantes*, a big wobbly pile of beer-flavoured custard and caramel topped with snowy meringue, without even breaking a sweat. That said, the walk home, moon hanging high above huddled sheep, is silent. Both of us, perhaps, have reached our elastic limits.

Fortunately, we bounce back quickly, because the next morning Nathalie presents us with a breakfast of raw-milk Camembert from the next village ('It's the best around here'), toasted on nubbly brown homemade bread with a few slices of apple: I'll give it to the French, they really get behind their regional specialities.

Powered by cheese, it's a fast run down to Créances, home of all those sandy carrots (and a few leeks, too, if the enormous mosaic of them on a roundabout is to be believed), where we join the coast road, looking out over vast empty beaches and seas of wind-blown grass that remind me strongly of North Norfolk. There, the rush is to get a good spot outside the pub for a few pints of Wherry and some whitebait; here, I'm quietly nudging the pace to taste what it's claimed are the best moules frites in France. Not only is it a sunny Sunday, but it's slowly dawned on me through the drip feed of roadside advertising that it's Mothers' Day here, and if I were a Norman *maman*, I'd be dropping hints about this place from Boxing Day onwards.

The road narrows as we approach the spit of land on which La Cale perches, and suddenly every car that overtakes us feels like a potential rival. At 11.15 a.m., a time when I'd barely be thinking about a mid-morning coffee at home, the beach car park is almost full. I wonder how many of those loitering I could see off should it come to fisticuffs over the last table: a lot of them look quite old, and there's a fair smattering of infants, so I'm fairly confident of our chances. Perhaps, I think, if it comes to pleading our case, I could pretend to be Matt's mother.

The restaurant itself, still firmly shuttered, is a utilitarian shed of a place with a rickety collection of mismatched and largely unstable furniture outside. We retire to the café next door for a tense cup of coffee, interrupted when I spot someone emerge from La Cale with a cigarette. The veteran of a hundred 'no-reservations' London restaurant queues, I spring into action like a greased whippet, leaving Matt to pay up. Bursting through the doors, I ask one of the young men leaning casually against the counter if they're open, fumbling with the unfamiliar words in my nervousness. He looks startled. *'Oui, bien sûr, Madame!'*

I race out onto the sandy, and completely empty terrace, and fling myself dramatically over a table right on the edge of the beach, then semaphore frantically at Matt to make haste. After all this, it's somewhat embarrassing to discover there was no rush at all: though tables fill up quickly, no one else leaps across the decking as if fleeing from a fire and I suddenly feel a very long way from home.

Having ordered at the bar (underneath a cheerful sign assuring clients that all rats have passed a hygiene inspection), we can sit back and enjoy ourselves, making leisurely work of a cold beer and a dozen oysters between us. They're good, as oysters always are by the sea, plump and cool, with a marine tang answered by the air, but the real treat arrives afterwards: two huge pans of mussels in a heady, wine-soaked sauce with a great dollop of yellow crème fraîche left to melt on top.

The flesh is small and sweet, and we barely pause to pick at the hot crisp fries alongside. Perhaps it's also the location, seasoned by the wind sweeping off the beach, the smell of the lamb shoulder cooking on the wood fire inside, or the sense of satisfaction as latecomers hang around waiting disconsolately for a table, but I don't think I've ever tasted mussels so good. Here's a recipe anyway:

Moules Marinières

Such a simple dish, but such a delicious one, with the added theatre of the whole shelling operation, which I never tire of. I like to use Norman cider and drink the rest with it, but if you prefer, you can use a dry white wine as at La Cale. Chunks of baguette or (or preferably and) hot salty fries to mop up the liquid are, however, mandatory.

Serves 2
1kg mussels
4 long shallots, finely chopped
300ml dry cider or white wine, e.g. Muscadet
50g crème fraîche
A small bunch of flat-leaf parsley, finely chopped
Baguette or chips, to serve (or both)

1 Rinse the mussels in cold running water, then give them a good scrub and scrape to remove any barnacles or dirt. Discard any with broken shells, and give any open ones a sharp tap: if they don't close, throw them away too. Pull out the beards – the fibrous little appendages which the mussels use to attach themselves to ropes or rocks – by pulling them sharply towards the hinge end of the mussel. If you want to prep them ahead, leave them in a sink of cold water until ready to cook.

2 Put the chopped shallots and the cider or wine into a large pan and cook gently for 10 minutes, then turn up the heat to medium-high.

3 Drain the mussels and tip into the pan. Cover and cook until most of them have opened: about 3 minutes.

4 Add the crème fraîche and put the lid back on for 30 seconds to allow it to melt. Add the parsley and shake the pan well to distribute, then season gently and serve immediately, discarding any mussels which remain closed.

Matt professes himself defeated by this point, but having spotted the children on the table next door chasing their oysters down with bowls of the mysterious orange dessert from the market in Cherbourg, I remember some unfinished business. Teurgoule, the man behind the bar tells me, means 'twisted mouth' – he purses his lips like a baby given a lemon – in Norman dialect, 'because it's very spicy!' What arrives is a very slow-cooked rice pudding coloured with liberal amounts of cinnamon and nutmeg that sits like a stone in my stomach all afternoon. It's too delicious to leave, however, and La Cale's owner Remi, who lives up gratifyingly to his eccentric TripAdvisor reputation, is visibly impressed by my greed. 'Welcome the English!' he shouts happily as he threads his way among the tangle of tables. 'We love you!' On the way out of the car park, I notice he's not joking: La Cale's van, a huge battered Renault, has been graffitied with the legend 'Rosbeefs welcome ... Frogs too'.

The afternoon continues to heat up as we turn in from the coast, and there's a lot of ground to cover after a relatively leisurely morning. I've already warned Matt that our destination for the evening is up a huge and sadly unavoidable hill, hoping the unbeatable views of the majestic Mont-Saint-Michel will soften the blow, but along the way there are other, unannounced hillocks that Google has hidden from me, and about four o'clock, he screeches to an emergency stop in a small town. 'I need a drink,' he says firmly and, like a homing pigeon, heads to the nearest bar.

While I vainly try to prop the ungainly Eddy upright against a house, he tosses his gloves and helmet onto a nearby table and goes in to order. I seat myself and regard the woman boldly doing justice to a large glass of red in the 30°C heat. So French, I think admiringly – so I'm startled when her husband comes back with a beer and broad Kent accent.

Two days away from home, and I can't resist striking up a conversation with my long-lost countrymen; turns out they've been here over a decade, and have no plans to return to the UK, though their older daughter is about to move back because she can't find work. I ask, in what I hope is a neutral tone, if the prospect of Brexit in less than 12 months' time worries them. 'No,' the lady says, with commendable sanguinity, 'we don't hear much about it here. I suppose it will be okay.'

They're more anxious about us getting run over by what they call 'milk floats' – the tiny, whining *voiturettes* you can drive in France without a licence, making them, they claim, popular with those banned for drink driving. 'They're lethal, those things,' she tells me as we leave. 'Watch your back.'

This slightly sinister warning, as well as a vast, bloated dead cow I spot out of the corner of my eye as I roll past a farmyard on the outskirts of town, make me feel quite nervous and when I lose Matt on a long climb shortly afterwards, I become positively paranoid. Just as I'm about to turn around to see if he's been flattened by a drunkard on a milk float, he comes round the corner looking a bit pink, and asks, very politely, how many more mountains we have to climb before the big one. I have to confess I have no idea, but there's certainly no mistaking the thing when we finally reach it: Avranches is a very pretty town, if you don't mind heights.

The road in winds up round the lower suburbs like a snake, though this gradient is at least preferable to the shortcuts Google Maps keeps trying to divert me onto, all of which appear near vertical. When I finally make it to our budget hotel, I'm puce, and there's no sign of Matt. 'Do you have a bar?' I ask Madame, sweating onto her registration forms. She looks genuinely apologetic as she shakes her head, so I head upstairs for a cold shower instead.

Somewhat revived, I look out of the window to check Eddy is still in the courtyard three storeys below, and see Matt sitting on the terrace sipping a large glass of orange juice and looking rather pink. 'She just offered it to me,' he shouts up in response to my aggrieved question. 'I think she went to get it from her own kitchen. I must have looked like I was having a heart attack.'

In the circumstances, it seems wise to head no further than the café across the square lest we lose even an inch of gradient before dinner. I happily put away yet more potatoey pizza, and Matt polishes off not only a sausage version, but a big bowl of 'pasta General Patton', named after the leader of the US liberating forces in 1944, which might also explain, now I come to think of it, the large tank parked up on the roundabout opposite our table. With a fair quantity of carb to walk off, we stroll through the town to try to find that famous view of Mont-Saint-Michel before the sun goes down.

As it sinks lower in the sky, almost bouncing against the horizon, we force our protesting legs into a final dash through the botanic gardens, tripping over bits of ancient stonework in our hurry, and just manage to catch a glimpse of the celebrity island across the bay before it disappears into the darkness. The sea is silvery under an apricot sky, and from here, on the edge of Normandy, we can see the Breton coast stretching away westwards in the sunset.

Give or take the odd farmhouse, it's a landscape that doesn't look much like it's changed in centuries. 'Nice and flat anyway,' says Matt with some satisfaction as we turn for home.

Km: 157.5

Croissants: 0 (Camembert on toast not a bad substitute, though)

High: Moules frites

Low: Thinking Matt had been squashed by a milk float

STAGE 3

AVRANCHES TO DOL-DE-BRETAGNE

Omelette Soufflée

The omelette is an ancient dish, known and loved long before Mont-Saint-Michel was even a twinkle in a monkish eye, but the island has been famous for 'the exquisite lightness and beauty' of its version for over a century. These are not the creamy baveuse omelettes of classical French cookery, but puffy soufflés, whipped until they rear from the pan like sea foam, and finished over a wood fire with copious amounts of Norman butter.

One of the benefits of staying at the top of a huge hill, of course, becomes evident the next morning, when we speed out of town like racing demons, Matt shooting past too fast for me to see the smile on his face. We've already learnt one valuable lesson today: many things in France, including, incredibly, boulangeries that even open on Christmas morning, are closed on Mondays (see page 95, *Pause-Café – French Opening Hours*). How I've never realised this before is unclear, but after wandering disconsolately around the shuttered streets for half an hour, we finally spot a man with a baguette under his arm and sprint to catch up. My reward for accosting a complete stranger in a foreign language before I've had so much as a coffee: a pretty decent, very flaky 8/10 croissant. Coffee, however, remains a distant dream.

After crossing the handsome stone bridge at Pontaubault where we finally wave goodbye to the Cotentin Peninsula, the road swings right and climbs briefly out of town before dropping abruptly down into the bay of Mont-Saint-Michel. Suddenly we find ourselves pedalling into a sea mist; the only sounds the plaintive bleating of sheep somewhere to our left and, briefly, the hullabaloo of a convoy of Americans on hire bikes too busy complaining about their 'sore asses' to greet us as they pass. As the sound of their protests recedes into the gloom, and I shrug on my jacket for the first time, things begin to feel a little bit creepy.

On the plus side, when the Mont does finally show itself to us, it seems gratifyingly close – until we notice the cycle route sign: 17km. 'Hang on a minute,' Matt calls to me. 'Didn't that last road say it was only 9km?' I check my phone, still wobbling slightly every time I take my hands from the bars of my poor, overladen steed. 'Yeah … I think possibly the cycle one takes the scenic route.' There's a short but loaded silence from behind, then, 'How scenic?'

He has a point: for all the Dutch caravans and British estate cars, these are hardly superhighways winding us through the polders, and I've made our lunch reservation on the Mont stupidly early for reasons I can't now remember, so we're easily persuaded off the bike route and on to the main road, which takes us past an enormous fragrant *biscuiterie* churning out delicious buttery galettes. Sadly, there's no time to stop and investigate the factory gift shop; I content myself with breathing in deeply instead.

Several kilometres from the island itself the road comes to an abrupt end in north-west France's largest car park. Once upon a time you could drive right up to the foot of the rock at low tide, and chance your vehicle being washed into the great beyond if you lingered too long over the postcards (indeed, as we discover later, there's still some very entertaining footage of exactly this online). These days, you have to park on the mainland and take a shuttle bus across the sands: visitors are allowed to cycle the 800-metre causeway before 10 a.m., but as you can't leave your bike at the other end it's a largely pointless exercise unless you're desperate to add another couple of kilometres to the day's total, and we're too late anyway, so we ditch them in the parking area, lugging our bags with us as the lockers are out of action 'due to high security level'.

Though the bike racks may be quiet, the bus is busy, and we cram on behind a great muscular man with a shih tzu in a rucksack, who tuts every time anyone inadvertently brushes against the dog, which, thanks to the density of humanity on board, is fairly often. I stack my mysteriously weighty panniers on my foot, hold on and pray that the bus moves swiftly, which of course it doesn't, stopping almost immediately at the row of rapacious gift shops a few hundred metres from the visitor centre, where more people attempt to squash in. It's amazing, I think, how quickly even a regular passenger on the Northern Line can get used to the glorious space and solitude of the open road.

The shuttle doesn't take us all the whole way to the Mont; it stops some distance from it, allowing everyone to rush over to the railings for snaps with the most famous island in France, a fortress that repelled every invasion attempt during the Hundred Years War with England. How things change; outside Paris, Mont-Saint-Michel is the most-visited site in the country.

Much as I love watching people pose for selfies, we're in a hurry, surging forward through the great stone arch at the vanguard of this particular wave of heathen marauders. The restaurant, La Mère Poulard, is easy to spot, thanks to the crowd standing outside with cameras, snapping the action in the open kitchen, where huge numbers of eggs are being beaten in copper bowls ready for the lunchtime rush.

This place has been known for its omelettes for over a century: the eponymous Mère Poulard set up shop cooking for pilgrims and tourists in the late 1800s, and gained a reputation for her omelettes in particular – an easy thing to put together on an island with no grazing or agricultural land. The hotel she ran with her husband, in a prime position just inside the gates, was perfectly placed to take advantage of the tourist boom, and her dining room was soon mentioned as a must-visit in contemporary travel guides (as, in fact, was the rival establishment run by her brother-in-law, though clearly he was less good at marketing).

Poulard is said to have ruled her establishment with an iron whisk: when King Leopold of Belgium demanded to eat outside, on a terrace reserved for the taking of coffee, he was apparently given short shrift by Madame. She must have been a tartar in the kitchen, too, because those omelettes look like bloody hard work. The recipe is a closely guarded secret; despite my best efforts in wheedling French, all I can get out of the wolfish young chef closest to me is that he has to beat the mixture for 15 minutes before it's ready. He winks – I'd make a joke about his wrist action if only I could remember the vocab.

Hanging around for slightly longer than feels entirely polite, I watch the process with a keen eye, taking notes as the team beat out a syncopated rhythm with their whisks. Each long-handled pan is heated in front of the massive fireplace until the butter inside sizzles, before the well-whisked mixture is added and the pan stacked neatly on a shelf at the side of the hearth. Once the omelette is cooked, it's briefly toasted in the flames, and then served immediately.

Having apparently learnt all that there is to be learnt from the tight-lipped staff, and shortly before someone calls security, I make my way up to the slightly sepulchral dining room, where Matt is sitting reading *The Times* in the company of a pair of Korean girls charging their phones on the table, a family of voluble Italians and a grumpy British couple who look like they'd dearly like to ask him for the features section. Almost every inch of wall is covered with photographs of grandees who have been lucky enough to feast on the famous Poulard hospitality, ranging from Trotsky to Marilyn Monroe and Margaret Thatcher, who came as a guest of President Mitterand, apparently to 'discuss the problems of the world over a good omelette' – one hopes they weren't served by the same rather pungent waiter that we've been assigned by the deliciously superior maître d'. 'I wouldn't mind,' Matt says in a manner that suggests that even if he did he'd be too well mannered to say so, 'but at this time of day surely it must be the beginning of his shift.' I'm just glad he smells worse than us, I say.

I open the menu and confirm what I already know: that at €34 this omelette is to be the single most expensive dish I will eat on my entire trip, and that includes a Michelin-starred birthday treat a month from now. (The price makes the three-course menu at €48 feel like a bargain, just as it's designed to, though in fact I probably don't need a poached egg and samphire salad and a frozen Calvados soufflé to push my egg consumption for the day into the danger zone.)

The American journalist and gourmand Waverley Root, recalling the 'luscious omelettes' of 1920s Normandy in his classic work *The Food of France*, feels confident enough to recommend the Mère Poulard version 30 years later, 'providing that the passage of time and of a good many thousand tourists has not wrought havoc on it'.

I can confirm that, almost a century later, mass production does not seem to have been to the detriment of quality. I suspect price inflation has been disproportionate, yet given the criminal mark-up, it's disappointingly delicious. The outer shell is almost leathery, in pleasurable contrast to the moussey interior, and gilded with salty, slightly burnt butter – it's almost like an American-style half-moon breakfast omelette rather than the classic runny French cigar, but stuffed with an egg-white foam rather than gooey cheese. A dish of potatoes and bacon fried in lard arrives on the side; for a few euros more I could have had scallops or foie gras instead, but, really, there are limits. My advice is, go to Mont-Saint-Michel, watch the spectacle, then go home and make one yourself.

Omelette Soufflée à la Mère Poularde

For all its carefully cultivated mystique, the world's most famous omelette is surprisingly easy to reproduce – all you need is a bit of elbow grease (or an electric whisk). I haven't suggested any fillings, as adding extra ingredients to the pan will knock the air out of the eggs, but a few chopped herbs on top are very welcome, and you can serve fried potatoes and cured ham, or sautéed mushrooms, or indeed foie gras if you must, on the side. I tried finishing it under the grill, to replicate the flashing of the pan through the fire, but concluded this was just for show, though if you want to get the blowtorch out, be my guest.

Per omelette
3 eggs
A pinch of salt
Oil, to grease
Generous 1 tbsp cold butter, cut into small dice

1 Crack the eggs into a large bowl with the salt, and begin whisking vigorously. Once they're fairly foamy, oil a heavy-based frying pan about 20cm wide and put it on a medium heat.

2 Keep whisking the eggs until they're very thick and bubbly, almost like a mousse. This will probably take just under 4 minutes with a hand whisk

3 Pour the mixture into the pan and leave to set until it begins to come away from the side of the pan, then gently loosen the edges with a spatula and slide the butter underneath, shaking to distribute it evenly beneath the omelette.

4 Once it's deep golden underneath but still foamy and wet above, carefully shake it on to a plate, fold over and serve immediately.

Almost €150 lighter, we stagger down the stairs with our panniers, the elegant maître d's eyes sliding tactfully away from us as we lurch in his rarefied direction, and attack the Mont proper, which is, even on a Monday afternoon in May, fairly swarming with visitors. The single street is one long gift shop, and it's a relief to pay the entrance fee for the abbey simply to shake off a few school parties – the man doing the bag search is all smiles when I explain we're cyclists, and lets us go through with our massive burdens, despite their bulk being in clear violation of the security regulations (to say nothing of the deadly salami slicer at the bottom of mine).

With such a burden, it makes sense to take turns in the church; I stand outside, enjoying the sea breeze and the relative peace and watching groups of excited human ants racing round on the treacherous sands below. Next to me, a British woman tells children more concerned with chasing seagulls that 'apparently the thing to do with quicksand is not to panic and try to move – it agitates the sand and turns it liquid so it sucks you down'. Clearly the ants didn't get that particular memo, I think, half hoping for a minor emergency to brighten the view. Suddenly an incongruous crocodile of heavily armed policeman, clad in what appears to be riot gear, march through the gardens beneath the wall on which I'm leaning. Be careful what you wish for, I think with a shiver, remembering the earlier warning about elevated security levels.

At that moment, Matt reappears blinking into the sunlight to rescue me from my morbid thoughts, and I slip into the abbey. I have a bit of a thing for monastic architecture (why, since you ask, I do have a favourite: the lovely light-filled Cistercian Abbaye du Thoronet in Provence), and this place delivers in spades, particularly in the quieter nooks and crannies, like the draughty room in the cliffside once reserved for the laying out of dead monks. I close my eyes and try to imagine the gloomy scene; the stinking guttering candles, hooded figures and howling winds. Above a child wails, 'Bird BIT ME!' The moment is lost. Time to go.

As we break free from the mercenary Mont without so much as a commemorative fridge magnet between us, clouds begin to gather above, and by the time we're back at the bikes, it's ominously dark. It's not far to Dol-de-Bretagne, our ultimate destination, barely 30km in fact, but shortly after leaving

Normandy, and well before we get there, the heavens open to discharge rain so hard and all encompassing that we're forced to seek refuge in a handily placed bus shelter until it slackens off. Parents waiting for the school bus in their warm, dry cars watch us watching the rain, and for the first time I wish I wasn't on a stupid bike. It certainly won't be the last.

Finally, we tell ourselves it's definitely getting lighter on the horizon and push off miserably into a road already lit for evening at 5 p.m. in the dying days of May, arriving in Dol-de-Bretagne damp rather than actively dripping, though clearly still a sufficiently tragic sight to merit the sympathetic offer of a hot coffee as we check in. Though our beds for the night are considerably cheaper than our lunch, the hostel is a sweet place: new and clean and cleverly designed, and Matt is even kind enough to let me have the top bunk, which immediately puts me in a good mood. If there's an age when you grow out of the thrill of sleeping near ceilings, I'm still waiting to reach it.

I duck into reception to ask about food. There's a terrifying pause as the staff confer, and then I hear the glorious word crêperie: ideal, given this is Matt's first and last night in Brittany. Monsieur is even kind enough to ring to check they're open on a Monday evening – 'you must hurry; they are open, but it is quiet, so they want to close soon'. In fact, once installed in the cosily lit, low-beamed dining room with the customary bowl of cider in front of us ('Are you sure we're meant to be drinking out of these?'), we prove to be quite the trendsetters, and thanks to the crowd that pour in after us, the poor proprietors of Le Dol'Mène aux Saveurs don't get their early night after all.

I order a galette with cheese, ham, egg (another egg! I think belatedly – why do I do this to myself?) and a local speciality, the andouille de Guémené, a sausage made from 25 layers of intestine and stomach, smoked, yet not sufficiently to mask the odour of its main ingredient. It looks strangely beautiful, like an optical illusion made from offal, but tastes more challenging – and I'm keen for Matt to at least smell it before he goes home.

He's not exactly effusive, but actually, fried until crisp, these andouilles are markedly more pleasant than my previous experience of them cold from the butchers, and they certainly don't dent my appetite for a sweet crêpe with apples and the famous Breton salted caramel sauce. Matt goes for one flambéed at the table with booze poured from a little copper pan, which embarrasses him no end to my actual and lasting delight, and we celebrate with a glass of cider brandy before wobbling back through Dol's charming half-timbered, solid little main street, with its medieval houses and plaques proudly celebrating the town's unlikely links to the Scottish House of Stewart. Haggis crêpes, there's an idea, I think as I fall asleep with my nose pressed up against the ceiling.

Km: 48.4

Croissants: 1 (8/10, flaky)

High: Jiggling the world's most expensive omelette like a comedy jelly

Low: The pouring rain

STAGE 4

DOL-DE-BRETAGNE TO SAINT-MALO

A Platter of Oysters

Oysters need little introduction, save to say that Brittany produces some exceptionally fine examples, which are best – as with all oysters in my opinion – served naked or perhaps with the merest dribble of shallot vinaigrette, preferably within sight of the salty waters from whence they came.

The next morning brings two excitements. Firstly, it's Matt's last day, a terrifying fact that I'm trying to avoid staring full in the face, and secondly, this comes just as he's proved himself indispensable with the information that there's a drive-through boulangerie round the corner. A DRIVE-THROUGH boulangerie. I literally could not be more thrilled if he'd added they were giving out free croissants.

The reality is even more perfect than I'd imagined: as a former petrol station repurposed to dispense human fuel, it even looks the part. Obviously I make Matt hang back to take a photo as I pedal up to the window. The girl serving seems amused to see me pop up in front of her: 'No, we don't get very many bikes!' she says cheerfully, handing over the goods for me to clutch awkwardly in one hand while steering with the other. Matt and I reconvene on the forecourt as a huge dog in the car behind actually attempts to climb over its owner and through the hatch: my croissant is a bit burnt, but I have absolutely no regrets – 10/10 for both novelty and practicality (and 7/10 for the actual goods).

That said, Matt's imminent departure seems a fair excuse for a second crack at a final breakfast, especially when we pass a boulangerie whose window proudly displays golden laurels for baking the second-best *baguette tradition* (see page 147, *Pause-Café – French Bread: A Bluffer's Guide*) in all of Brittany. Their croissant isn't bad either (7.5, well flavoured, let down by a slight sponginess in the middle), but it's overshadowed by my impulse purchase: a golden *kouign-amann* apiece, sporting a jaunty Breton flag, which I immediately stick on my handlebars.

If I think too hard about the 30-odd years of my life spent in ignorance of these unassuming-looking pastries, I start to feel a bit sad; like a sweeter, crunchier version of the best croissant you've ever eaten, soaked in buttery syrup and baked until crisp, they're incredibly rich and stupidly delicious, and I can't in all conscience let Matt leave Brittany without trying one. Even I struggle after two croissants, however, and the second half of the little cake ends up in the bag on my handlebars for later – something that will happen so often in the weeks to come I'm surprised I don't have a fully-formed bread-and-butter pudding in there by the time I get to Paris.

On the way out of Dol, wobbling through pretty but uncomfortably cobbled streets, we pass a huge cathedral with a tower that looks like it's been abruptly snapped off. Actually, as I discover from the information boards with which Dol is well furnished, it was never finished, due to 'insufficient funds' (or the devil throwing an enormous menhir in the works, depending on whose version you believe). The unexpected grandeur of the church is explained by the fact that, until drainage work took place in the 11th century, the sea reached as far as Dol-de-Bretagne, making this morning's route a ghostly seabed.

Having undergone serious adjustment at the hands of the hostel receptionist, who refuses to check us out until he's politely pooh-poohed my plans, this meanders towards the modern coast by way of Mont Dol, which, at 65 metres tall, counts as a significant peak in this part of the world. Indeed, once upon a time it was an island, just like Mont-Saint-Michel. Apparently, St Michael, patron saint of France as well as sensible knitwear, fought a duel with Satan at the top, but Matt doesn't show much enthusiasm for climbing it to see the 'certain curious marks' the battle left in the rock, so we leave it be and head for the sea instead.

The D155 is one of those glorious roads that spools out in front of your wheel, allowing you to see exactly where you're heading for miles before you get there, lined on one side with squat granite houses staring out across the marshes and clusters of corrugated sheds advertising '*creuses de Cancale: vente au detail*' (*creuses*, or hollow oysters, being the French name for what we call rock oysters).

The air is heavy with the iodine reek of shellfish, whetting my appetite for what I hope lies ahead of us in Cancale, known across France as the oyster capital of Brittany – though first we have to contend with one of Google Maps' helpful cycle routes, which takes us up a road at first stony, and then muddy, and finally all but impassable on a delicate beast like Eddy, whose mudguards quickly fill up with the stuff. Eventually I have to get off and push before I'm thrown off like a questing knight who has finally pushed his patient steed too far.

Though I haven't got round to mentioning it to Matt, I've plotted a course that just happens to pass right by La Ferme Marine de Cancale, which, its website promises, offers 'a fantastic one-hour-and-a-half tour!' Fortunately, it's well signposted from the road, allowing me to discover it with delighted surprise, a surprise that becomes all too real when I learn that it's closed, so instead of prying into 'the secrets of the oysters', we pedal on to the town of Cancale proper, and the not-so-secret oyster market at the end of the harbour ('#1 of 11 things to do in Cancale!'). The wide road along the bay is fringed with seafood restaurants gearing up for the Tuesday lunchtime trickle, culminating in the market, a clutch of striped tents above the concrete slipway, facing inwards against the wind.

PAUSE-CAFÉ – The Mysterious Fruits of the Sea

For some reason, this is the kind of vocabulary that runs in one ear and out of the other like the tide – possibly because I'm not quite sure what the name for all those little shells is in English, let alone French. Here's a crib sheet:

Coquillages – seafood
Moules – mussels
Huîtres – oysters (*creuses* are rock oysters, *plates* what we know
   as natives, the flatter, rounder shells that aficionados believe
   to boast a sweeter, more complex flavour than cheaper,
   pointier rocks)
Bulots – whelks

Bigorneaux – winkles

Coques – cockles (*amande de mer* is a common variety known in
   English as a dog cockle, though disappointingly it bears
   little resemblance to either a dog or an almond)

Crevettes – prawns (*géante tigrée* or *gambas* suggests the larger
   variety, *crevette rose* are average-sized North Atlantic prawns)

Crevettes gris – shrimps

Langoustine – Dublin Bay prawn (like a little lobster)

Palourdes – clams

Couteaux – razor clams

Homard – lobster

Crabe tourteau – brown crab (sometimes just listed as *tourteau*)

Araignée de mer – spider crab

Crabe mou – soft shell crab

Their custodians loiter in front, waiting for customers. I experience the same mild panic as when confronted by a weighty wine
list in a smart restaurant – how on earth is one supposed to
choose between baskets of bivalves? I do a slow circuit of the
stalls, trying hard, like everyone else, to look like I know what
I'm doing, and end up back at Aux Délices de Cancale, run by
two brothers, Fabien et Gildas Barbé, attracted not by the subtle
curve of the shells on display, or the quality of their barnacle
build-up, but by the fact that they have the largest oysters I have
ever seen, propped out front to draw in the kind of shallow
people impressed by size. People like me, in fact.

I go for half a dozen ordinary number 4s (they're graded by
size, from fat 00s to tiny 6s, and in general, I think smaller shellfish have a better flavour) and one complete beast of a *pied de
cheval*, or horse's hoof. Come on, it had to be done!

People gather round murmuring in wonderment as the stall-holder, who has opened the others as easily as a can of Coke, braces Monsieur Big against the back wall and sets about him with a chisel. 'How old is he?' I ask as he hammers away with gritted teeth. 'Oh, about 15.' Fifteen! I think. That's the same age as my oldest nephew! When this animal was born (spawned?) I still naively thought I was going to have a proper job by 30.

Holding his prize carefully lest it spill out, Gildas, victorious over the shellfish at last, explains that the creature weighs about 180g, well over twice as much as the others, and will need to be tackled with a special knife, which he will lend me for the purpose. The assembled crowd goggles as I escort my victim over to the sea wall, where Matt is already sitting with his slightly more modest order. He raises one eyebrow, which in Matt terms is pretty serious stuff, and don't I know it. I like oysters you can eat in one gulp, that are easy to chew and slip down as smoothly as an ice-cold martini, not ones with the strength to fight back in your digestive system. Nevertheless, I've paid to have this chap's shell wrenched off, and he deserves to be done justice, if you count being eaten alive as justice, though now definitely isn't the time to go into that particular argument.

I unfold the sturdy knife Gildas has provided and nervously begin to divide the creature into vaguely edible portions, silently begging for forgiveness as I perform this gruesome but neces-sary live butchery, and then, conscious of the expectant gaze of not just Matt, but several other diners, tip the first chunk into my mouth and begin to chew. It's better than I expect, more scallopy, but with a definite meaty texture, and a surprisingly harsh, almost tannic finish. Not unpleasant exactly, but for reasons as much psychological as gastronomic, I can't say I enjoy the remaining four bits. After a bit of a breather (if only I'd known you could buy chilled wine to take away at the shop round the corner), I tackle his smaller, sweeter relatives, who prove far more to my taste, though frankly, once the last shell is tossed onto the beach below, joining the thousands already piled up there, I feel I wouldn't be sorry not to see an oyster again for a good while.

A Platter of Oysters

Though fun to order in restaurants for the sheer decadence of it, it's far better value to eat oysters at home – they're not expensive. I like natives, which have a slightly sweeter, more complex flavour, but rocks are cheaper, and almost as good.

As many oysters as you feel you can eat (3 per person as an
  amuse-bouche, 6 for a starter, between you and your god for
  a feast)
2 banana shallots
100ml red wine vinegar
1 lemon per dozen oysters
Very thinly sliced brown bread, spread with unsalted butter
  and cut into decorous triangles

1 Keep the oysters, flat side up and tightly wrapped in damp newspaper, in the salad drawer of your fridge (between 1° and 4°C), refreshing the newspaper every couple of days as it dries out. In theory they'll be fine for 10 days, but the longer you leave them, the greater risk you'll have to chuck out some dead ones, so I'd advise eating them as soon as possible.
2 When you're ready to shuck them, if this is your first time, I'd highly advise watching a video online if possible. A stout

oyster knife will make life easier too. Wrap the oyster firmly in a damp tea-towel, as much to protect your hands as to provide a firm grip, then gently insert the tip of the knife into the hinge at the pointy end of the shell. Slowly work it in, twisting it slightly, until you hear the shell pop. Remove the top shell, cutting away at the oyster if it sticks, then slide the knife underneath its body to detach it from the bottom. Carefully place it on a platter, making sure not to spill any juices – if you're feeling fancy, the oysters look lovely on crushed ice, which seems less wasteful than rock salt.

3 To make the shallot vinaigrette, peel and finely chop the shallots and put them into a small bowl. Pour in the vinegar and season well with freshly ground black pepper (no need to add salt, the oysters will supply plenty). Cut the lemon into wedges and serve with the oysters, with the bread on the side (don't forget a little spoon for the vinaigrette, and somewhere for people to put the oyster and lemon shells if they're not sitting down).

We sit in the sun, quietly digesting, trying not to think of the bivalves splashing about inside, and watch the bustle on the beach below, which is less of a place for sunbathing and sandcastles, and more a giant oyster factory – long, low racks stretch right down to the low tide mark, laden with huge wire bags of bivalves. Workers in waders rolled down to their waists in the sunshine wander among them, turning the odd bag and loading a few that have clearly passed some mysterious test onto the tractors that chug in a steady train down the slipway behind us – one flops off onto the road with a great jolt, and a chino-clad tourist runs to the driver's aid. His spectacular failure to even get the bag off the ground, and the nonchalance with which she picks it up and tosses it back onto the trailer, have us cheering like a seaside Punch and Judy show.

In fact, all this activity proves sufficiently fascinating to persuade Matt to cycle back to check on the museum before we head on to Saint-Malo – at which point it begins to rain, and not just rain, but pour. Shoving our bikes hastily behind an abandoned boat, we rush in the direction of the entrance, only to find it still locked up. When I eventually locate a living being in a shed nearby, she tells me, and a vexed-looking French couple who have followed me in, that they're not actually opening for another 30 minutes. The French observe this is not what's printed on the board outside. She happily agrees it isn't

The terror of missing out on the opportunity to get better acquainted with the many creatures currently dying a horrible death in my stomach must show on my face, because Madame suddenly relents and offers to let us into the museum early instead. I'm delighted: not only will this offer entertainment (though, given that it turns out to be largely devoted to a collection of seashells from around the globe, it doesn't actually provide very much of that), but it's warm and dry, too. Perfect.

Once we've exhausted the gruesomely detailed biological diagrams of the oyster and mussel, both of which make me heartily regret my dietary choices over the last 24 hours, we stand and watch the rain until a sufficiently large number of pensioners in sensible waterproof clothing have gathered to make a tour. This begins with a lengthy video in French, during which I think I learn that the bay of Mont-Saint-Michel produces about 15,000 tonnes of oysters a year. Their superior quality is attributed to the dramatic tides, which work the muscle holding the shells shut, rather like one of those electric six-pack machines advertised on daytime television: 'Strong muscles are important,' the narrator explains 'as they might be in transit for up to three days if they're destined for Japanese tables.' Things could have turned out worse for my 15-year-old, all things considered.

I read on the way out that oysters are 'your best friends if you are slimming ... the queen of all diets, with only 70 calories per 100g'. So French.

Outside, the rain losing heart now, we squelch down to the shoreline to peer at the racks in the distance, where bags of tiny oysters grow into adults, helped by the farmers, who regularly turn and move them to more spacious accommodation to encourage expansion. Once they're big enough for sale, the oysters are brought up to spend a week or so in an oxygenated, temperature-controlled tank (5–8°C is apparently optimal) to ensure they're in tip-top health before they're sorted, with workers weighing each shell in their hands to check they're heavy, and thus full of water – any suspiciously light ones are discarded as probably dead.

'In the run-up to Christmas, we employ 69 people here, and they grade 1,800 an hour,' our guide explains, 'so they don't have much time to chat.' Matt shoots me a meaningful look as the party moves on to the climax of the tour: the *dégustation*, the oysters already laid out on long tables for our gustatory pleasure. Frankly, I'm relieved to make our excuses and hurry off, though Madame is shocked that we'll miss the best bit. '*Ah, les fous Anglais,*' I imagine her muttering as we hastily exit through the gift shop, but I'm content to live up to the national stereotype if it means I don't have to look another oyster in the frilly gills for a day or so.

Though his check-in opens in half an hour, and we're still 15km away from the port, Matt confidently assures me as we unlock our sodden steeds that his ship doesn't actually sail for hours, so until Google Maps sends us down the side of a farmer's field with mud as deep as our pedals, we make a fairly leisurely pace west.

Fortunately, once we divert on to the main road my phone is so keen to avoid, it's a fast run into Saint-Malo, although the town sprawls wider than I remember, and the ferry terminal sits bleakly, in the manner of such places, on a dual carriageway with nowhere for a farewell drink but a warehouse advertising cheap crates of beer to British booze cruisers. For the last time, I give thanks for my companion's unerring nose for 'just a quick one', which leads us up the hill to the distinctly un-Gallic Cunningham's Bar from where we can enjoy the sight of Matt's boat patiently waiting for him as we raise a cider to my continuing adventures.

When the funnel begins to smoke, I reluctantly suggest we should probably make a move and insist on chaperoning him all the way to the ticket gates, more for my benefit than his. As he disappears cheerily through them on his way to that much-anticipated buffet, I feel cast adrift like a tiny oyster larvae floating free in the bay. Here I am, on my own, in a strange place, not knowing where I'm going to stay or eat tonight, and a whole month stretching terrifyingly ahead of me. Well, nearly alone. I still have that *pied de cheval* to keep me company.

Km: 51.8

Croissants: 2 (average score, 7.25/10)

High: The *kouign-amman*

Low: The final bite of that massive oyster

STAGE 5
SAINT-MALO TO REDON

Crêpes Complètes

Buckwheat crêpes were once the bread of Brittany, a region too poor
and damp to support much in the way of wheat cultivation.
Indeed, Anne Willan claims in her excellent guide French
Regional Cooking *that they formed the basis of whole meals,*
starting with yesterday's crumbled into soup, followed by a main
course of fresh pancakes spread with salted butter, and concluding
with a second filled with butter and sugar or jam. They remain
incredibly popular, though buckwheat is now generally saved for
savoury dishes: look out for the galette-saucisse, the Breton
equivalent of a hot dog, at markets throughout the region.

It feels weird not to have someone behind me as I pedal
towards my first campsite; terrifying yet also strangely exhil-
arating. If the last five days have been half-holiday, a gradual
easing into this new normality, then the tour proper starts now
– and a wet evening in a tent feels like an appropriate baptism
of fire, or damp squib, depending on your perspective.

Riding past Bernard Hinault's son's bike shop, which saved
my silly bacon in 2016, when I'd brought a bike with no func-
tioning brakes on a cycling holiday, I thank God I have no need

of it today. I do, however, need somewhere to lay my head before the rain starts again.

Saint-Malo's municipal campsite may be some way outside the city limits, but to my relief it is at least open, something not entirely clear from its website. The nice chap behind the desk, visibly surprised at a lone female camper, directs me to 'a very quiet' pitch behind a hedge, among the trees, which is kind of him, except, as I realise when I get there, it's overrun with mosquitoes and separated from the rest of the site by a small but significant bog. No matter. I open the pannier with the camping stuff in it for the first time since KnifeGate at Portsmouth, and merrily tip the contents out on the wet grass. Rookie error, but I'm so proud that it only takes me 10 minutes to pitch my tiny tent that I promptly message last summer's touring buddies to tell them so. 'Challenge: down to 8 mins in a week,' one of them responds immediately. Tough crowd.

As it's raining again, I repair to the *bloc sanitaire* to wash almost everything I own, and in the meantime, perch stylishly on a plastic chair in nothing but a waterproof jacket and towel, taking advantage of the warmth and free electricity offered by an unplugged* tumble drier to try to plan ahead. There's nothing to eat on site, and the huge oyster is still making itself comfortable in my stomach, so I end up spending about three hours in there, squinting at train timetables and maps, before finally dousing myself in mosquito repellent and taking my bundle of clean laundry to bed. It occurs to me as I lie there in the dark that perhaps a secluded corner of the campsite is not the best place for a single woman to pass the night, but to be honest, I'm too sleepy to care.

Something I'd conveniently forgotten about camping, though, is that however tired you are, the local birds will still be

---

* By me, obviously.

up with the lark. In fact, given the noise they make from 5 a.m. onwards, possibly they are all larks – in any case, my bijou residence, which has in the past been unkindly compared to a body bag, isn't really somewhere for a luxuriant lie-in, so after taking at least three times as long to strike camp as to set it, and allowing myself five minutes to sit on a pannier and eat the other half of yesterday's *kouign-amann*, I make my way back to Saint-Malo, where I have a reservation on my first train of the trip to Finistère, home to the best crêperie in Brittany, and thus France, and so, I think it's fairly safe to say, the world.

The department takes its name from the Latin *finis* and *terre*, or 'end of the earth'. Unsurprisingly, it's not the easiest place to get to, and last night's reality check in the laundry has put paid to any fantasies of exploring mysterious Arthurian forests. It's a shame; Brittany, which feels a lot to me like Cornwall – it even has a region called Cornouaille – is a place with a lot to offer the greedy visitor: apart from the aforementioned oysters and *kouign-amann*, and the inevitable crêpes, its rocky coastline gives forth fabulous fish and seafood, and the land is famous for its butter and cream (though, interestingly, Brittany does not have a great history of cheesemaking: indeed, the old Breton word for cheese was *lait pourri*, or 'putrid milk'. Yum!).

Instead I'll be whizzing through all that on a TGV bound for the port city of Brest, on Brittany's westernmost tip. It doesn't leave Saint-Malo until mid-afternoon, leaving me with a lot of time to kill, and not a boulangerie, café or restaurant in sight. For all my grand plans of reacquainting myself with the old town, the remarkably persistent rain makes me disinclined to explore much further afield than the immediate vicinity of the railway station, which is how I end up sitting in the Relay convenience store with an acrid espresso, an Innocent smoothie (the closest thing I can find to fresh fruit) and a family packet of

St Michel *galettes au bon beurre* for breakfast, probably produced in the *biscuiterie* we passed near the Mont.

After waiting in vain for the sky to brighten, I make an executive decision to retire to the *médiathèque* round the corner for an executive planning meeting. Even in the May gloom it's a lovely light-filled building that would be a peaceful place to wile away a few hours if it wasn't filled with gossiping, flirting teenagers from the local college, fortunately too absorbed with each other to notice me and my very loud shoes. It's amazing how long everything seems to take – I'm in there four hours, and come away with three restaurant reservations, a campsite for tomorrow night, a strange apartment-hotel for this evening, and some train times scribbled in my journal. All in all, it's not a great start to my first day on my own. I'd hoped to feel like Paddy Leigh Fermor; instead, I just feel like myself, in a bad mood.

On the plus side, the train is a swanky new one, and I seem to be the only bike booked on it – fortunately, as on locating the correct carriage I realise there's only one space.

PAUSE-CAFÉ –
French Trains

I'm not saying I'm an expert – the French railway is a byzantine operation – but it may be helpful to pass on some of the scanty wisdom I acquired after six weeks of travelling the network.

First off, if possible, speak to an actual human being rather than doing battle with the SNCF website or (even worse) one of their various apps, all of which are hard to navigate, even in French, and can be temperamental.

Secondly, if you're taking a non-folding bike, you'll need a reservation for it (€10) on high-speed TGV and other *grandes lignes* – unless, that is, you want to take it apart and transport it in a *housse*, or bike bag, maximum dimensions 120 x 90cm, in which case it travels free. Though the website makes great claims about how many spaces each train has (marked with a blue bicycle symbol on timetables), I found they were rarely available, so make sure you check ahead.

That said, if you don't mind travelling at a snail's pace, you can take your bike on any regional TER service for free – the bike carriage is usually at the far end of the train, and newer ones have hooks to hang your front wheel from (top tip: take your panniers off first). Though the steps can be a nuisance to navigate on older rolling stock, there's almost always staff around to help. Try to lock the bike to something, or itself, if you're going to sit elsewhere; it's generally safe, but I have seen things stolen in the past.

Both ferries and Eurostar require separate bike reservations – the latter may claim you'll need to take the bike apart for travel, but quite often they don't when you actually get there. Bear in mind that the place you'll need to collect the bike from or drop it off at Paris's Gare du Nord is so far down the left-hand side you'll think you've gone wrong – follow signs to '*Bagages Enregistrés Eurostar/Geoparts*'. (Note that, at the moment at least, they only take bikes between London, Paris, Lille and Brussels.)

As I gaze out at the countryside through the steady stream of water running down the window, I'm reminded of an old joke from Robb's book in which a visitor to Brittany demands of a passing infant, 'Boy, tell me, does it always rain like this here?' 'I don't know, sir,' replies the child. 'I'm only eight.'

It only gets worse as darkness falls, and thanks to the sea mist smothering Brest to its damp bosom, I end up seeing little of the city beyond my front wheel. The 'apart-hotel', the cheapest of my very few options for tonight, is clearly aimed at commercial travellers, perhaps staying a week or two, and its strip-lit corridors are full of the smells of cooking. When I ask if there's a garage for my bike, the lady behind the desk shakes her head in apology, before adding, almost as an afterthought, 'Of course, you're welcome to take it up to your room if you don't mind that.' I can't believe I've heard right – really? She looks puzzled by my reaction and points out the lift as if I might be above hoiking him upstairs. I don't need telling twice, and Eddy spends his evening in three-star comfort, propped against a trouser press. The French know how to treat a bike.

Having patted him dry with a hotel towel, I turn to the urgent matter of sustenance: I haven't eaten a proper meal since the crêperie in Dol-de-Bretagne, but this is not a neighbourhood replete with restaurants, and having lugged Eddy all the way up here, I'm loath to take him out foraging in the rain. Thankfully, Madame at the desk saves my bacon for the second time by pointing me in the direction of a supermarket, which, small as it is, offers an embarrassment of options for anyone as easily thrilled by food shopping as me.

I wander its aisles in a distinctly suspicious daze, picking things up, putting them down, goggling at the possibilities (Provençal fish soup! Microwave tartiflette! Instant noodles!). Experience has taught me that the opportunity to ingest vegetables is not one to be sniffed at in France though, so after about half an hour, and just before they chuck me out, I approach the checkout with half a kilo of spinach, a packet of potato pancakes, some salted cream cheese and a block of Brittany butter, and then go back for a bottle of local cider, because I feel like I deserve a drink.

I won't pretend it's the most gourmet feast I've ever prepared but I do feel better for having swallowed almost an entire bag of spinach drowned in butter and cheese, even if Eddy doesn't prove the most loquacious of dining companions. It's nice to see him there when I wake up at some ungodly hour though (curtain check: still raining, but perhaps a little less), and at least I don't have to share the rest of the powdery pancakes, which are, as with so many things, much better slathered in butter and Marmite.

My first proper solo ride is to Le Faou, a 'village of character' about 30km south-east of Brest whose chief attraction is La Frégate crêperie, run by Christophe Beuriot, three times crowned the best crêpier in Brittany. As it's closed from Sunday to Thursday in winter (which apparently lasts until June here), I've grabbed the first free table they had, and after reading woeful reports of people being turned away, even out of season ('Drove 150km for a nice lunch ...'), I'm keen to be on time, which means an early start – it's not far, but I have no idea of the gradients along the way, and of course the weather still doesn't look too jolly.

Though it's rarely pleasant cycling into or out of a city, Brest has the great advantage of being on the coast; even I would struggle to get lost following water, despite the fact I can't see more than a couple of metres beyond my handlebars. A huge bridge gradually looms out of the fog: the pedestrianised Pont Albert-Louppe, partially destroyed by the German Army in 1944 to halt the Allied advance, has a satisfying 888-metre span, bookended with rather grand 1920s gatehouses – and, on a wet Thursday morning, I have it entirely to myself. Though the tarmac is slick with standing water, and the views all but non-existent, it's still a buzz to look out and imagine Newfoundland somewhere out there to the west, though in fact, when I look at a map that evening, I realise a fair bit more of Brittany stands between me and my romantic Canadian dreams.

On the other side, I discover that Finistère is a spiky place – the highest hill may be a mere 163 metres, but it gets there with commendable rapidity, and by the time I reach the top, it's so muggy I tear my waterproof off with claws of desperation. While stuffing the damp garment into a pannier, I get the funny feeling I'm being watched and look up to find myself an object of intense interest for a field of cows, who have silently gathered near the fence for a better look. I feel the weight of their judgement upon my red face, and hastily move on.

Now that it's finally stopped raining, I can see what I'm riding through: a landscape of stone walls and dripping trees and old-fashioned blue-and-white enamel signs to places with too many vowels stuffed into them – Kerouant, Goarem Goz, Stangmeur, Squivit.

The constant up and down slows the pace, and I succumb to low-level but mounting anxiety regarding my 12 o'clock reservation. The last 10km or so seem to stretch out forever, so I'm relieved to finally see the magic sign proclaiming I'm in Le Faou, twinned with Modbury, UK, and somewhere else in France, just in case Devon proves too exotic. I cross a medieval bridge, pass a 16th-century church and there, at the end of the main street, is the equally ancient-looking building housing La Frégate, the first floor overhanging the ground floor, and the second floor overhanging that, all rising to a slate-tiled point. A wrought-iron frigate in full sail dangles from the corner gable, and outside, men from the town hall are installing great boxes of flowers ready for the summer season.

As I tie Eddy to the tiny stretch of railings they've left unencumbered, I watch an elderly couple slowly peruse the menu outside. Had they then walked away, I would have been tempted to run after them to stop them making a terrible mistake, but fortunately they're already seated by the time I bumble in, covered in chain grease.

Though the restaurant is otherwise deserted at 12.01, I'm still gratified when Madame remembers my reservation, and leads me to a table right by the open kitchen. Perfect. Once furnished with a bowl of cider, I turn my attention to the weighty menu, which kicks off with a lengthy mission statement outlining the criteria La Frégate has had to fulfil to be recognised as a Crêperie Gourmande. These include devoting at least 76 per cent of the menu (!) to crêpes and galettes, and retaining a crêpier with a solid knowledge of local and regional products, such as those provided by the list of suppliers underneath. It concludes with the plaintive note that 'a Crêperie Gourmande is not a fast-food restaurant – thank you for your understanding'.

There are a handful of seasonal specials – a crêpe with wild asparagus, locally cured coppa pork and Parmesan, and one with abalone (ormeau, a new piece of vocabulary for me), purée of chervil root and more of that asparagus – on top of the standard menu, which offers 48 different possibilities, from ham and egg to seaweed and scallops. I feel panicky, much as I did when confronted with all those oysters, and briefly flirt with the idea of ordering them all in the name of research.

Fortunately, help is on his way, in the form of Christophe himself, who is doing the rounds of the rapidly filling restaurant to greet his guests and show off the ingredients of the moment

– the spindly asparagus and fleshy abalone, a sea beast popular in Asia, though these hail from nearby Plouguerneau – '€75 a box, shell-on!' – and a box of the chervil root: 'Very, very rare!' he says excitedly. 'Not common at all.' I agree I've never heard of it. Should I have it? Well, he says, abalone is abalone (unarguable); me, I'd have the asparagus and coppa. It's made by a friend of mine up the road, and it's really good.

I feel a great weight lift from my shoulders; the asparagus it is. Relieved, I sit back and indulge in a bit of people watching. There's a party of pensioners, arguing over who's going to order what, and a couple next to me signing at each other, which is annoying, because I can't earwig on their conversation. Opposite is a lone man who looks like he's on his lunchbreak. I smile tentatively, and then remember I'm covered in mud and oil, and go and discreetly try to mop some from my legs in the loo.

To be honest, he doesn't look much more impressed on my return, but I don't care because Madame has brought my crêpe, whose dark golden colour reveals the principal ingredient to be buckwheat. It's a particularly fine-looking example, a neat triangle, with leggy stalks of asparagus snaking out from underneath a blanket of crisply fried coppa on a mattress of melted Parmesan. There's even a proper salad, with batons of candy beetroot and discs of purple radish, rather than the usual limp green leaves. God, it's good – the crêpe itself the best I've ever tasted, crisp on both sides, but soft within, its earthy flavour gilded with generous amounts of butter. I think I'd love it even without all the bells and whistles on top, delicious as they are.

I confirm to the young waiter that, yes, as the empty plate suggests, I enjoyed it very much, and naturally I have room for pudding, thank you for asking. On the sweet crêpe menu, which is barely less extensive than the savoury one, a summer special of local Plougastel strawberries with vanilla ice cream tempts me, but then my eye alights upon the Bretonne: a scoop of Breton butter biscuit ice cream, sautéed apples and salted caramel sauce, a description that suggests copious amounts of butter. The reality proves even better: there's a shard of unadvertised almond brittle, plus a buttery little biscuit that crumbles in the mouth like a sweet and salty sandcastle. The crêpe, finer textured and softer than the buckwheat version, is consequently less interesting, though I still manage to polish it off without too much trouble.

After ordering a coffee for the road, I ask if I can go and have a look in the kitchen. Of course, Madame says, no problem. Christophe is gently tending one of four hot plates, sweeping the batter across the smoking surface in elegant half-moons as calmly as if he was buttering toast. 'You can have a go if you want,' he says, 'once I've finished these orders.' I smile nervously and hope he's joking.

In the meantime, we chat about how he, a Normand no less, ended up as the *meilleur crêpier de Bretagne* – a turn of events he still seems faintly baffled by. Having worked in Switzerland as a baker for 18 years (and winning several awards for it, I discover later), and with a young daughter, 'I wanted a change. We were actually looking for a boulangerie in another part of Brittany ... and we ended up with this.' He shrugs; La Frégate found him, it seems.

You must have made pancakes before, though, to have taken on a crêperie. 'Oh, occasionally,' he says modestly, 'but it's all just luck, really. Good cooking is always about the ingredients you use, that's the difference. The buckwheat batter is just flour and eggs – I don't put milk in the savoury ones, though some people do ... Actually,' he neatly folds something startling involving chicken and pineapple, 'maybe there is a secret. Well, not a secret, but watch, I cook them on both sides. Not everyone does. Lots of people just do the bottom, then add the toppings. Cook them on both sides, with plenty of butter like this, that's how you do it.'

The thing is, Christophe muses, cleaning the hot plates, it's great to be so popular – 'we turn away 200 people a summer, people have come from Australia, from Réunion, it's madness. We're full every night!' – but the problem is that not everyone ('Especially you English – it's always time, time, time! with you') understands that real crêpes have to be made to order, and good ingredients need cooking with care. 'It's not like a restaurant where you can prepare the starters and desserts in advance,' he points out, 'we only have the batter!' Being so busy, he rarely gets to bed before 3 a.m., he says, though he admits he now allows himself the luxury of a day off a week, even in summer: 'We're getting old.' (He's 52.)

Eventually, the orders stop coming in, and he persuades me behind the counter. Which do you want to make, buckwheat or wheat? Buckwheat, I say. Much nicer. He demonstrates the technique to me: using a little metal spreading tool to drag the mixture to the edge of the hotplate before it sets, first anti-clockwise and then, with a deft flick (it's all in the wrist apparently), the other way – 'and not too hard or you'll rip them!' I'm so anxious by this point I can't find the words in French to explain to him how hopeless I am at following physical instructions, so instead I demonstrate it with a ragged shroud of a pancake. 'Not bad,' he says kindly, scraping it off for me, 'but you can do better.'

For the next attempt, I have an audience: a fellow crêpier from Dinan on a busman's holiday, who sweetly offers me the chance to come and do some work experience with him, too, if I have time. His wife merely giggles behind her hand, and frankly, I don't blame her.

Eventually I manage one that's almost intact. Christophe kindly folds all my burnt offerings up in clingfilm for me to take away (possibly he's too ashamed to put them in his own compost) and pops in an old jam jar of his award-winning salted caramel sauce, sticky with promise. I pose for photos with Sylvie, his delightful wife, who is so petite that I feel like an Anglo-Saxon ogre beside her (there's nowhere to hide in Lycra) – and then ask them the best way to the station.

'It will only take you 20 minutes, max,' the waiter says confidently.

Christophe shakes his head. 'I'd leave an hour if I were you. He's young ... I mean, you're young too ...'

'Non, mais elle est sportive!' Sylvie says encouragingly. Still, I think, best be off, just in case.

Crêpes Complètes (buckwheat pancakes with ham, cheese and egg)

Known as galettes elsewhere in France, these emphatically savoury pancakes get their earthy, slightly bitter flavour from the buckwheat (sarrasin or blé noir), which sustained generations of Breton peasants, for whom imported wheat flour would have been an unthinkable luxury. Because of its lack of gluten, buckwheat is harder to work with than ordinary flour, but it's well worth persevering, as the finished pancakes have a lovely crisp texture and a far more interesting flavour that, to my mind at least, pairs particularly well with cheese.

Makes about 20 galettes
500g buckwheat flour
2 tsp coarse salt
1 egg, beaten

Per galette
1 tbsp butter, plus extra to serve
1 egg
50g grated cheese (I like Gruyère)
1 slice of ham, torn

1 Mix the flour and salt together in a large bowl, then gradually whisk in 1 litre of water until bubbly and the consistency of single cream. Beat in the egg, and ideally leave to rest, if possible, for a couple of hours – but it's no disaster if you don't, it just gives a better final consistency.

2 Grease a flattish, heavy-based frying pan (you want to mimic the professional *billig* hotplates as closely as possible) with half the butter and put over a high heat. Pour some of the batter into a jug.

3 When the pan starts to smoke, pour in just enough batter to cover the base, quickly swirling to coat it evenly but as thinly as possible, using a palette knife to help spread it if you find that helpful (if it's too thick to swirl, add more water), and cook until it begins to come away from the base. Loosen and turn it, adding the rest of the butter underneath.

4 Once cooked, break the egg in the centre and spread out the egg white. Sprinkle the grated cheese around the white and top with the ham. Fold each side of the galette into the centre, so only the yolk is exposed, and cook for another 3 minutes.

I can't resist popping my head round the door of the church on my way out of town and then, on reading that there's a statue of St Anthony and his pig, seeking it out to pay homage – in the process I manage to leave the bag with my passport and money on his altar rail, remembering it only as I cycle out of town. Fortunately, it's still sitting there in front of the pig's beneficent gaze when I rush back in – which, given how tight my schedule is, does feel a bit like divine intervention.

Huffing my way up a couple of hilariously steep hills between Le Faou and Pont-de-Buis, where the nearest station is located, I'm relieved not to have lost too much time to my own foolishness. In fact, I'm there early enough (so *sportif!*) to make a detour up yet another hill to a supermarket, where I shelter from the rain, which has returned with vigour, and buy an emergency packet of peanuts before heading back to await the service to Quimper.

The station is a one-platform affair, with a timetable at the entrance, but nothing in the way of announcements or other signs to help the visitor. Trains in both directions just appear without warning, which is how I find myself inadvertently heading not south to Quimper, Nantes and the Loire Valley to meet my friends, but back to Brest, the city I cycled out of six hours before, and very much the end of the line. Not that I realise for the first 20 minutes of the journey as I change out of my wet Lycra in the loo and relax into the dry warmth: in fact, the ticket collector who gently points out my mistake has to then sit down himself, so serious is my error. He sucks his pencil, removes several timetables from his breast pocket and makes many little calculations on my ticket, sighing heavily. Eventually, he looks up sorrowfully and says, 'Mademoiselle,' (as if I could love him any more), 'I'm afraid there is no way for you to get to Nantes tonight.' He explains the furthest I'll be able to get is Redon, if I get off at the next stop, and that he's written on my ticket to explain the situation. He takes out a weighty silver stamp to authenticate this and leaves me to my misery.

My next problem, apart from the fact that nothing at Landerneau – my connecting station, where I am condemned to spend two tedious hours – is open, is the paucity of accommodation in Redon. The name also sounds oddly familiar. A nasty suspicion begins to take shape at the back of my brain. I flick through my photos from last year's cycling trip and realise Redon is indeed the place where we finally got fed up of the relentless damp, and after being lightly pelted with stones by gypsy children, camping in an industrial estate where a strange man haunted the ladies loos and being turned away from a potato-themed restaurant in the pouring rain, decided to skip Brittany altogether. This memory does not fill me with hope, so I pick the closest free room to the station to enable a quick exit tomorrow morning.

When I arrive, the two-star Hotel Asther is locked up and deserted. Nothing Redon throws at me can surprise me, so I'm almost disappointed when the lady who answers the phone says she'll be down in a jiffy … and actually is. The hotel itself is worn, but comfortable, all rickety stairs and wheezy beds – more characterful, I think, than a modern chain, as long as I don't end up with bedbugs. Then a thought strikes me. I run back downstairs – is there anywhere open for dinner? Not even a supermarket? There is not, Madame says regretfully.

Back in my creaky palace, I unwrap the damp excuses for crêpes that Christophe packed for me, and smear them with salted caramel sauce and some of the emergency peanuts. They're not the best crêpes in the world, but right now, in Redon, they'll do.

Km: 53.5

Croissants: 0 (potato pancakes with Marmite: 2)

High: Eventually producing a half-decent crêpe

Low: Nearly making a ticket inspector cry with pity

STAGE 6

A STAGE IN TWO PARTS: REDON TO TOURS, PARIS TO LAMOTTE-BEUVRON

Tarte Tatin

The tarte Tatin, perhaps the most famous apple pie in the world, is at its most basic, a simple upside-down apple cake made with pastry instead of batter. What sets it apart from its many rivals, however, is that the fruit is slow-cooked with copious amounts of butter and sugar until it becomes deliciously caramelised. Trust the French to come up with that particular stroke of genius.

PART ONE: REDON TO TOURS

Having already been caught out once too often by the idiosyncratic opening hours of the French boulangerie, and not wanting to rely on Redon for anything but bitter disappointment, I've signed on for breakfast at the Hotel Asther, served in a windowless room behind reception, where two workmen sit on the same side of a scuffed banquette, gloomily watching a TV on the wall showing a rolling montage of cars floating in flooded streets across France. We greet each other politely (a lovely French custom that's hard to adjust to after 15 years strenuously avoiding eye contact with London's other eight million residents) and I grab a kiwi and an orange from the buffet (vitamins!) and find a spot in the opposite corner.

Madame, who has single-handedly redeemed Redon in my eyes, brings over a basket containing half a baguette, a plump golden croissant and four little pats of Paysan Breton *beurre demi-sel*, which does actually appear to be 50 per cent salt, 50 per cent delicious dairy fat – I end up eating everything, just so I have an excuse to finish the butter. The men watch me curiously as I take a picture of the croissant (whose slightly bland flavour is offset by an excellent crisp texture and layers like a seashell – 7/10), but I don't try to explain; being British is surely a get-out-of-jail-free card, given everyone now thinks we're mad anyway.

As I'm a day's ride – or a morning's train-ride – north-west of where I'm supposed to be this morning, and have friends arriving in the Loire Valley for lunch, I don't really have time to feel sad about leaving Brittany until the lush, rain-soaked countryside rolls past the train window, and I wish I'd seen more of it. Regret is tempered with relief: my biggest worry for the last few months – travelling on my own – looks as if it might turn out to be no more than a classic monster under the bed, and I'm pleased to have slain it.

I have about an hour to kill in Nantes between trains, which is just enough time for a quick, roadwork-dodging tour of the centre, but sadly not quite sufficient for a ride on the giant shiny steel slide that tumbles from the top of the castle walls into the moat below. I'm dying for a go, but instead content myself with a nose round the cathedral, which boasts a clam-shell stoup of holy water of such magnificent proportions it properly belongs in the Cancale shell museum, and a magnificent carved marble tomb described by Henry James as 'one of the most brilliant works of the French Renaissance'. It is indeed striking; a rather elegant hound lies bravely alongside a lion at the shrouded feet of the deceased: François II, the last Duke of Brittany, and his second wife, Marguerite de Foix, who wear suspiciously beatific expressions, as if at any minute they might leap up and shout GOTCHA!

Rather oddly, François's first wife, also called Marguerite – a 12-year-old who also happens to have been his first cousin – is buried in the same grave, but as the whole monument was commissioned by the second one's daughter, Anne of Brittany (later Queen of France), she doesn't get so much as a name-check, let alone a flattering effigy or a dog to accompany her to eternity.

On the way out, I stop to read a printed notice in several languages telling visitors they are 'entering the House of GOD!' and requesting 'respectful silence and proper dress' before invit-ing 'Brother Believers' to attend prayers in the Chapel of the Holy Sacrament '(near the Tomb of François II)'. Some fair-minded visitor has added to this last, in pencil, 'and Marguerite of Foix' in every language: a small victory for feminism which puts a spring in my step as I return to my bike, even if, I note, poor old Wife One has been forgotten yet again.

My second train of the day runs along the length of the Loire Valley, and I find myself back on the tourist trail for the first time since Mont-Saint-Michel, sharing a bike carriage with an elderly couple who seem to have strapped their entire lives and a squashed baguette to their back wheels. They're a type I'll see again and again on the roads: retired couples with skin as tanned and creased as mountaineers, placidly covering vast distances in no particular hurry. I'd envy them if it didn't look like such hard work.

They're going to Tours. I get off at Saumur, where I'm meeting my weekend companions, Tess and her husband Tor. I have a good feeling about this place from the moment I spot a baguette vending machine outside the station. Crossing the Loire for the first time, I stop to take a picture; this is the longest river in France, running over 1,000km from the high, stony gorges of the Massif Centrale via this pretty valley full of fairytale chateaux and limpid wines to placidly discharge into the Bay of Biscay. Sadly, we'll only be cycling a tiny part of its course.

With the others en route from the airport, and our hotel reception closed for lunch, I take refuge in the Tourist Information Centre to try to secure a back-up plan should my companions find, belatedly, that cycling is not their idea of mini-break fun. Neither of them so much as own a bike back in the UK, so their willingness to even give it a go demonstrates the kind of loyalty old François II's first wife could only dream of.

I ask the lady behind the desk if the train is the only transport option between Saumur and Tours, given that tomorrow is a strike day and, according to the SNCF website, not much seems likely to be running on this particular line. She confirms the worst: they're going to have to cycle the whole lot with me tomorrow.

Just then I get a text from Tess: 'We're in the first bar we saw! What do you want to drink?' Perfect, I think, nothing like booze to bury bad news. I find them round the corner with a beer and a glass of wine. Two rounds later, I gently suggest we should perhaps think about lunch, as it's nearly two o'clock. A couple of restaurants nearby claim to serve until 2.30 p.m., though of course in reality they all but laugh in our faces. '*Non, Madame!*' the waiter chortles, stacking chairs. 'Too late!' while in the second, the maitre d' scowlingly shakes his head as soon as I cross the threshold. The crêperie we end up in is definitely not one that would meet the strict definition of Crêperie Gourmande on Christophe's menu, but it's in a sweet little square, they serve Loire wine by the carafe and the waitress is so grumpy at having to work past the designated lunch hour that it becomes almost funny ... though not quite as funny as the burger Tor orders that arrives unexpectedly swaddled in a soggy crêpe instead of a bun. 'It's all right, I guess,' he says bravely. 'Bit of a weird texture.'

Unable to face the rest now I've tasted the best, I bypass the pancakes in favour of a salad in the traditional French style, the few leaves hidden beneath curls of cured ham and chunky toasts topped with rounds of creamy local Sainte-Maure goat's cheese. Tess's comes with another Loire speciality: *rillons*, or pork belly, slowly cooked in its own lard until it melts into a deliciously fatty pâté. 'I love France,' she says happily, demolishing the lot.

We share another carafe of thin wine for dessert, and halfway down it, I hear my name shouted from somewhere behind me. It's startling in a country where I know no one but these two for about 400 miles, and I turn around to see a blonde woman flying across the square in my direction. 'I thought it was you!' she squeals delightedly. Fortunately, the Muscadet is innocuous enough that I immediately recognise Martine, an art director who I last saw at a photoshoot six weeks ago attempting to make Bermondsey look like Brittany for a French recipe feature I'd written for her magazine: 'And now we're here in the real thing!' she squeals – and in true Brits Abroad fashion, we're both a bit tiddly at four in the afternoon. I feel a warm flush of national pride, though to be honest, it could just be the wine.

Martine explains she's here with a group of friends for a big birthday and sweetly urges me to stop at their villa for a few

Campari and sodas on my way south. With the sun out again, the idea is incredibly tempting, and I curse my tight schedule, before reminding myself I'm here for a reason, and that reason is definitely not drinking by the pool (though what an idea for a book, eh?).

This pleasant interruption breaks the spell of the wine list, reminding us that we should probably go and check into our hotel so Tess and Tor can pick up their hire bikes, given we're fresh out of other travel options for tomorrow (not that I've told them this in so many words – I vaguely say something about possible strikes, and playing it by ear. No sense in scaring the horses). They're away a long time with the rental bloke, and I get into a conversation with the man at reception about the rail strikes (not a fan), and then, inevitably, despite my best efforts to avoid it, Brexit (also not a fan). At this point, thank goodness, the pair return, Tess looking a bit nervous. 'Are the bikes all right?' I ask, without knowing quite what to say if the answer's no. 'They'll do, I guess,' Tor says ominously. 'I think I need another drink.'

Of the rest of the evening, which we spend at an apparently excellent little wine bar on the waterfront, probably the less said the better, mostly because my memories of it extend only as far as the first bottle of delicious Saumur white and a board of superlative charcuterie. A receipt I find the next day assures me we only have this one bottle, and then a glass each of dessert wine with the cheese board, but frankly none of us believe this.

After downing three pints of water, I find my new companions – who, in the harsh sunshine of morning (naturally it's come out in time for my first hangover), I'm inclined to regard as a Bad Influence – already in the boulangerie across the street, looking even worse than I feel. Tor in particular can't work out what on earth will make him feel better, and then once Tess has ordered him something – 'Anything!' – sits there looking glum as I work my way steadily through an unremarkable but vast croissant (6/10, doughy, dull) and a cardboard cup of bad coffee. United in misery, there doesn't seem much point in putting off the inevitable any longer. A big group in high-vis with matching city bikes is dawdling on the kerb and, as it seems a fair assumption that they'll also be following the same cycleway along the valley floor, I'm keen to be off before them lest they set an inconveniently slow pace.

The route immediately takes us back past the scene of last night's crime ('Remember when he shouted at us because he didn't believe we hadn't ordered that seafood platter?' Tess giggles. I don't) and then, as punishment, through a street market. When James Bond rides a scooter through a market, people get out of his way. This does not happen to us, but on the plus side, none of us overturns a stall of oranges either, and soon we're following the river out of town, past a large and impressive castle. 'Not sure how we missed that yesterday,' says Tor.

The cycle route soon turns steeply off the main road and climbs up through the village of Souzay-Champigny, then turns along a narrow path, rather than street, flanked with houses built into the soft pale-yellow cliffs. A sign points us in the direction of the *circuit troglodyte*, which, despite the huge potholes en route, proves a detour I can't resist. We wobble through pitch-black caverns it's hard to imagine anyone ever having lived in until we find ourselves in a clearing where sunlight pours through the rock and fairy lights are strung up between the cliffs, as if for a local fête, but the place is eerily deserted, with a pervasive damp smell that gives me the shivers.

We press on, cycling away from the river now, and past a handsome church. Twenty minutes later we see what appears to be the same church from the opposite direction. 'Aren't we supposed to be following the river?' Tor asks. It's a fair point and, looking at the map, I see that we are victims of yet another scenic cycle route. Given the heat, the hangovers and the two people who scoffed in the face of padded shorts, a more direct course feels strongly advisable.

There's one more stop I'm keen to make first, though – lovely as the Loire is, this entire leg was designed to end with the world's most famous apple tart at the restaurant that created it, only for me to discover, sitting in the library in Saint-Malo, that its opening hours are somewhat less liberal than listed in the *Michelin Guide*. Whichever way I looked at it, given that they're closed half the week, dinner at the Hotel Tatin would now be impossible on this trip without throwing my entire itinerary into chaos. From here, I head due south to meet friends, and then hard east to meet more, before making my way back up the other side of the country to Strasbourg, Paris and home – so there's not the faintest chance of zig-zagging back to the leafy Loire for a piece of pie, however famous.

Not for the first time, I curse the sheer scale of this country, but it can't be helped: the Eurostar is booked for 2 July, and that's that. I'll just have to come back later in the year, because I won't be getting a slice today, that's for certain.

PAUSE-CAFÉ – French Opening Hours: A Fun Guessing Game for all the Family

A subject so esoteric it deserves a nice sit down with a *café crème* – though, really, the general rule can be summed up in three words: trust no one. French opening hours are a law unto themselves, and even when they are available online, or printed on the door of the actual establishment, they're rarely respected, so this can only ever be a rough guide, and I will accept no responsibility for starvation due to reliance on it.

French bakeries and cafés tend to open early, around 6.30–7 a.m., for obvious reasons, but like most shops, banks and even post offices they close somewhere between 12 and 1 p.m., and don't re-open until 3.30 at the earliest. The same goes for most tourist attractions, save churches. The last are, of course, open on Sunday, but many shops aren't, and even big supermarkets that boast of being 7j / 7 are actually only open on Sunday morning, because the French take the work–life balance seriously, and so should you. Even if it takes you three weeks to appreciate three hours of enforced idleness in the middle of the day.

Restaurants keep opposite hours – they will generally open for lunch at noon, or shortly beforehand (the sanctity of *l'heure de déjeuner* between 12 and 2 p.m. is very noticeable for anyone travelling on French roads – more than once I nearly got run over by the lunchtime rush to get home to eat), and will usually stop serving at about 1.30 p.m., so unless you're in a big city with a brasserie 'non-stop', or can find a McDonald's, don't expect to get fed after that time. Dinner is usually eaten between 7 and 9 p.m., though people in cities and further south may push this slightly later.

Many smaller shops and bakeries are closed on Mondays as well, and the entire country seems to take its summer holiday in August. Be aware: most things will be shut on May Day, Bastille Day (14 July) and, to a lesser extent, the Feast of the Ascension (a movable feast, 39 days after Easter Sunday), in addition to the usual Christmas, New Year and Easter holidays ... and there are a couple more regional feasts in Alsace, too.

Apart from that little list, though, you ought to find at least half the places you want to visit open.

(Note: I always find counting to 10 before kicking a shuttered door very calming.)

———————————————————————

With the Tatin off the menu for now, I've identified another apple-themed attraction to make up for it: the museum of *pommes tapées* in the village of Turquant, which promises, rather excitingly, to tell us 'the story of a passion' ... for preserved fruit. I have absolutely no idea what a tapped apple might be, but I'm game for finding out, and Tess and Tor can barely contain themselves, especially when we discover a small group already in the modest car park, patiently waiting for the gates to open.

So eager are these others to see the apple artefacts that by the time we've taken a few star-struck selfies with the rain-blasted mannequins that stare blankly from the caves above the entrance, they've already zoomed off on a guided tour. A private guided tour. Thus, after paying the princely sum of €6.50 per person ('My treat!' I call merrily from the counter), Madame leads us to the back of a very dark cave, hands us a stack of fleece blankets decorated with cartoon dogs for warmth and abandons us to a surprisingly slick film about the history of the apple-tapping trade in the Loire Valley, complete with lavish aerial shots of chateaux that played no part in the industry as far as any of us can tell. Suddenly the British narrator, who appears to have taken acting lessons from Brian Blessed himself, drops his tone to a confidential whisper. 'Come closer,' he breathes seductively, 'as I tell you the story of the *pommes tapées*' – we lean in, interested despite ourselves, and then jump back as he booms, 'BUT I WILL NOT REVEAL THE VARIETY, THAT'S A SECRET!'

Any plans of making our fortunes abruptly crushed, we concentrate instead on the meagre facts available: that, after the phylloxera bug devastated the Loire Valley's vines in the late 19th century, enterprising local *vignerons* turned to apples and pears instead. Cider and perry would have seemed the obvious choice in the circumstances, but instead they decided to go big on preserving, hoping to sell the fruit, once dried and squashed, to sailors as a portable, durable source of vitamin C.

The apple-tapping process seems as pointlessly labour-intensive as any work-creation scheme: the fruit is peeled and then dried in a low oven for about five days, during which time someone occasionally hits it with a special hammer until it becomes a travel-size apple – each one is, we're solemnly assured, tapped an amazing 60 times in the pursuit of maximum space efficiency. The end result is like an apple that someone has let all the air out of – a wrinkled beige disc a centimetre or so high with a stalk sticking out of the top.

Not the most appetising of prospects, but the pay-off for all this labour is that it can then be stored for up to a decade, ready for those moments when you really fancy some vitamin C but find yourself fighting an imperial war in the South Seas. The

Brian-a-like even reads a little poem in praise of the pioneering apple tappers, which deserves to be recorded for posterity:

> *Once upon a time there was a funny man,*
> *Who liked his apples plump and crisp, like a small behind.*
> *Unceasingly he flattens, flattens*
> *– he has only one goal, to fill his jars!*

Perhaps it scans better in the original French.

Apple tapping was indeed a thriving industry in the region, with over 200 ovens operating in 1914 in this village alone, but one that, of course, was easy prey to advances in refrigeration technology. These days, you're only really likely to come across *pommes tapées* in the museum shop, where they're €8 for six – as one TripAdvisor review observes, 'Not the best value for money, but you can dine out on the experience for months.'

I'm getting ahead of myself, though, because before we get to the gift shop, we have the museum to enjoy. The French group are being taken through the display of apple-coring machines through the ages in agonising detail, so we're left to wander the caves alone, admiring exhibits of varying degrees of relevance with which they've struggled to fill the echoing space. Alongside the usual rusty farm machinery and house-of-horrors mannequins engaged in mysterious rustic tasks is a semi-circle of champagne bottles from the largest, the Nebuchadnezzar, to the smallest … a plastic fridge magnet.

Trying hard to wipe the smirks from our faces, we re-emerge into the light, startling Madame, who had clearly expected us to take rather longer to appreciate the treasures within. 'Would you like to taste a *pomme tapée*?' she asks hopefully. '*Bien sûr!*' I reply, thinking of the almost €20 I've just dropped on this quarter of an hour of entertainment. She proudly sets three dishes, each containing half a squashed apple fresh from the micro-wave, in front of us. I'm struggling to contain myself, but Tess is right in there, and following her lead, once I've eaten the apple, which is surprisingly pleasant – like a marshmallowy version of those dried apple rings beloved of middle-class parents – I pick up the bowl and drain the spiced red wine it sits in. Our hostess looks a little surprised, but waste not want not, as my grandmother used to say.

After we've all but licked the bowls, and Tess has gamely bought a souvenir jar of the things to atone for our hoots of laughter at the video, which, we sense, did not go down well, we attempt to make some progress in the direction of Tours. Along the way, we're accosted by a group of giggling men dressed as pirates, flying Jolly Rogers from their handlebars and towing two of their number in a child's trailer decked out as a galleon – whether they're blind drunk, or merely French, we can't quite tell, but Tor does his bit for international relations by lending them a pump for nautical repairs. While they're busy with that, Tess and I pop into a small supermarket to try to buy a drink, only to find almost every shelf empty, apart from one, which contains a large comatose Labrador. God knows where anyone buys anything except for cigarettes and lottery tickets round here. Perhaps that's all they need.

Weird, and only getting weirder: given the number of tourists who must cycle along this route on a summer weekend, I've naively assumed lunch won't be a problem today, yet the town I've been aiming for, which we hit just after noon, turns out to boast only a takeaway pizza joint (shut) and a dusty truckers' café on the main road out. Every space on the latter's cramped terrace is occupied, which feels like a good sign, so we perch ourselves at a flimsy plastic table on the sun-baked verge and order a carafe of wine and some water. Almost 40, very thirsty minutes later, we're still waiting – and every time I wave at Madame she assures me it's coming in an aggrieved fashion, which suggests my impatience does not do me or my nation any credit.

'I have a good feeling about this place,' I tell the others, in the face of all available evidence; after all, such charmless rustic joints always come up trumps in the work of people like Elizabeth David or M. F. K. Fisher – undiscovered gems! they trill. This is where the real people eat!

Unfortunately, however, this one is just an ugly roadside joint: my *truite aux amandes* has been cremated rather than cooked, and Tess's crème caramel is so tough we can, and do, stand a spoon up in it. With no one else left to talk to, Madame comes to chat to us about the weather – a mini tornado last week! – and we decide, as we wait for the bill with not much hope of seeing it before sunset, that she's just hopelessly inefficient, rather than actively rude, which is at least slightly mollifying, even if every wasted meal in France still feels like a tiny tragedy.

The rest of the afternoon is, from my point of view at least, uneventfully pleasant cycling, trying to adjust our paces to poor Tess, who has, it seems, been saddled with a bike so bad that even pedalling at full speed she's unable to keep up with our careless freewheeling. We have a cold and silent beer at Villandry, with barely a glance at its famous fairy-tale castle, and make it into Tours about 50 minutes after everyone loses patience with the entire enterprise. The first thing Tess and Tor do, as I'm busy stowing Eddy in an underground garage for the night, is rid themselves of their hated charges, after which they fairly skip into town with the air of people liberated from a great burden.

Over some local gooseberry-flavoured aperitifs, I tell them we've cycled 82.1km, which cheers the mood a bit, especially given that it's the biggest distance I've covered so far. 'Bloody HELL,' says Tess, draining the glass with gusto. 'No wonder I feel like this.'

In the circumstances, I feel justified in choosing a starter, the *tourte tourangelle*, a sturdy pastry case stuffed full of more confit pork belly and goat's cheese, which would certainly have done as a meal for three. This is followed by *sandre* from the Loire, which, despite Tor's scepticism about a fish Google translates as 'pike perch', turns out to not only exist, but taste delicious, meaty and firm. I think the chocolate pot with salted caramel might finish me off, though. No one even mentions stopping at a bar on the way home, and I fret, as I lie in bed plagued by indigestion, that I might have dampened my companions' considerable joie de vivre.

But no, the next morning they're keen to go large before they go home, and we find a café in a medieval square offering a *formule* of baguette, butter, jam and coffee, which hits the spot nicely – for me at least. Once the crumbs are cleared, Tess looks thoughtful. I beckon the rather jaded-looking waiter over to order another coffee.

'What beers do you have?' she asks. Suddenly, he perks up. What strength beer was Madame after on this fine morning? 'Quite … strong?' ventures Tor. Why, he has just the thing: a Mort Subite, delicious at a mere 9 per cent! They settle for something named after a troll, at a more respectable 5 per cent, and though I'll miss them, my liver gives grateful thanks that they have to be back at work tomorrow.

Km: 89.3

Croissants: 2 (average score, 6.5)

High: The apple-tapping museum continues to cheer me up for weeks

Low: First hangover

PART TWO, THREE MONTHS LATER: PARIS TO LAMOTTE-BEUVRON (TARTE TATIN AT LAST)

Good as the tapped apples were, perhaps unjustly they're hardly in the same league as the tarte Tatin, which continues to annoy me as unfinished business for the rest of the tour, and the rest of the sweltering summer. Back in a sun-bleached London, I eat Calippos and dream of caramelised apples. Finally, in mid-September, I get my chance to return to France, bleary-eyed on the first train of the morning, this time with rather less in the way of luggage, Eddy having gone ahead of me the night before. As I get changed in yet another station loo, yanking awkwardly at freshly laundered Lycra as the queue builds disapprovingly behind the door, it's as if I've never been away.

Once I've hoofed down a quick croissant from Maison Pradier's Gare du Nord branch, crouched over a bin (8/10: ends as dry as my hair after months sticking out of a cycle helmet; excellent, rich, almost dulce-de-leche-like flavour), the bike lanes of Paris, with their idling lorries and idle strollers, feel like coming home. And it's good to be back, not least because cycling is a lot more fun than actual work; for all the weaving and dodging and holding my breath to squeeze through traffic,

I slip gratefully back into the rhythm of the bike like a hot body into a cool pool.

My new peloton is waiting for me on the bench outside the Ten Belles coffee shop just off the Canal Saint-Martin: the two girls, Harry and Caroline, looking somewhat jaded, Harry's boyfriend Jay somewhere beyond that, in his own private pit of despair. Harry, a fellow food writer, is based in Paris; Caroline lives in Provence, where she's been writing a book of her family's recipes, and poor Jay – nothing to do with food – only arrived from Birmingham the night before, and explains, without opening his eyes, that he found the other two in a state of some inebriation. In lieu of further details, Harry hands me a jerky video of the pair of them riding around Paris on the front of a cargo bike pedalled by her sister Georgie, whooping and drinking claret (Harry and Caroline, not Georgie, who was apparently on the way to a parents' evening at her children's new school). If Jay's face this morning is anything to go by, he quickly made up for lost time, and they make a sorry sight, even to someone who got up at 3.45 a.m. to catch a train.

More pertinently, though they'd planned to pick them up as soon as the rental shop opened at 10 a.m., I see no likely-looking bikes. My weary gaze slides along the railings that shield the pavement from traffic before pausing at three heavy city shoppers with generous baskets on the front. Triathlete Jay and I exchange grim glances, and silently I thank God I've planned a relatively gentle route based on Harry's protests that, despite her boyfriend's prowess on two wheels, she rarely cycles further than the market, which is exactly what these beasts are designed for.

The Sunday-driver tone of the expedition is confirmed when Harry sees the brand-new shorts I've selflessly donated to the cause of her posterior comfort and dissolves into helpless giggles, gasping for breath as I waggle them around by their bright pink straps. I have to say, once she's got over their ridiculousness, she does them justice by putting on a neon pink bra and declaring it too warm for further clothing. We may be going slowly, I think, but we'll certainly turn some heads.

This quickly proves to be the case, but sadly for all the wrong reasons: as Harry fearlessly leads the way through her home city, a shiny black Mercedes swings suddenly into the bike lane, forcing her to brake so suddenly she falls off. A bearded hipster smoking outside a vintage vinyl shop runs to her aid as the Merc, unconcerned, speeds through the lights and disappears. Fortunately, she's fine; the Yann Couvreur croissant she's carrying for me has taken the brunt of her fall. After wiggling her wrist experimentally, Jay declares us fit to proceed in the direction of the Gare d'Austerlitz, where we're taking a train to the winningly named small town of Lardy, about 40km from the capital.

We get there eventually, after forcibly charging a ticket gate like a Lycra-clad battering ram (a ram with valid tickets, I might point out), and then spending 37 minutes sitting on a dirty subterranean platform waiting for a train and sharing the squashed croissant (a 7.5/10, sweet, ultra-crisp and so well cooked it looks like it's had a spray tan) as stylish Parisians step over us in disgust.

After the drama of Paris, Lardy proves a sleepy place, where the only thing open is a station bar, which looks perfect for lunch. No, Madame behind the bar explains, they're not serving food, but there's a bakery and an épicerie just down the road. She's right, there are ... and they're both firmly shut up against the mid-afternoon sun – after all, who would want to do any shopping at 3 p.m.?

Just as I'm beginning to foresee disaster ahead, I spot a roadside poster for a hypermarket, three minutes' drive away. My heart fairly leaps with joy at this golden opportunity for reacquaintance with my beloved French supermarkets with their obscure regional specialities and endless boxes of toast, though as poor Jay – waiting outside with the bikes with his eyes closed again – discovers, it's actually impossible for three food writers to get in and out of any supermarket within half an hour, even if they're ostensibly only buying enough for a quick snack.

I bump into Harry at the checkout clutching a pot of pickled garlic and a large sheep cheese, both of which are destined to travel with us all day before being invaded by ants overnight and chucked, while my greengages turn to compôte in Caroline's basket, though we do manage to finish the 'amazing' own brand biscuits she's desperate for us to try – 'so much nicer than Choco Leibniz!' Blissfully ignorant of these facts, we sit cross-legged on the warm concrete of the car park and shove ham and cornichon baguettes into our faces until I suddenly realise, with a start, that it's already 4 p.m. and we have 50km to do – a total that seemed leisurely back in London with a whole day to play with, but now feels formidable, though I keep quiet about this in order to maintain team morale for as long as possible.

The first half of the journey is glorious; it's hard to suppress irritating sighs of profound contentment at being back on the road as we pedal through the reassuringly flat, lightly forested countryside, passing the odd modest chateau, raptors of some sort wheeling overhead. On the long, straight B-road that will take us to Pithiviers, however, I sense morale is beginning to flag; even the glorious sight of a hare leaping across the fields beside us, effortless at full tilt, can barely distract them from the muted screams of their undercarriages. Even the smallest rises in the distance look like mountains, and I'm forced to play the underhand game of knocking 5km off every progress report I make, figuring that by the time we're a mere 5km away, things won't seem too bad.

Nevertheless, it's a slightly glum group that picks its way through the backstreets and allotments of Pithiviers to the campsite where a bored woman slouches on a white plastic chair, smoking and pointedly ignoring our arrival. '*Bonsoir!*' a man whom we take to be in charge shouts from a distant pitch where he appears to be supervising some Dutch people driving into a tree: '*J'arrive!*' I'm not saying we look exhausted, but as we're negotiating the unfamiliar tangle of lines and poles, he reappears with four bottles of cold beer. I'm surprised Harry doesn't kiss him, but also a bit relieved, given the mood of his wife.

He also makes it clear time is of the essence in the dinner department, and as we waddle into town, still in our kit, it's clear he's right, because everything is shut. A woman Harry corners in a car park claims there's a pizzeria nearby, which turns out to be a kebab shop, and eventually I reluctantly concede that the strip-lit Japanese restaurant might be our only option. As we trudge back along the dark, shuttered streets towards it, there's a quiet burble of life from somewhere nearby, and then, round a corner, the glad sight of the Relais de la Poste, a solid coaching inn with a terrace so full they can't accommodate us, and a painfully bright dining room with an enormous Rotary Club insignia over the massive fireplace.

If conversation pauses as we troop in wearing our unusual garb, we're too tired to notice – I blush to recount the scenes when the young waiter brings a plate of warm puff-pastry pieces with our drinks. The Relais isn't anything fancy, but the €19 menu, once I've allowed myself to dodge the terrifying-sounding chicken carpaccio, is a straightforward choice: a melon salad, a bavette steak with gloopy mustard sauce and a big pile of chips fresh from the freezer and, of course, a pithiviers, the sweet pastry that drew me to this town in the first place. Rather than the circle of stuffed puff usually sold under the name in the UK, however, this is a dense little almond cake topped with white icing, which the waitress confirms is something called a 'pithiviers fondant', a new one on all of us. Washed down with an absurdly generous measure of raspberry eau de vie, it does the job in the sugar department though, and we return to our wonky tents in rather better spirits than we left them.

The town looks more welcoming in the warm light of morning – things are at least open, including a bakery whose windows proudly display a long list of awards, from 'Best Baguette Tradition in the Ile de Loire 2009' to more recent accolades, including several from the 2018 Concours Confrérie de Pithiviers, in which they seem to have scooped the gold medal for their pithiviers fondant and various other gongs too. The trophies themselves are inside the shop, next to framed certificates solemnly declaring the owners to be knights of the Brotherhood of Pithiviers and big tempting jars full of boozy rum baba.

Talking to Madame behind the counter, I learn that the more familiar puff-pastry pithiviers is a johnny-come-lately, created in the 18th century, while the almond kind we had last night is said to have Gaulish origins, reflecting the town's former importance on various ancient trading routes, carrying things like almonds from the balmy South. She apologises that the puff version isn't out of the oven yet, so I take another fondant pithiviers for the road – much moister than the last and full of tiny air bubbles, rather like a crumpet – plus the inevitable croissant (sweet and yeasty, let down by a slightly too doughy centre, 7.5/10).

After a *café crème* in the bar opposite, run by a very jolly lady who positively insists we spread crumbs all over her clean tables – 'Oh, don't worry about that, *messieurs-dames*!' – we balance the remainder of our purchases on our panniers and ride out of town, with only the briefest of detours to the little supermarket, outside which several men drinking cans see fit to pass comment on our Lycra-clad bottoms. Whereas in Britain I'd give them short shrift, in France they seem almost charming, though I'm still pleased to be able to pedal off at speed with a merry *bonne journée* before Harry hears and is less charmed.

The morning is a cloudy one and, powered by pastry, we make good progress – after about 13km, just as we're about to enter the forest, I pull in by a roadside inn to remove some layers, and before I know it the others are inside, ordering beers: 'Just small ones, to keep us hydrated.' Monsieur behind the bar, accompanied by a single gloomy customer watching the television, and himself observed by various taxidermied pieces of game, is delighted to see us, and in deference to our achievement, brings us out a plate of cured ham, which we quickly devour, for all the world like we haven't just put away half a bakery.

An hour and a half of trees later, after passing a centre for the care of wild fawns, which would seem to have its work cut out given the number of 'private hunting' signs in the vicinity, I spy a riverside picnic site, deserted apart from a hatchback, which has disregarded the designated car park to position itself right on the water's edge, doors open, music blaring. We lay out our feast on the grass: a cheese-laden *fougasse*, more ham sandwiches and some slightly furry squashed tomatoes from yesterday, plus a tot of whisky apiece from Jay's handy hipflask, and I am profoundly happy.

It's very tempting to stretch out for a post-prandial nap to the relaxing sounds of French hip-hop, but time marches on and we still have some way to go if we're to make Orléans tonight. After rallying the troops by threatening a repeat of yesterday evening's route march, I generously allow a detour via the canal, whose tree-lined, gravelled towpaths encourage a leisurely pace in the others, and send my wrists, which absorb every vibration from my narrow tyres, completely numb. When this waterway suddenly meets the Loire, the great river I left three months previously, still there, still flowing lazily towards the sea, I forgive it everything. The scale is stunning.

We stop by a geranium-covered lock and take a moment to sit with our legs dangling over the edge, watching a huge fish loiter in the shallows, arguing about how best to cook him (Jay retreats to the loo at this point, possibly to scream silently at the wall), before continuing westwards along the river's spacious banks into the city, where we chase an ever-elusive campsite sign through subways and across retail estates.

By the time we get there and get in line behind a group of elderly and impressively whiskered Ukrainian cyclists who meet every language the receptionist tries with blank incomprehension, it's 7 p.m., and even I can't muster the enthusiasm to suggest we cycle back into Orléans for dinner. Instead, we sit and drink acidic local wine from the campsite shop with doughy but delicious pizzas topped with merguez or tartiflette, according to taste, from the 'Indian Pizza Van' parked by the ping-pong tables (Indian, in this sense, appears to mean Native American judging by the fellow in the feathered headdress on the back) before retiring to an early bed. I sleep better in a tent than my own room these days, but the others are kept awake by the Ukrainians having an argument – and then, according to a furious Caroline, getting up in the night to wee in the hedge just by her head.

I wake up quite excited by the prospect of finally getting my tarte Tatin on to find a grumpy little group of campers waiting outside – the ground was like bedrock, Caroline's venerable air bed has developed a leak and Harry has spent much of the last 10 hours awake and watching *Seinfeld* – so thank God we've pre-ordered our croissants (savoury and very bready, with a good crisp base, 7/10), and there's a proper coffee machine behind the bar. We bump down the unmade and barely maintained road that leads to every self-respecting French campsite feeling very slightly chirpier.

Following a brief detour to a sports superstore to purchase Caroline a new bed, we're on our way in the sunshine – good roads running arrow straight through fields and forests, quiet enough to cycle two abreast, shooting the breeze, and it almost feels like cheating to stop after 20km in the handsome village of Marcilly-en-Villette for a coffee. There's a little café on the Place de l'Église with tables outside in such a sunny spot that it seems a shame not to have a beer, too (after all, they come in such very modest measures in France), and suddenly it's lunchtime and Madame is warning us we'll have to hurry if we want to catch the bakery before it closes for the afternoon.

Though the flaccid cheesy pastries and cloying rum babas we manage to scavenge aren't much cop, the setting for our picnic is so lovely that the only fly in the ointment is the loss of a bottle of wine we've purchased for later on the cobbles as we stagger back to our bikes, sleepy with the sun. It runs down towards the war memorial like blood between the stones, and suddenly awake and full of remorse, we hastily deploy all our newly filled bidons to slosh away our shame and get on the road.

It's not far to our dinner destination, Lamotte-Beuvron, which proves to be a surprisingly busy little place with the air of a home-counties market town, full of chic clothes shops and expensive stationers – and, on the outskirts, where the restaurants have turned to shuttered bars, I suddenly spy a familiar name, painted in faded lettering on the side of a *fin-de-siècle* mansion facing the railway. 'TATIN!' I shout. 'We're here!' I swerve dangerously across the carriageway and haul Eddy up to meet his destiny.

Like many great dishes, the tarte Tatin is claimed to have been born out of culinary clumsiness. At the end of the 19th century, this place was in the hands of the two Tatin sisters, the older of whom, Stéphanie, was in charge of the food. Perhaps a little flustered by the orders flying in from the mob of braying Parisian hunters who still frequent the forests of the Sologne in autumn, she shoved a tart into the oven upside down, or possibly without its pastry base, depending on which account you believe. Neither, to be honest, sound very likely to me, but nevertheless it's claimed that she decided to make the best of a bad job and serve it anyway. Maybe she reasoned that, by the time the tweed brigade got to dessert, they'd be too merry to notice the difference – but someone did, approved and a classic was born.

In dull truth, fruit tarts are an ancient speciality of the Sologne region, and the *gâteau renversé* (upside-down cake) existed long before the Tatin sisters themselves, yet, by 1903, their tarts were well known enough to merit a mention in the journals of the local geological society, which describe them, in an account of a field trip in the area, as 'a speciality of the house' and 'famous all over Sologne' – suggesting that, even in the homeland of apple tarts, Stéphanie's version was in some way special.

By the 1920s, word had spread far enough for the celebrated French critic Curnonsky, 'Prince of Gastronomes' (goals), to recommend 'The Famous Apple or Pear Tarte from the

Demoiselles Tatin of La Motte-Beuvron' in his travel guide, and by the late 1930s, it was a fixture on the menu at Maxim's, the Parisian institution that has played host to everyone from Marcel Proust to Lady Gaga. The owner at the time claimed to have stolen the secret recipe from Stéphanie herself after posing as a gardener at the hotel in his youth – the fact that he was only four when the sisters retired in 1906 makes this about as likely as anyone in their right mind putting a tart in the oven upside down, but to be honest, I'm not here for the history, I'm here for dessert.

It must be said that the hotel looks firmly closed to me, but, I reflect, as I pose for a victory photo (having waited three whole months, and an entire lifetime, for this moment), we're in France, where no doubt it's perfectly normal for a hotel to be shut mid-afternoon on a Friday, so instead, we push on to the nearest campsite. It's only 7.5km away, but the idea of cycling back to Lamotte for dinner is not a popular one; indeed, the peloton has already decided among themselves that they're not doing it, they tell me firmly as we stop to pick up some vital provisions at the village shop. Harry even goes so far as to ask the girl on the till for taxi numbers, which, as we're the only customers, she happily googles and writes down for us on a length of receipt.

Once safely installed in *le camping*, a lovely, if deathly quiet place at this point in the season, set around a large lake stupidly devoted to fishing rather than swimming, the ever-efficient Harry rings them all, and eventually makes contact with a man called Jean-Paul, who may or may not be able to pick us up after dinner, he says, he'll have to see. As every other number, including something which claims to double as an ambulance service, responds with a flat no, he has us over an apple-shaped barrel.

Fortunately, a train does run between the two places regularly enough to at least get us to Lamotte in time for our reservation without having to fall on JP's mercy for the outward leg – but when we arrive at the station, dolled up for this very special occasion, there's no sign of the 18.06 and, of course, no information either. A woman sweeping her steps by the level crossing notices us standing around and cheerfully tells us we've missed it – it came two minutes early … 10 minutes ago.

Panicking, we rush across the road to the bus stop: mysteriously, no service appears to run to the nearest town, and a very drunk man staggering away from the station bar is unable to suggest any alternatives (actually, he's unable to do anything but look terrified, possibly that one of us might ask him to drive us).

We sit sadly in the bus shelter while Harry calls every number we can find (thank God, I think, for fluent Francophones on this particular leg). Jay suggests cycling and picking up the bikes by train the next morning, Caroline hitchhiking – quite the done thing in France apparently – and, seeing my mythical tarte Tatin receding once again into the ether, I just sit there miserably, kicking the dust with my sandal.

But, from the jaws of defeat, the heroic Harry wrenches victory. A distant taxi operator says he does have an employee in this very village who might be able to help us out – and sure enough, a slightly battered estate car swings round the corner not five minutes later. I think Hélène – who explains as she moves a pile of shopping off the back seat, that she was just on her way back from the supermarket: 'My daughter wanted pizza for dinner' – is somewhat bemused by our effusive gratitude: I'm almost crying with joy, even when it turns out as we enter Lamotte that Harry has left all her worldly possessions in the bus shelter and we have to turn back to rescue them.

Hélène, like many people round here, she says, is a hunter –
'Bow and arrow, that's my thing.' Deer, hare, wild boar, she has
a freezer full. The Hotel Tatin? No, she hasn't been recently. Not
really her kind of place, though she won't elaborate, presumably reluctant to dampen our evident excitement. Certainly, the
place doesn't look too welcoming – the front door is still firmly
closed, so in the end we find our way in round the back, up what
look like they were once the kitchen stairs.

Madame inside, all smiles, thank God, is of course expecting
us – little wonder as I booked two months ago. Could we have
a drink at the bar first, we ask, as we're early. You can sit down
if you like, she replies. The table's ready.

In fact, it's one of the few actually laid for dinner in a rather
sepulchral dining room, an odd mix of faded tapestries, heavy
wooden furniture and bad art. We're in the corner, right by the
massive marble fireplace – the only other diners, two elderly
couples at the window tables, eye us anxiously as we chink
glasses in celebration of our achievement. Initially I put this
emptiness down to the hour – it's barely 7.30 p.m. – but to my
surprise, no one else arrives all evening. On a Friday in sunny
September, this ought to be a place of patisserie pilgrimage, yet
tonight it's just us and retirees here for the fishing, if the conversation I can hear is anything to go by.

The *menu du terroir* isn't terrible value, at €29 for three
courses, but there's not much of the *terroir* on there – no duck
or freshwater fish, and though nicely presented, the chilly
tomato carpaccio lacks the advertised 'flavours of yesteryear',
unless yesteryear was last February. My *tête de veau* is better:
lumps of soft and perfectly bland beige meat, with boiled
spuds and a punchy, lumpy ravigote sauce – and far better,
it seems, than the dry filet mignon of pork the others have
gone for.

We're not really here for the savoury stuff, though: it's a mere warm up act for the slices of tarte Tatin that arrive naked and unadorned in obedience to tradition. 'No cream, no,' says Madame firmly. 'This is how it's served.' I almost feel like a cliché for ordering it, but really, why else would you come here?

Perhaps anything would be a let-down after such a build-up, but I must confess to a slight disappointment: my piece is a little burnt on one side, and missing a chunk of pastry, too. The fruit itself is soft and jammy, caramelised rather than caramelly, and the pastry – shortcrust, I note with interest – is soft and almost spongey: pleasant enough, but no patisserie epiphany.

We quiz Madame on her return with glasses of local pear eau de vie (so excellent we persuade her to sell us some to take away in plastic cups). 'We cook it – all together, yes, pastry and fruit – in a very low oven for about an hour, maybe a bit less, and then we put it on a high heat on the hob, just to caramelise the apples, you know.' Everyone but Jay looks sceptical as we try to imagine this, but before we can ask any more technical questions, she's disappeared to talk about Labradors with the remaining couple by the window.

The Brotherhood of Tarte Tatin Lovers' Official Recipe for Tarte Tatin

Though the Hotel's version is nothing like the way I'd cook a tarte Tatin, it does sound fairly similar to the closest thing we have to an original recipe, from the handwritten notes of Marie Souchon, a friend of the Tatin sisters. These cooks, however, would have used a copper pan piled with coals on top so it was heated from all sides: Souchon notes that 'you will need equal heat from above and below to be successful', which is not terribly practical today, and may explain the disappointing pastry on the current Hotel Tatin menu.

A better approach, for those of us without embers to chuck around, comes from Jean-Paul Cousin-Martin, current Grand Master of the Brotherhood of Tarte Tatin Lovers, who cooks his apples for an hour before even so much as rolling out the pastry. Instead of the firm, caramel-slicked apples I've aimed for in the past, this yields a richly flavoured compôte much like the Hotel Tatin's, which can then be topped with very short, very buttery pastry. Here's my take, only modestly adjusted to my own experience. You can make it up to the end of step 3 a couple of days ahead.

Serves 6
8 small apples (I like Cox's or Russets), about 725g in total
100g sugar
70g butter, cut into pieces

For the pastry (or use 350g shortcrust, but it won't be as good)
210g flour
100g cold butter
1 egg yolk

1 Preheat the oven to 200°C/180°C fan/gas 6. Peel and quarter the apples, removing the cores. Put a heavy-based ovenproof pan about 20cm in diameter on the hob over a medium heat and add the sugar and butter. Melt together, then take off the heat and carefully pack the apples into the pan in two layers so they cover the base – I like to put the slices on their sides and arrange them in two concentric circles – remembering the sugar will be hot. Bake for 30 minutes.

2 Meanwhile, make the pastry by putting the flour into a large bowl with a generous pinch of fine salt and grating the butter into it. Rub in until well coated, then stir in the egg yolk and just enough cold water (about 3 tablespoons) to bring it together into a slightly crumbly dough. Shape into a disc, wrap well and chill.

3 After 30 minutes in the oven, put the pan on the hob (don't touch the handle!) for about 20–30 minutes over a low heat until the liquid round the edges is caramel-coloured. If towards the end of this time it shows no sign of browning, turn up the heat slightly, but be careful it doesn't burn.

4 Take off the heat and allow to cool slightly. Meanwhile, roll out the pastry until just large enough to cover the pan; it should be quite thick. Once the apples are cool enough (or you can leave them to cool completely at this point if you prefer), put the pastry on top, tucking it in round the sides, and bake for about 35 minutes again in the preheated oven before loosening around the edges and turning out on to a serving plate, again remembering the pan will be hot!

Km: 192.3

Croissants: 4, average score 7.5 (Note: I have a much nicer Yann Couvreur croissant on my return to Paris, which scores a 9/10, so possibly it didn't like having a Harry fall on top of it)

High: Finally making it to the Hotel Tatin

Low: Harry nearly getting squashed before we'd even left Paris

LIMOGES (CIRCUIT)

Clafoutis aux Cerises

A speciality of the Limousin (a rural region with a big fruit business), it seems early clafoutis were baked custards studded with purplish fruit, though many modern recipes are batter based, rather like sweet Yorkshire puddings. I found both on my greedy travels, and can happily report that, though almost two different desserts, they're equally delicious. The Limousin is also famous for the quality of its beef, and it even has its own breed of red cattle, which you'll find on menus all over France.

Backpedal, if you will, to early June in the Loire Valley where, 117km west of Lamotte Beuvron in the ancient city of Tours, I'm waving goodbye to the terrible two, Tess and Tor, who, having achieved their oft-stated aim of going big, are now going home, leaving me to my first full week on my own.

I turn my front wheel towards the railway station. Tours, like many provincial French towns I pass through, has a stunningly grand example, in this case designed by Victor Laloux, also responsible for the Beaux Arts Gare d'Orsay in Paris – now, of course, a fine museum with an excellent polar bear sculpture. In fact, the station is so lovely and I'm so uncharacteristically early that I do a circuit of its glorious tiled murals advertising the boundless possibilities of rail travel – a daring *belle-époque* couple ride a tandem through snow-capped Pyrenean peaks, a woman feeds geese by a stream in the Auvergne and a family promenades along the beach at Biarritz. The images are so thrillingly evocative they make my footloose heart throb, so God knows what they did to your average *fin-de-siècle* peasant.

I hotfoot it guiltily back to Eddy, whom I've left looking after the luggage, and make myself comfortable on the grindingly slow regional service to Limoges, including a bonus hour and a half at somewhere called Vierzon, which looks so unpromising in the pouring rain that I stick my head briefly outside and then beat a hasty retreat to my old friend the Relay café. Feeling a bit sorry for myself, I ogle a pack of Cadbury's chocolate fingers – *'Croquez, vous allez fondre! Encore plus de Finger!'* ('Bite it, you will melt! Yet more Finger!') – but instead, mindful I'm en route to the capital of the French beef industry, I grimly munch my way through a lentil salad and an enormous, unnervingly fizzy, pot of carrot vinaigrette instead.

It's merely drizzling in Limoges when I finally arrive and I'm disposed to like the place, until, on my way to the municipal campsite, I turn up yet another Avenue du Général Leclerc (one day I will write a fascinating thesis on why the French name things after national heroes while we commemorate local councillors) and see the road ahead climbing into the clouds.

As I quickly discover, the city is built on seven enormous hills, and it appears my campsite is on the other side of one of them while my dinner reservation is back in the centre. Having berated myself, the relevant tectonic plates and the world in general, there's nothing to be done but push on up and try to forget I'll have to do it all again in a few hours' time.

Not only is Camping Uzurat up a mountain, but out of town, too, down a side road past an enormous hypermarket and a Roman fort; handy for all the attractions, basically. Most of it is given over to campervans and the ramshackle cabins popular with gangs of contractors working away from home, but I manage to score a space that's only half waterlogged and comes with its own bone, half buried in the shadow of the hedge. This slightly sinister state of affairs makes more sense when a Yorkshire terrier leaps out of the Belgian-registered caravan opposite and makes straight for its treasure, ignoring the pleas of its owner, who comes running after it in a dressing gown. The dog eyes me suspiciously as it is forcibly removed from my pitch, leaving me contemplating the happy prospect of a night with half a lamb leg next to my head.

Limoges's promotional literature claims that 'Arts of fire deeply mark the city's identity, at the crossroads of artistic creation and industrial innovation,' which sounds marvellous if you're into floral porcelain. The capital of the old Limousin region, a mecca of metropolitan sophistication in a vast wilderness of fruit farms and cattle ranches, the city sits just west of the Plateau de Millevaches, though a thousand cows is a rather conservative estimate given that over a third of the Limousin is grazing land with one of the lowest (human) population densities in the country.

Unsurprisingly, given its prime position, it has been a centre for butchery since the Middle Ages: indeed, their trade guild was once so wealthy that it is said to have lent money to kings, and so powerful that the butchers received Henry IV when he visited the city in the 17th century, rather than the other way round. (Possibly the King was having problems with his repayments.) It feels today like a pleasant but rather slow place, though perhaps no city is at its vibrant, multicultural best on a wet Sunday evening.

Neither, of course, is this the best time for dinner anywhere, let alone provincial France, but a place going by the name of La Vache au Plafond (The Cow on the Ceiling) at least sounds like a safe bet for beef. Even in the tipping rain, it's hard to miss, thanks to a life-sized model cow standing outside, placidly allowing a bickering couple to flick their ash onto its back. To my disappointment, I'm seated by the bar, so I have to go to the loo twice in order to admire its fibreglass friend rearing out of a painted grass ceiling in the main dining room, brown-and-white head stretched out plaintively towards the table below, where they're busy tucking into steak. Reading the menu, I discover her name is Marguerite, the French for Daisy. It's all pretty weird to be honest, but after the carrot salad, it'll take more than that to put me off.

PAUSE-CAFÉ – Black or Blue?

Interestingly, it seems that the simple grilled steak is an idea adopted from the British – early French recipes are called things like 'beeft steks à l'Angloise'. Unlike our own, rather bloodless scale of rare, medium and well done, however, the French terms for cooked meat are far more evocative:

Bleu: very rare – lightly coloured on the outside, still mooing (or bleating) within.
Saignant: literally, bloody – what in the UK would be regarded as rare.
À point: medium-rare – perfectly cooked.

Bien cuit: medium – likely to still be pink inside, though there's always the risk, when ordering with a British accent, of receiving it incinerated instead, so proceed with caution. If you like them well done, however, emphasise the point with *très bien cuit* ... or, perhaps more safely, order something else.

Note that unless the cut is listed (*entrecôte* is rib-eye, and *faux-filet* sirloin; *filet* and *rumsteck* what they sound like), the steak will probably be the cheaper *bavette*/flank, or *onglet*/hanger, both of which are completely delicious but don't lend themselves to being served anything more than '*à point*' unless you really love chewing.

After lingering pleasurably over the many cuts on offer, I go for the *Assiette Madame La Vache*, a kind of Limousin Greatest Hits compilation of (raw) carpaccio, (rare) onglet and (braised) oxtail. And because you can't have steak without wine, and like many French restaurants they don't, somewhat cunningly, offer it by the glass, I order a half-bottle of Haute Gravières from nearby Bordeaux as well (half, it turns out, actually means two-thirds). Just as I'm tucking into both, mopping up the shallot sauce with crispy chips and feeling pretty pleased with myself, a large British party arrives.

'Do you speak English?' one demands at the bar, with not so much as a pre-emptory *Bonsoir*. The proprietor seems to take some pleasure in mutely shaking his head, and then abandoning them to a younger, slightly more polyglot waiter, who is immediately bombarded with questions – 'Diet Coke? Do you have Diet Coke? I want vodka and Diet Coke, but it has to be Diet, you understand?' 'Don't you have any fish?' and so on.

Suddenly a woman pops up in front of my book and points at my plate. 'Excuse me,' she asks loudly and slowly. 'Do you speak English?' I admit I do. 'OH MY GOD, you ARE English!' she hoots. 'What are you eating?' Having explained, and recommended it, I finish my wine and do a runner – I'm sure I hear one of them order kidneys and I'm not sure I want to be there when they arrive. As divine retribution, on my way back up to the campsite, it starts raining again, and I'm kept awake half the night by a plague of noisy frogs.

Worrying about what to do next doesn't help: groggy and grumpy, I lie in my dark prison the next morning listening to the rain, watching cheering YouTube compilations of people slipping over on ice and pondering my options. It's Monday, and I have to be in a little village near Carcassonne the following Saturday morning – via Bayonne, Pau, Toulouse and Castelnaudary, which is a punchy enough itinerary in itself but, satisfying as last night's dinner was, I don't feel like I've got the best of the beef yet.

On the other hand, none of the farms that open for visitors do so on a Monday, and I really need to head south tomorrow to have even the slimmest chance of keeping to schedule. I had considered trying to get to Périgueux in the Dordogne in time for its famous Wednesday market, but as it's neither foie gras nor truffle season, wisdom suggests there's not much point in cycling 100km to a place I'd have to leave by 11 a.m.

Impulsively, I log on to the SNCF site from my sleeping bag, book a morning train from Limoges to Bayonne for the following morning and immediately feel a lot better – thank goodness, I think for the hundredth time, for the abolition of European mobile roaming charges. That done, ice videos exhausted, I decide to spend the day hunting for some Limousin cattle, which feels like a pleasant enough plan if the sky ever stops leaking.

I literally cannot convey how great it feels to pedal off without my panniers, leaving the tent standing in its puddle of rainwater. Despite the weather, I have a glorious morning in the saddle, though I quickly regret snootily dismissing the one shopping centre bakery I pass early on, as this empty landscape is not replete with breakfast options.

It's not long before I spot my rusty red prey and stop to take a long-distance fuzzy pap shot of them, which proves unnecessary as soon they're everywhere. I even surprise a couple in an intimate moment, though neither of them seems that into it, if I'm honest.

I've scouted a promising-sounding lunch venue, Le Boeuf Rouge, from a little booklet put out by the French Association of Master Restaurateurs, and given to me by my friend Christophe the crêpier back in Brittany. Maître Restaurateur is a state-awarded title guaranteeing that the holder has the appropriate culinary qualifications, and that their food is cooked from scratch, using fresh ingredients, in an environment that meets national health and safety standards. The FAMR's website makes much of the fact that membership is 'VALIDATED, RECOGNISED AND CONTROLLED by the State'. Theresa May can't even work out the right meat for a lasagne.

The clouds are almost lowering themselves onto the church spires of Saint-Junien as I bowl down the hill and I only just make it into the squat Inter-Hotel, situated handily on an unprepossessing roundabout on the main road into town, before the heavens open in earnest again. Once more, I'm surprised by the lack of eyelids batted at a woman tipping up on her own for lunch on a Monday in full Lycra and gratified to find

I'm by no means the only solo diner: there are several smartly dressed people already installed who look like they've just stepped out of their offices for lunch. I blend right in.

The menu exceeds my highest hopes, with an entire section devoted to *le boeuf de race Limousine Blason Prestige* – I go for a sirloin, which comes punctured with a little flag showing it to be a pure-bred bovine aristo, some slightly soggy, deliciously potatoey chips and a generous pot of homemade béarnaise sauce, and, of course, it's delicious. Like the onglet the night before, however, it has the pale beige exterior of a piece of seared tuna – master restaurateurs or not, I reckon they could do with turning up the heat a bit underneath their pans.

I ask the waitress about what makes the beef so special. She replies as if it's completely obvious: 'Well, it's the very best, Madame. The flavour' – hands spread as if mere words are inadequate to describe its qualities – 'you won't taste better. The Limousin, it's the king of beef.' I tell her we have some pretty good stuff in Britain, too, and she generously acknowledges that she's heard of Scottish beef, but perhaps the spectre of BSE still hangs heavy, for she denies ever having tried it. Maybe one day, she smiles, somewhat unconvincingly. I say she really should and, having done my bit for the British beef industry, sit back to finish my lunch.

Earwigging on the next-door table as I eat the remaining béarnaise with a spoon, I'm delighted to hear her mention the magic word clafoutis while reeling off the list of desserts – they're another local speciality, and I'd feared I was too early in the year for the classic cherry variety, but it seems not. It's an unusual one, too, like a crisp Yorkshire pudding in texture rather than the usual wobbly flan, topped with berries and Chantilly cream.

As I polish off a double espresso to fortify me for the afternoon ahead, I get chatting to the men opposite, who work in an office nearby. 'Do you always come out for a proper lunch?' I ask, curious. They laugh; oh yes – 'Normally,' the younger one says, 'we have champagne, white wine, red wine, Cognac, the works.' Then straight back to work, his companion adds, chuckling.

'No, seriously, though, sandwiches, fast food, they're no good for you. You need a proper lunch. It's normal here.' I tell them that when I worked in offices in the UK, most people would eat lunch at their desks, Tupperware by the keyboard. They visibly shudder at the prospect, delighted by this tale of barbarism across the Channel.

The coffee feels like necessary fortification: seeing that I'm in Limoges from my endless cow photos on social media online, several people have strongly recommended a visit to Oradour-sur-Glane, the site of a Nazi massacre in June 1944 – and, according to one friend, 'a place everyone should visit once in their lifetime'. To be honest, I've always had mixed feelings about the idea of including such places in a tourist itinerary, but to swerve it now feels cowardly, so I set off, dragging my pedals with reluctance to face the horrors ahead.

I'm not wrong either – this isn't the right place to even try to sum up the experience, but I'm glad I went; the village has been left exactly as it was at the end of the war by order of General de Gaulle, as a permanent reminder of the barbarity that happened there, the entrance marked by a huge stone plaque bearing the words, '*Souviens Toi*. Remember'. Beyond sit roofless houses, tangles of rusted bicycles and cars, a baker's shop with powdery coals still in the oven, melted telegraph wires, and streets marked by familiar blue-and-white enamel signs. There's no real need for the notices requesting silence: it's impossible not to come out deep in brooding thought.

The cycle home proves a good time for reflection; the lush, almost-mountain pastures and gentle wooded hills round here are kind on the mind, and I'm so deep in thought that I don't see the snake basking in the sudden sunshine ahead of me until I almost run over it. I yelp with fear, it accelerates with what I assume is similar emotion and disappears into the bushes, though I catch a glimpse of black and yellow, and fancy it fairly large, perhaps a foot or so long. A few villages further on, I see my first lizard on a stone wall while trying to take a photo of an enormous cat lying supine in the middle of the road. By the time I make it back to Limoges, having not passed a single place selling Orangina in 27km, I feel ready enough for human company to brave the hypermarket in search of drinks and dinner.

As usual, food shopping cheers me right up. Who could fail to be happy in a place with maroon bananas from the French Caribbean, Breton intestine sausages and 75 varieties of espadrille? I buy a monstrously ugly tomato the size of a guinea pig for dinner along with a hunk of *tomme de Limousin* cheese, stick in a bottle of local cider and a packet of paprika crisps for a civilised aperitif, and leave feeling quite perky again – I even consider calling in on the Roman remains next door, but they're closed. Perhaps I've had enough history for one day.

Not quite enough drama, however: as I'm attempting to pay for my extra night at the campsite, loftily ignoring the group of workmen sitting around in reception staring at my Lycra-clad bum, there are sudden shrieks of alarm, and the young man at the desk immediately evacuates us all, indicating what looks to me very much like a hornet. '*Non, non, c'est vraiment dangereux!*' a woman tells me seriously as she cradles a small white dog protectively in her arms. We watch Monsieur enter stage left with his T-shirt held over his nose and mouth, and pursue the hefty insect across the room with some sort of spray before it visibly drops to the floor and we all excitedly cheer its demise. He opens the door again, and there's much head-shaking and hand-wringing from the assembled company, all of whom are clearly enjoying the theatre immensely.

As I study the feebly twitching corpse, the receptionist comes to drop a box over the evidence – explaining it's an Asian hornet, though this one, which must be two inches long even in death, is a mere tiddler. 'We are getting them more and more here: last year, we had a nest of over 1,000 of them on this roof!' he complains. 'One time, I went camping with my girlfriend and got stung by one and had to go to hospital – my whole arm swelled up.' Plus, he adds with some venom, they kill my bees. 'These things are not natural,' he concludes with force, selling me a washing-machine token. 'Man-made. MUTANTS.'

With which sobering thought I return to the tent, giving any flying objects in my path a wide berth, to begin my picnic. Though the bone has disappeared, I have new neighbours in its place: a middle-aged couple sitting around a camp stove on what look like proper chairs, though how they got them here on the two bikes propped against the hedge is a puzzle.

The man comes over to chat, and I feel briefly ashamed of myself, sitting on the wet grass eating crisps and drinking cider straight from the bottle while his wife barbecues sausages next door – for a moment I think that they might be about to invite me to join them, and then feel faintly aggrieved when they don't. Nevertheless, it's nice to have an exchange that doesn't peter out when I forget a vital piece of vocabulary, and I discover they're South Africans on a clockwise tour of France. They did a similar trip 30 years ago, he tells me, with a lot less luggage – he glances at my tent, which is about the same size as their porch. 'This is a lot more comfortable, though. If I sit down like you, I'll never get up!'

What with the excitement of conversation, cider and a fresh load of clean, dry washing, not even the frogs can keep me awake, though they do wake me up about 10 times between midnight and 5 a.m. instead.

Having packed up, eaten about three pounds of cherries straight from the bag and waved goodbye to my intrepid friends already busy frying bacon on their stove, I head back down the Avenue Leclerc for the final time to pay Limoges's old butcher's quarter a visit before I get on the train. The half-timbered Rue de la Boucherie is immediately identifiable by the fact that it's blocked by workmen engaged in stringing a banner across its narrow width, welcoming tourists to what is currently a building site, and the 15th-century Maison de la Boucherie, the only surviving example of the traditional butcher's dwelling (shop at the front, abattoir at the back, accommodation jutting out above), which is very much out of action behind safety barriers.

Squeezing past the scaffolding, I push Eddy round the corner and find myself in a little square, facing a stubby chapel standing all on its own, with the kind of *Frankenstein*-ish architecture that suggests extreme age. The sign outside identifies it as the chapel of Saint Aurélien, patron saint of butchers, and still the property of his Brotherhood, formed after the powerful medieval guilds were outlawed in the aftermath of the Revolution. Membership was once restricted to a group of six families, who guarded this power so jealously that they obtained special dispensation from the Church to intermarry within themselves, rather than admit outsiders; and until the 1960s, it was still limited to male, Roman Catholic butchers and their sons or sons-in-law.

Inside, the chapel is pleasingly gloomy, the better to show off the dramatically lit altar, with its flying saints and hanging cherubs suspended beneath a ceiling painted the brightest shade of sky. The Brotherhood's green-and-white processional flag hangs to one side, overlooked by a statue of the Virgin holding the infant Jesus, who's clutching something rosy red to his mouth that I initially take to be the sacred heart but is, according to the church guide, a kidney – traditionally given by butchers to customers as a children's treat, the way my butcher never lets me leave without a bone for the dog.

As I'm tragically four months too early for the annual *Frairie des Petits Ventres*, the Brotherhood's charmingly named 'Festival of Little Bellies', my next stop is Les Halles, the city's indoor market, which, I discover, is currently a building site too. The traders have moved temporarily into a collection of Portakabins next door, which don't have quite the atmosphere of the late-19th-century original, with its decorative tiling of fish and fowl, but wandering round, the variety of meat specialists – from the inevitable *triperies* to the chicken and rabbit merchants, the pork butchers and the many businesses proudly displaying the Limousin *Label Rouge* alongside photos of happy red cows – give me a flavour of the place … and that flavour is flesh.

Having had enough of that for a bit, and finding the bakers opposite inexplicably out of croissants at 9 a.m., I pick up an enormous slab of more familiar-looking clafoutis for the road: absurdly cheap, at €2.30 for about half a kilo, it's a dense yellow flan of a thing and (I can't resist a bite before cramming it on top of my panniers) almost like a chewy custard, with a slightly caramelised underside. This recipe, based on some hurried questioning of the girl behind the counter, comes pretty close.

Clafoutis aux Cerises

This creamy, chunky version is very much in the same flan tradition of those I saw in bakeries in the region, rather than the crisp clafoutis served hot for dessert in restaurants and after dinner: sturdy and surprisingly portable, it's a good choice for a picnic at the height of cherry season … though make sure you warn people to watch out for stones. Leaving them in may seem like the height of laziness on my part, but in fact adds to the fruit's flavour as well as making life considerably easier for the cook. (The demerara sugar isn't something I came across there, but a tip from fellow food writer Sarah Beattie, who lives in the south-west of France.)

Serves 6–8
Butter, to grease
3 tbsp demerara sugar
600g cherries
4 eggs
100g caster sugar
A pinch of salt
100g plain flour
500ml whipping cream
150ml milk
A dash of vanilla extract
50ml rum or brandy

1 Grease a deep roasting dish about 25 x 20cm wide with butter and sprinkle with the demerara sugar. Preheat the oven to 180°C/160°C fan/gas 4.

2 Remove the stalks from the cherries, but don't bother to stone them unless you're feeling very energetic. Put them in the base of the dish – they should cover the base in a single layer. Eat any extra.
3 Whisk together the eggs, caster sugar and salt well, then whisk in the flour until smooth, followed by the cream and milk. Finally, stir in the vanilla and rum or brandy.
4 Pour on top of the cherries, carefully put into the hot oven and bake for about 50–65 minutes, until firm on top with a slight wobble in the middle.
5 Allow to cool to warm before serving – though it's also very good cold.

Km: 95.6

Croissants: 0 (but not for want of trying)

High: My first lizard!

**Low: Oradour-sur-Glane would take
some beating**

LIMOGES TO BAYONNE

Chocolat Chaud

Hot chocolate may seem an odd choice on the Franco-Spanish border in midsummer, but Bayonne is the historic capital of the French chocolate industry   and this isn't any old hot chocolate.

Limoges station is just as impressive the second time round – so much so, in fact, that I lose my footing on the stairs as I'm gawping at the cupola, and fall painfully onto Eddy's sharp left pedal, the clafoutis in my pocket bouncing merrily to the floor before it can cushion the blow.

When I assure the guard who kindly helps me up that I'm honestly fine, just in a hurry, he directs me to platform 3 in pure Brummie; apparently, my accent needs work. Sadly, I don't have time to investigate why he swapped the stygian gloom of New Street for the stained glass of Limoges-Bénédictins, because I have a train to catch down to the Spanish border, via Bordeaux, world capital of wine.

I spend a grand total of seven minutes in this *cité du vin*, all of them stressful; the French may build beautiful stations, but their signage is no work of art, and I end up hauling Eddy and panniers up and down four further flights of slippery steps before practically hurling myself onto the Bayonne service, swearing under my breath.

Breathing a sigh of relief, I sit back, get my book out and am immediately accosted by a group of Americans who, in that lovely open fashion so suspiciously foreign to us northern Europeans, are keen to offer the hand of friendship to a lone traveller. They're from Chicago, over for a month on a vacation to celebrate their retirement, and they make me feel both extremely daring, especially when I mention camping (I do point out that there aren't many bears wandering around provincial France) and cycling. 'My, you are brave,' one says. 'I'd be terrified on these roads.'

Apart from the traffic, however (so fast!), they're enjoying themselves. The people are so nice, and the food – well, the pastries – the older man whistles through his teeth in quiet admiration. They kindly tell me if I ever decide to do a similar ride in the States, I should look them up. A vision of an 18-wheeler truck whistling past me on a lonely freeway as coyotes howl in the distance passes before my eyes. I shiver involuntarily. Sure, I say. I will definitely do that.

As we chat the train whips through the endless flat pine forests of the Landes, and when it finally pops out, it's into steep, almost fortified architecture of the Basque country, all whitewash and timbers and overhanging roofs in the same vivid red as the local spice, *piment d'Espelette*, and the traditional Basque beret. Sadly, it's still raining, though.

As I reluctantly wheel Eddy in the direction of the deluge, a man stops me and points to a small train on the far platform. 'That one!' he says. Whatever expression my face assumes at this point prompts him to add, 'Saint-Jean?' and then, more uncertainly, 'Are you a pilgrim?' and I realise my bedraggled appearance and air of beatific serenity has led him mistakenly to assume that I'm about to embark on the Camino de Santiago pilgrimage route across the Pyrenees, and I start hooting with laughter, at which point he backs away nervously.

In truth, I had seriously considered walking the ancient Way of St James to Santiago de Compostela with a friend a few years ago, excited by the idea of bringing Wilf along as a tiny pilgrim, but then got put off by the idea of 10kg of Scottish fluff being eaten by a Pyrenean shepherd dog along the way. Right now, however, another train is a tempting prospect given the weather outside, and I regret my hasty '*Non, Monsieur!*' even more when I step out of the station and realise that Bayonne is currently undergoing the same extensive programme of civic remodelling as Limoges and Nantes.

Even better, tonight's hotel is on a pedestrianised street and up a vertiginously steep flight of stairs. I abandon Eddy round the corner, and dash through the downpour, hauling my soaking panniers up to a rather grand salon, where several policemen are sitting on plump sofas drinking coffee with a man I assume to be the owner. They look round in surprise as I drop my worldly belongings on the carpet and brandish my passport – I'll be honest, the whole place feels a bit strange, but given the weather, I'd happily sit down with them for a cuppa, if only I didn't have an hour to get to the chocolate museum before it closes.

PAUSE-CAFÉ – Chocolat

One might assume that the French chocolate industry was centred around the chic boutiques of Paris, or perhaps somewhere slightly closer to Belgium, but it's Bayonne's location on the opposite side and end of the country, barely 30km from the Spanish border, that led to its historic status as the national capital of cocoa.

The Spanish, who first brought cacao beans to Europe, guarded the secrets of chocolate production jealously, and though a port like Bayonne would have received shipments of the precious cargo, it was Portugal, a country which did a spot of South American marauding of its own, which inadvertently exported the craft across the Pyrenees along with its Jews. By 1687 Bayonne's nascent chocolate industry seems to have been in the hands of these religious refugees, based in their ghetto of Saint-Esprit, across the river from Bayonne proper.

Municipal authorities were initially suspicious of the novel substance, but locals were quick to see its financial potential and, having learnt the process, attempted to wrest control from the very people who'd taught it to them by banning them from the industry.

For all this ugly business, trade thrived – Bayonne exported chocolate nationwide, though nowhere was it more popular than in the city itself. By 1830, more people were employed in chocolate-making there than in the whole of Switzerland, and today, though somewhat smaller, its producers still specialise in what they claim is a Spanish style of chocolate, more bitter, less sweet, with notes of cinnamon and other warm spices, and the city is stuffed with aromatic boutiques.

I wish I could tell you I learnt all of this from the Atelier du Chocolat museum, but, somewhat inevitably, having dodged barriers and pneumatic drills, hauled my bike over a pedestrian bridge, done several turns of a large and busy roundabout and eventually found the place in a scrubby backstreet, they won't let me in – 'Too late, Madame! You can come back tomorrow afternoon.'

Naturally, the museum shop is still open for business, so much as I dearly wish to burst into tears in a soggy heap on the floor, I decide to take solace in sugar – my misery is clearly embarrassingly obvious, because as I stare balefully at the selection, sniffing loudly, the lady from reception taps me on the shoulder and holds out some samples. It's small consolation, frankly, but I'm not proud: I take two.

After a glum selfie outside with my purchase, a slab of 70 per cent cocoa flavoured with vivid stripes of *piment d'Espelette*, I head for the more welcoming embrace of Chocolat Cazenave, tucked away in the arcades underneath the old town's huddle of half-timbered townhouses. This glittery Art Nouveau tearoom has played host to everyone from the Duchess of Windsor to Roland Barthes, and now, desperately trying not to drip on the immaculate mosaic tiling, me.

A lady perched on a stool behind a till appears to be in charge of both restaurant and shop, alternately placing orders on a large spike and weighing purchases on a huge silver scale. Everything is displayed beneath glass cloches or in the kind of wooden cabinets more usually seen in Victorian museums, the bars of chocolate in their colourful paper wrappings arranged in rainbow order from Number 1 (milk chocolate, pale blue) to 12 (dark chocolate and almonds, leaf green), and the whole effect is more like an old-fashioned apothecary than a temple to pleasure.

Eventually, I'm led to a seat next to a fantastically old couple both glaring at the Pekinese winding itself around the table leg opposite as its buxom owner gathers up her many scarves for departure. Though the menu lists teas and coffee, beer and ice cream, everyone's really here for one thing: the famous Cazenave hot chocolate, served rich and frothy in the traditional fashion. The usual accompaniment, I learn, is 'toasts', but I decide to buck the trend and try a gâteau Basque, a shortcrust tart filled with almond frangipane or black cherry jam, while I'm here. *Non, Madame*, not possible, the white-aproned waitress says, without further explanation. Perhaps the toasts? As I don't seem to have a choice in this matter, I nod meekly and await what she deigns to bring me.

I must concede, perhaps she was right. For someone brought up on Cadbury's drinking powder, this hot chocolate is barely recognisable as the same drink. Intensely bittersweet, rich but not creamy, with a handsome mousse of cocoa bubbles rising out of the rose-patterned Limoges porcelain like a crown, it's exactly what I need today, and the comfort of the accompanying thickly sliced, generously buttered brioche toast feels like a big, warm hug. Cake would, I see now, have been entirely de trop.

That said, I slightly regret having declined the customary accompaniment of whipped cream as a waste of calories as I see the scowls of my pensioner companions relax into grins of sheer childish joy as they stir the towering mounds into their cups. Emboldened by this change, I venture to ask, ever so politely, if they're regulars here. Oh no, the lady says. She looks at me closely and then helpfully tells me that too much chocolate makes you fat. Her husband adds firmly, 'Once a week. That's all.' To be fair, they're both birdlike, albeit of the angry variety.

Hot Chocolate and Buttered Brioche (in the style of Maison Cazenave)

Perhaps the ultimate afternoon tea on a cold, wet day, the original relies on a special long-handled wooden tool called a *moussoir*, but you can replicate it fairly satisfactorily at home with a whisk.

Makes 2
100g 70% cocoa chocolate
200ml whole milk
A dash of vanilla extract
2 thick slices of brioche
Salted butter, to spread

1 Grate the chocolate or cut into small pieces. Meanwhile, heat the milk in a medium pan over a medium heat until steaming, then take off the heat and add the chocolate. Leave for 2 minutes, then stir until melted.
2 Add a dash of vanilla extract, then put on a very low heat and beat for about 15 minutes by hand, or rather less if using electric beaters, until very light and moussy.
3 Scoop the foam into two small cups, then pour the hot chocolate on top. Lightly toast the brioche, spread with the butter, and serve the two together.

As I wait for Madame at the desk to tot up my bill, I ask how they make the hot chocolate – is it possible to buy the ingredients here or look into the kitchen? As she smilingly shakes her head I suddenly realise that I've left my wallet sitting on my bike for the last 30 minutes and dash off in a panic, flinging my phone at her as security (London habits die hard). When I come back, damp with relief, I give up any attempt at cross-examination and buy a bar of Number 12 for the road instead. I'm rewarded by hearing, as she hands over the phone, that I have a very pretty dog. I do, I think proudly, looking at Wilf's furry tummy on the lock screen, though he feels a very long way away right now, sunning himself in the Home Counties while I'm shivering in the South of France.

With hot chocolate warming me from the inside out, and the rain slowed to an exhausted drizzle, I make a pilgrimage to the cathedral and then enjoy a pleasant squelch around the little nooks and crannies of Bayonne, some of the lanes between the houses so narrow I have to flatten myself against one wall if I meet someone coming from the other direction. I pass shops selling Basque berets and colourful tinned fish and duck into a boutique offering the one local speciality I can happily invest in: the *kanouga*, a delicious squidgy chocolate caramel created in 1905, apparently inspired by the wealthy Russian visitors who flocked to the nearby seaside resort of Biarritz. (The name is claimed to be a bastardisation of the Russian city of Kaluga, south-west of Moscow.)

Still licking the sugar from my lips, I stumble upon a ham museum, attracted by the pair of cartoon pigs outside through which some British children are happily poking their faces as their mother takes a photograph. 'Museum's closed,' her husband reports, coming out of the shop. The kids wail, I sigh and, as the charcuterie in front still looks open (*quelle surprise*), decide to go in anyway to buy some *jambon de Bayonne* for tomorrow's lunch. The lights still seem to be on out back, so I ask Madame behind the till whether I can have a very quick look before paying. 'Of course!' she says, taking my ham from me. 'Take as long as you like!'

The man may not have been impressed, but I'm enraptured by this glorious display of photographs of happy black-and-pink pigs captioned by inspirational quotes such as 'Age doesn't matter. Unless you're a ham'. The text underneath explains that the Basque country has a micro-climate ideal for the ageing of hams – slightly unnervingly described as 'the period in which they develop their personality' – and that, in 1981, the Basque Kintoa was declared on the path to extinction, thanks to more productive English breeds', before being saved by, who else but the Brotherhood of Basque Pork. It is now, the boards proudly declare, 'an ambassador' for the region. What a build-up! I exit both excited about making the Kintoa's acquaintance, and strongly considering getting a tattoo of my new favourite proverb, '*Lou jamboû pertout que hé boû*' in Basque – 'Ham goes with everything'.

Naturally all the restaurants I've earmarked as potential ham providers are closed for their annual holidays, and after wandering around furiously for a bit, huffing to myself, I end up in a cider and tapas place with a promising number of Xs in its name and the atmosphere of a brightly lit Basque Harvester. No sparse carvery here though: in fact, the ham arrives in such quantity that I suspect, indeed hope, that no rare Kintoa pigs have been harmed in its production. I follow it with a slightly chewy salt cod and red pepper stew and a delicate, barely set sheep's milk junket with *piment d'Espelette* jam, plus a bottle of acidic local cider that reminds me of the stuff served with such great theatre across the border in San Sebastián.

The moon is rising over the river as I pick my way home through the puddles, and the half-timbered houses on the other side shimmer in its light. I haven't seen the best of this place, I think. And next time I'm definitely buying a beret.

Km: 16.6

Croissants: 0 (but, to be fair, this stage didn't include breakfast)

High: Drinking the world's finest hot chocolate in a tearoom stuck in time

Low: Being turned away from the chocolate museum in the rain

STAGE 9

BAYONNE TO PAU

Poule au Pot

Though associated with royalty, poule au pot, a stuffed chicken poached in a simple, vegetable-studded broth, is good wholesome fare for princes and peasants alike, and an excellent way to make a decent bird stretch a bit further, too.

It's started raining again by the time I gingerly unlock my bike from the narrow stairwell of the slumbering hotel and make my way out of Bayonne the next morning, early enough that the lights of the rush-hour traffic shimmer on the wet road, and the broad, sluggish River Adour shines the same grey as the pre-dawn sky. My route follows its banks more or less closely all day, which sounds like it ought to guarantee a fast, flat ride, but, of course, as any GCSE geographer will tell you, rivers descend towards the sea, while I'm travelling inland towards the city of Pau, 120 or so kilometres to the east, on the edge of the Pyrenees. This makes for a completely terrifying gradient profile on my route-planning app, yet, thanks to the river, it climbs so gradually at first that I barely notice it as the main road out of town turns off into autoroutes and dual carriageways. I continue to meander along the river's increasingly wooded shores, past fishermen in flat-bottomed boats casting nets into the glassy water, shuttered restaurants advertising eels and lampreys and thrillingly Pyrenean-looking farmhouses as I head straight for the hills on the horizon.

At one point a high-speed train shatters the placid peace, but otherwise I see little traffic, only kiwi orchards (having only lately learnt that kiwis grow in Europe, rather than tropical jungles, I'm excited enough by these to stop to take a photo of their trailing vines) and a field of punky-looking goats, who watch with quiet satisfaction as I electrocute myself on the fence trying to get a good shot of their grumpy faces, which remind me fondly of the dog. After yowling at the swift kick of pain, which feels almost as if someone's flicked an elastic band hard at my heel, I find myself helplessly humming 'That Don't Impress Me Much' over and over as I push on to the town of Peyrehorade before stopping for breakfast. Fortunately, I'm already close enough that Shania doesn't quite succeed in sending me over the edge.

Pedalling into the centre, I'm annoyed to find the way blocked by an all-too-familiar yellow *route barrée* sign before realising, having slid discreetly past it, that the road is closed for market day – an event I'm only too happy to dismount for. Like many of the best markets, this isn't the most scenic of affairs, sprawling scruffily out of a long narrow place that clearly functions as a car park for the rest of the week, but it's full of stuff to look at. There's a donkey-milk soap stall, and a donkey salami stall (the two face each other, but it's not immediately clear if they're the same operation, or sworn enemies), piles of greyish tripe and strings of fresh garlic, as mild and milky as a spring onion.

Thinking already of lunch, I buy the smallest, heaviest melon I can find, a stick of almost black rye bread that looks promisingly fibrous and, more importantly, is half the size of everything else on the stall, and a croissant (7/10: bit soft on top, but excellent flavour) and retire to the Bayonne Bar for a *café crème* and a spot of idle gawping – one of the lesser-sung pleasures of such slow travel.

PAUSE-CAFÉ – French Bread: A Bluffer's Guide

First, choose your bakery. To be honest, you probably won't have much choice, and the French appetite for fresh bread means they're rarely terrible, but look for the blue-and-yellow sign of a baker putting a loaf into the oven under the words '*Artisan Boulangère*', which indicates the bread is made on the premises (a '*dépôt de pain*' means they sell someone else's bread, which is harder to judge).

The baker's name on the sign is often a good omen: if they're proud enough to boast, they're probably doing something right (and if the acronym MOF, or Meilleurs Ouvriers de France, 'best craftsmen of France', appears after their name, even better). As part of the national drive to promote the work of skilled artisans, France is home to any number of regional and national baking competitions, so indications of success may be listed on the window.

Once inside, quietly greet the queue and, as anywhere, if it's busy, try to work out what you want before getting to the front. Feel free to ask for it '*bien cuit*' (well cooked) if you like it crusty, or '*pas trop cuit*' if you prefer it soft and fluffy, and even to ask for just a half or '*demi*' baguette (though they may have smaller *bâtard* available, too).

Baguette tradition/à l'ancienne must, by law, be made using just
flour, water, salt and sourdough levain (or sometimes yeast)
and then hand-formed. They're usually the ones with the
pointy ends.

Baguette ordinaire/classique/normal is usually cheaper, fluffier
(so lasts a bit longer) and made with yeast. They have
round ends.

A *flûte* is a slightly thicker baguette, which is ideal for
sandwiches.

A *ficelle*, literally string, is a very skinny baguette, which is very
crunchy and completely useless for sandwiches, but find a
cheese or lardon one and they make a very decent lunch on
their own.

Pain de campagne is a round sourdough loaf, usually made with
a proportion of wholemeal flour.

Pain de mie is a soft white tin loaf, rather like a British sandwich
loaf, but generally slightly sweeter and thus, in my opinion,
to be avoided unless making bread and butter pudding.

Pain complet is a brown loaf.

Pain aux céréales is a multigrain loaf: *seigle* is rye, *avoine* oat, *blé
noir* or *sarrasin* buckwheat and *orge* barley.

Pain cuit au feu de bois means it's been baked in a wood oven,
and *au levain* is sourdough.

Fougasse is a Provençal shaped loaf that is found in bakeries
all over the country, usually stuffed or flavoured with
something. Because it's both crusty and rich in olive oil, it
keeps relatively well, and is a good thing to buy with your
morning croissant just in case you don't find any lunch.

I'm always astounded by the feast of humanity that populates the average French market, even on a Wednesday morning, and as I wobble back down to the main road, having stashed the melon awkwardly on top of a pannier and buried the bread deep in anticipation of further rain, I can't help wondering, does no one round here have a job to go to? (A 21st-century job, I mean: there's a woman plaiting a chair next to a display of wicker baskets, a man sharpening knives and, underneath a concrete shelter, various old men selling chickens and rabbits from cages, including one particularly magnificent cockerel that I regret I just don't have room for today.) Though looking it up later, I discover that France currently has one of the highest unemployment rates in Western Europe, at 9 per cent; in fact, I suspect many of these people are small farmers for whom this is part of the weekly routine. Certainly, there's an air of happy purpose about both shoppers and stallholders as they chit chat their way through the morning, poking fruit and squinting at nylon housecoats like they're the new season's collection from Paris.

As I climb, still ever so gradually, the villages begin to feel more closed in, the houses sturdier, the windows smaller, almost fortified against the weather, and deserted save for the crowds of house martins I chase down the silent streets, swooping to catch insects in front of my wheel. I pass another of my favourite roadside animals, the donkey, and a huge free-range dog, which trots down the road in complete oblivion to my hopeful attempts to woo it, though as its shaggy coat completely covers its eyes, it's unclear if it can actually see me.

My journey soon takes me off the grandly named Route Impériale, to my slight disappointment, and on to the D187, a fast, busy and strikingly straight road lined on one side by the usual parade of plane trees. Just as I'm cursing the dramatic effect their roots have wrought on the tarmac, it begins to rain again, and I suddenly appreciate the brief intervals of cover the trees provide. A passing lorry-load of sheep, their woolly haunches pressed against the slats, sprays me with what could be mud, but smells ominously like something worse, and I'm relieved to eventually reach Orthez, more for the shelter it provides for consuming a couple of squares of Bayonne chocolate than for its handsome 14th-century bridge or 12th-century church, neither of which I notice in my soggy despondency. The chocolate's good, though. Extra good, possibly, in the circumstances.

From here on, the road begins to ascend more noticeably, culminating in an absolute beast of a hill coming out of Maslacq, which rears up to the horizon so dramatically that I pull over to remove my rain jacket and, waiting for a break in the traffic to spare my blushes, have time to observe a mobile home labouring on its 10.7-per-cent upper flanks. Thankfully, once I've conquered the first bit, it turns out to be one of those climbs whose bark is worse than its bite and I'm rewarded by a joyous downhill into the village of Lagor, where I screech to an abrupt halt by the world's most perfect picnic stop: a table by the church overlooking the valley below, with a water tap and a bin.

I literally could not have designed it better given that it's also, at 1.30 p.m., empty save for a couple smoking on a bench who look, I decide as I cut into the melon with my contraband knife, like they're having an affair and it's not quite working out as they'd hoped. Though almost devoid of perfume, the fruit proves nectarous in its sweetness and, squashed into my rye bread with a fistful of savoury, nutty jambon de Bayonne, tastes like manna from heaven, though I regret not removing my gloves before engaging with its sticky juices. Why have I never thought of putting melon in a sandwich before, I wonder? – it's a game changer. Unable to live in the moment, I can't help then thinking how perfect this whole set-up is going to look on Instagram – and indeed, I don't want to boast, but it did get 564 likes, even though I can't resist mentioning the business with the sheep shit.

As I leave Lagor, I notice the valley on the other side of the ridge is far more heavily populated than the one I've left, and realise to my slight shock that I'm nearer to Pau than I'd dared hope – it almost looks as though it's at the bottom of the hill. In fact, adding a slight detour into the disappointingly workaday suburb of Jurançon in the hope of tasting their famous honeyed wine, which results in a scolding from the satnav and not so much as a single bar open for business, I actually have another 40km to go, much of which seems to be through the endless roadworks of Pau itself. May and June appear to be Digging Season on the French transport network.

When I finally reach my hotel I'm so damp and cross with the potholes and erratic diversions that even the pleasing Del Boy connotations of the address, Rue Nelson Mandela, fail to raise a smile. Though not quite Peckham, it is a tower block, and after impressing the receptionists with my serviceable but really quite modest French, I immediately blot my copybook by coming back down to complain that the key they've given me doesn't work. They try it in the machine, confused, and one of them accompanies me back to the room to see for herself – quite a trek – only to announce, in the slow and kindly manner of someone addressing a small and particularly simple child, '*Non, 229 BIS, Madame!*'

Bis? I query as she unlocks the room next door. What's that? She shrugs – it's just *bis*. We reach a linguistic impasse, and I thank her and go in and look it up. It has the same meaning as 229A would in a British address. So that's a useful piece of

French vocabulary I've learnt, and finally explains what all those 'itinéraires bis' mean on signposts – alternative routes. Every day's a school day here.

Though I'm sure it's a great city with all manner of attractions, I'm in Pau for one reason, and one reason only: poule au pot, a dish associated with Pau as the birthplace of Good King Henri, who is said to have declared, 'If God grants me life, I will see to it that there will be no labourer in all my kingdom without the means to have a chicken in his pot,' a sentiment echoed by Louis XVIII, two centuries later. A laudable ambition, but given the average diet in the 17th century was mostly black bread and the rest vegetables, with only the occasional treat of salt pork or pig fat, poached chicken for all has a certain Marie Antoinette-ish quality to my British ears.

Nevertheless, in keeping with its proud heritage as the food of working people, poule au pot is usually consumed at lunchtime only. Fortunately for me and my dwindling store of Anglo-Saxon patience, I find one local institution that dares to serve its much-acclaimed chicken in the evening, too, and I can't think of a nicer way to spend a dark, rainy night after a mighty 133km in the saddle (a trip record!) than sitting in the warm dining room at Chez Olive, tucking into a cold glass of sweet Jurançon wine with buttery goose liver pâté on hot toast, followed by a steaming bowl of intensely savoury chicken broth replete with the golden floating coins of fat so esteemed by Jewish mothers. Also in the bowl is a great ball of forcemeat-stuffed cabbage resting on a bed of poached chicken and vegetables.

I'm not the only woman in there eating chicken alone; there's a Japanese lady who takes even more photographs than me, and the restaurant is obviously used to being a place of pilgrimage.

The waiter who delivers this unapologetically beige dollop of pure comfort takes the time to talk me through its constituent parts: the forcemeat contains the chicken innards, and the broth leeks and turnips, too, as well as peppercorns and bay, and I should eat it with the rice and these two sauces, one of which is tomato-based, and the other creamy. He beams like a proud father.

Though I must confess that I have been thinking quite a lot about hot curries and spicy noodles for the past few days, I find that I really enjoy the soothing blandness of it all; it's just so wonderfully simple: chicken, broth, root veg and plain rice – it needs nothing more, not even lime pickle. In fact, it's the kind of thing I can imagine craving were I a 17th-century French peasant miserably chewing on a crust of old bread.

Poule au Pot à la Façon de Chez Olive

The stuffing, and the generous vegetable elements of this dish, are designed to stretch out the weekly chicken yet further, but in fact make it a complete dish in its own right, though at Chez Olive they serve it with rice, which is also a nice way to soak up the copious broth. This is a dish that it's well worth buying a good chicken for if you can – by which I mean a chicken that's lived life a bit, and had a chance to develop some flavour. It doesn't need to be huge, because there's enough other stuff here to keep everyone happy; and though they're much harder to find in the UK than France, it is possible, if not at a butcher's or farm shop, then online (I found one with feet! Which was thrilling, but not strictly necessary). Note that you'll need a poultry needle and thread, or some cocktail sticks, for this recipe.

Serves 4

1 good chicken, about 1.8kg

2 litres chicken stock

1 tsp peppercorns

4 small leeks, trimmed, or 2 large ones, cut into thick chunks

4 small carrots, scrubbed, or 2 large ones, cut into thick
chunks

12–16 small new potatoes

4 small turnips, cut in half if on the larger side, or 1 large one,
cut into chunks

6 large Savoy cabbage leaves

For the stuffing

A knob of butter

2 banana or 4 round shallots, finely chopped

2 plump garlic cloves, finely chopped

2 sprigs of thyme, leaves picked

A good grating of nutmeg

4 chicken livers

420g sausage meat (about 6 sausages' worth)

75g fresh white breadcrumbs

2 tbsp Armagnac or other brandy

For the sauce blanche (optional)

1 tbsp butter

1 tbsp flour

2 tbsp crème fraîche

1   Start with the stuffing. Melt the butter in a small frying pan
     over a medium-low heat and sauté the shallots until soft, then
     add the garlic, thyme leaves and nutmeg. Fry for a couple
     more minutes, then allow to cool.

2 Meanwhile, finely chop the livers, discarding any stringy bits, and put them into a large bowl. Add the sausage meat and breadcrumbs and stir in, then add the brandy and season. Mix well.

3 Put roughly two-thirds of the stuffing inside the chicken, then either sew the neck up, or use cocktail sticks to secure it (my preferred method).

4 Bring 1.75 litres of chicken stock to the boil in a large pot with the peppercorns, and add the chicken. Bring back to the boil, turn down the heat and simmer very gently for 45 minutes, then add the vegetables apart from the cabbage leaves and cook for 30–45 minutes, until both the chicken and the vegetables are done (if the chicken's juices run clear, from the thickest part of the thigh, before the veg are done, lift it carefully out of the pot and set aside to keep warm, then turn the heat up under the pan to finish cooking the vegetables).

5 While the chicken is cooking, bring a pan of salted boiling water to the boil. Carefully cut out the base of the tough central core from the cabbage leaves and discard, then blanch them for 2 minutes, drain the pan (no need to wash it up at this point) and cool the leaves under cold running water to stop them cooking any further. Dry well.

6 Stuff the cabbage leaves by rolling a generous tablespoon of the remaining stuffing mixture into a short cylinder at the base of one of the leaves, above the cut stem, then tuck in both sides and continue rolling up to the top of the leaf. Put, seam down, in the base of the same large saucepan you used to blanch the cabbage, and repeat. Tip in the remaining 250ml of stock and bring to a simmer. Cover with a lid and turn the heat down very low. Cook for 45 minutes, then turn off the heat but leave covered to keep warm.

7 Once the chicken is done, keep warm while you make the white sauce, if serving. Melt the butter in a small saucepan, then stir in the flour and cook for a couple of minutes. Gradually, spoonful by spoonful, whisk in the chicken stock the cabbage rolls were cooked in. Once smooth, take off the heat and stir in the crème fraîche. Season to taste.

8 Carve the chicken and divide between shallow bowls with the stuffing, the cabbage rolls, the vegetables and a good ladleful of broth. (If the middle of the stuffing looks pink, and this worries you, fry it briefly in a hot pan first.) Serve with the white sauce, and steamed rice if you'd like to bulk it out further.

I order a pastis béarnais for pudding, after establishing, to my disappointment, that it's a local cake rather than a boldly boozy take on a hollandaise – the pastis part of the name apparently comes from its anise flavouring. Not that I'm complaining, given that it comes with both crème anglaise and ice cream – the actual dream team.

The rain is making a night of it, which makes navigating an utter misery – I have to pull into a drive-through McDonald's at one point to check the map on my phone – and by the time I haul the bike into our little room, there's so much water dripping off my helmet that I can barely see to find the light switch. I hang my sodden clothing up in the hope that it will at least dry to damp overnight, give Eddy an apologetic pat, and get into bed, feeling fairly buoyant, to check train times for tomorrow, when I'm planning to travel to Toulouse.

But not, it seems, by train. It's my first strike day in the South, and while this hasn't proved too great a problem thus far, down here – as I discover now that they've released details for tomorrow's action – when they strike, they really go for it. After spending 45 minutes trying to find a work-around to the problem, I reluctantly realise I have absolutely no choice but to cycle there instead – about 160km. I check the gradient. It looks like a seismograph record of an earthquake. I check the weather. More rain. I quickly turn off the light before anything else can go wrong.

Lying awake, I fret about whether I can even cycle that far – I've done 100 miles before, but not with this much stuff, in unknown territory, without people handing out energy drinks and bananas at regular intervals. With the dismal weather added into the equation, it feels like the universe is ganging up on me, and it's annoying. But the fact is, I don't have any other choice: it's Wednesday, I have a lunch date on Saturday of the kind you'd cycle twice as far for and two cassoulets to put away first. This realisation is oddly comforting – there's no point in worrying, so I may as well get as much sleep as I can. Which, exhausted by today's exertions, I promptly do, watched over by a silent Eddy, who seems to be undaunted by the day ahead. To be fair, he hasn't seen the route.

Km: 133.1

Croissants: 1 (7/10)

High: That cold glass of sweet wine in a warm restaurant

Low: Being sprayed in the face with sheep dung

STAGE 10

PAU TO CARCASSONNE

Cassoulet

Cassoulet, a 'voluptuous monument to rustic tradition' as Richard Olney describes this unapologetically rich gratin of beans and animal fat, studded with various meats and served hotter than the southern sun, is the star turn of Gascon cuisine. Many claims are made about the different versions native to its three epicentres, Castelnaudary, Carcassonne and Toulouse, but in truth they are all delicious.

As I set off through the drizzly grey suburbs of Pau at dawn, I have a nasty premonition I'm about to work up a serious appetite, something that proves correct the moment my app demands a sharp left turn off the main road and up a single-track road through the woods. Glancing down at my bar computer, I'm startled to realise the gradient has quickly escalated to an unprecedented 15 per cent. Though it's still damp, trees dripping around me, the day is surprisingly warm, and by the time I pop out at the top (NB: 'Pop' may be too energetic a verb), I'm sticky and more than a little cross with life – until, turning round to pack my jacket, I see the Pyrenees behind me, rearing snow-capped out of the fog settled in the Pau valley. It's a truly thrilling moment – and even better, the view stays with me for much of the morning, becoming increasingly wreathed in cloud as the day wears on.

I stop for breakfast in a dilapidated little town where the only café open is full of old men smoking and watching the lottery results – I sit outside in the gloom and can't even be bothered to finish my croissant (3/10, yeasty, puffy, almost unpleasant). Instead, I put two lumps of sugar into a fierce little coffee, and take a swig from my hip flask.

Though this is ultimately to prove one of the worst rides of the entire tour, for a few hours it's hard to feel glum with a mountain range over my shoulder, with its bears (respectfully referred to in Basque as *lo moussu*, or 'the Sir'), goats and ski slopes to daydream about.

The topography and the weather do their un-level best to keep me interested in my more immediate environment, though – both are almost comically up and down, and it takes little things like a poster for a bovine beauty contest (outside a butcher's, of all places) to keep me going, especially once the sun comes out in earnest and the route abandons main roads in favour of tiny twisty ones that rise and fall with merciless regularity. After four or five hills, I detect a pattern – a steep, tortuous ascent through the trees, a little turn at the top to show off the demoralising view of similar climbs ahead, and then back down, with just enough time on the flat to lose any speed before hitting the next lump on the landscape. The routine grinds me down, and by mid-afternoon, picnicking on yesterday's bread and ham in a village full of flies but with no apparent source of water, I'm running low on liquids and feeling furious. Where's a goddamn Spar when you need one? I cry plaintively, to myself.

Indeed, my only consolation, strange as it may sound, is that I'm on my own, which means there's nothing to do but push on

– I may feel like crying (though I have to keep reminding myself that would be a foolish waste of liquids), but though there's no one to comfort me, or even to rail at, there's also no one to apologise to, and no one to suggest giving up either. Plus, I'm on my own, but never entirely alone. There are rabbits everywhere, running kamikaze-like in front of my wheels, and the joyous sight of a deer, leaping through a cornfield by the side of the road in one of the valleys, makes me smile in spite of myself.

Nevertheless, I plumb some very dark depths of the soul, and find them desiccated – stopping in the town of Lombez, which would sound thrillingly Spanish if I wasn't so jaded, I down an entire bottle of aggressively fizzy Badoit outside a supermarket and then feel very sick. A wise person would also have picked up some supplies because by the time I reach my target campsite, everything in the village of Saint-Lys has closed for the evening, including the campsite itself, but sadly I'm well beyond rational thought at this point, so I don't.

Filthy and exhausted, having been on the road since before dawn, I ring the number pinned to the door of the shed marked reception and croak my desperation down the phone. Fortunately, Madame is an utter delight, offering me a special cyclist's rate of a laughable €5, '*pour courage*' (a phrase that's becoming increasingly familiar), warning me about the mosquitoes the rain has brought out (no need, their tinny whine was the first thing I heard when I took off my helmet and sat down in the dust to wait for her arrival) and quizzing me about my trip as she takes down my details.

This being France, she doesn't seem overly surprised to discover I'm on a culinary pilgrimage, and, more specifically, on the trail of cassoulet. Pooh-poohing everything I've read on the subject (and believe me, there's a lot to read about this cult dish), she assures me cassoulet isn't really about the ingredients, the mutton or the sausages – it's about the person making it.

Unlike poule au pot, me and cassoulet have what could be coyly described as 'history', ever since it first bubbled onto my radar during a previous tour of France in a borrowed Nissan Primera, the summer before university. I'd like to say I and my boyfriend at the time happened upon it in a little trucker's café run by a gruff but ultimately charming Gascon with a yard full of fat, happy ducks, but in fact, if memory serves me correctly, we developed a taste for the tinned variety – cassoulet is an excellent thing to cook up on a camping stove, if you happen to have a car to carry one in.

The release of the *River Cottage Meat Book* a couple of years later, with its recipe to serve ten, only fuelled the flames of this passion, and there is a part of my memory forever stained with the goose fat and cheap red wine of twentysomething dinner parties. I can assure you, it's impossible to have a hangover once you've lined your stomach with cassoulet. Or perhaps that's just youth.

If I've made a lot of cassoulet in my time, I've eaten even more. Indeed, in 2017 I managed to do the treble, eating one in each of the three towns associated with the dish – Toulouse, Castelnaudary and Carcassonne. Time for a repeat performance – and this time, it's professional.

PAUSE-CAFÉ – Cassoulet: When Baked Beans Go to Heaven

Joël Robuchon, the most Michelin-starred chef on earth (who died during the writing of this book), explains in *French Regional Food*, co-authored with food historian Loïc Bienassis, that 'when we speak of cassoulet country, we speak in the plural of several different farming areas that lend themselves to the production of cassoulet's key ingredients. You might ask whether this ... categorisation is born of cowardice – yes, a certain lack of courage in choosing decisively between the three famous cities that have compelling claims to be the authentic home and guardian of this most famous dish of French gastronomic history'.

You might well, and if Robuchon doesn't dare choose between them, it would certainly be more than my life is worth. The celebrated chef and writer Prosper Montagné, himself a Carcassonne man, famously defined the cassoulet as 'the God of the cuisine of South-West France', claiming 'God the Father is the cassoulet of Castelnaudary; God the Son, the cassoulet of Carcassonne, and God the Holy Spirit the cassoulet of Toulouse', which, even for a subject so shrouded in myth, is a strikingly unhelpful clarification.

The three are often claimed to contain slightly different ingredients: according to *French Regional Food*, Castelnaudary generally includes confit goose or duck, Carcassonne pork cutlets and Toulouse mutton and, of course, its world-famous sausage. 'These distinctions', Robuchon explains, 'mask numerous other debates about the length of cooking and the addition of this and that ingredient.'

Though few books admit it, even this is up for debate – I find each of these ingredients attributed to all three places, including the Toulouse sausage, which mysteriously puts in an appearance in the official recipe of the Brotherhood of the Cassoulet of Castelnaudary. One thing is certain: cassoulet is a symbol of a region that prizes duck fat over olive oil and knows the value of a hearty stew. As Robuchon says, perhaps it's best described as 'the God of the inland cuisine of southwest France, where the influence of the Mediterranean evaporates, then finally vanishes'. And that's as far as he or I am going to go.

Madame, after warmly urging me to try the duck-fat fries in Toulouse, suddenly stops – 'But what are you going to eat tonight?'

When I confess that I was hoping she might be able to tell me, she seems genuinely heartbroken that her little épicerie behind the till is bare apart from a bottle of ketchup and some scouring pads. Even the pizzeria in the village will have closed by now. What were you after? I shrug. After 157km, my expectations are very low. A bag of crisps or something, I say miserably. But don't worry, I have chocolate.

Just as I'm hammering the final tent peg into what appears to be an all-you-can-eat buffet for biting insects, she appears again, clutching a large bag of crisps she's brought me from home. I'm almost overwhelmed by her kindness – 'It's not really French gastronomy,' she says, 'but it'll do the trick.' So, exhausted, and with a phone that seems to have taken this morning's rainstorm to heart, jumping madly between apps and refusing to respond to even the angriest jabbed finger, I dine on salty potato crisps and sugary Milka Daim clusters, and go to bed with 2 litres of gloriously cold, fresh water and a lungful of Deet.

Though the phone is a worry, given how much I rely on it for navigation and research, I feel oddly elated at having got through today, and as the terrible details recede, I pick over them like someone worrying at a mosquito bite, taking a perverse pleasure in their awfulness. I did it, and lived to tell the tale, and there's satisfaction in that.

The next morning it's sunny again, and, to my slight astonishment, my legs feel pretty fresh as I pedal the 30km into Toulouse, stopping for a leisurely and surprisingly decent croissant in a roadside boulangerie: a good lesson, never discount these, however unprepossessing they look. Treasure can sometimes be found in the most unlikely places, and this is the best I've eaten so far: very buttery, very crisp, with a definite but not overpowering sweetness, I give it a 9/10. (NB: Do not discount the power of a sunny terrace and a good lunch ahead either.)

Croissant dispatched, it's fun to be in a big city again, especially a southern one, glowing pink in the heat, with people drinking pastis with their morning coffee, and old men playing boules in the dust. I'm making good time as I speed into the centre, the roads quiet in the minutes before the lunchtime rush, straight as an arrow towards the 'beating heart' of the city's food scene, as *Lonely Planet* bills it, the Marché Victor Hugo. It's a striking white 1960s edifice whose winding multi-storey car-park ramp puts me in mind of the old penguin pool at London Zoo, but with quite a bit more scaffolding. In fact, the whole place is covered in the stuff (like most of France, it seems to my jaded eye) and it takes me quite some time to find my way in, which panics me, because it's already 12.10, and everything I've read suggests that I'll be lucky to get a table at the market restaurants on a Friday lunchtime.

Though there are a handful on the upper level above the trading hall, I've chosen Le Louchebem for the fact that it reached the finals of the world cassoulet championships a couple of months before (the winner, Café Francis, doesn't appear to have cassoulet on its menu for some arcane but no doubt entirely logical French reason) with a recipe using broad beans, which were apparently the local pulse of choice before the new-fangled haricot arrived from the New World to take their jobs. Of course, on opening the menu, I discover that the broad bean version is only available on the first weekend of every month, but no matter: I have a prime spot on the balcony overlooking the square, the sky is azure and the first glass of rosé of the trip on order. I'm pretty happy with the situation, despite a vocabulary failure, which means I'm not exactly sure what I've ordered. The cassoulet that is on offer comes with a *manchon de canard*, which, the waitress tells me, is a bit of the leg, but no, not the thigh … she doesn't seem able to point it out on herself, which makes more sense when Google suggests the word means 'muff', which doesn't sound right (do ducks have muffs?), but also makes me very nervous.

To my relief, what arrives beneath the bubbling dish of beans appears to be nothing more sinister than the top of the wing, along with the requisite helping of fat Toulouse sausage, so packed with meat it's almost, but not quite, dry and another, pinker, juicier sausage lurking beneath. The flavour of the whole is creamy and mildly herbaceous, but the overwhelming effect is of heat – thick, gluey beans, fatty meat, pure pleasure, even on this unexpectedly sweltering day. A revelation: cassoulet is as much about the texture as the taste – something I'd never realised, for all the cassoulets I've put away over the years.

Maybe it's just that I've never eaten it alone before. That said, I can't help but notice that the two men jammed in next to me – father and son, I assume – also take an interest in my lunch. I make eye contact and they look away hastily, almost embarrassed, which is so unusual in France I'm slightly perturbed. When the waitress comes to take my coffee order, they have a word with her, slightly too quietly for me to hear, and she looks over, obviously taken aback. I have a moment of terror, wondering what mad Toulousian by-law I've contravened (was it the salad I insisted on ordering on the side?), before the older man addresses me directly.

'Mademoiselle,' he begins politely, 'how was the cassoulet?'

It was good, I tell him. He shakes his head, kindly but dismissively – 'It wasn't dry?' And not waiting for an answer, he turns to the waitress. 'It looked dry.'

She looks at me. I shrug. 'Well, maybe a bit, but I enjoyed it,' I admit.

Ah, he says, slowly, kindly, as if to a child – but was it your first cassoulet? They shouldn't be dry, they should be more … more like a soup in fact. As he warms to his theme, the waitress slips away, and I learn that despite this setback ('Usually it is very good here, you know, you made a good choice'), Toulouse is still the place to come for bean stew. Sure, he says, you can get decent cassoulet in those other places (he manages Castelnaudary, but apparently can't quite bring himself to pronounce the name Carcassonne), but here is the best. It's all in the sausage, you know. He winks. His son, fiddling with his phone, looks embarrassed as they get up to pay the bill, bidding me farewell, and good luck with my quest.

Wandering round the market downstairs as it winds down for lunch, I get a text from my editor at the *Guardian* telling me

Tony Bourdain is dead. Cassoulet is perhaps the quintessential Bourdain dish – gutsy, ballsy French, the kind of peasant recipe that doesn't shirk from hard work. His recipe takes three days, because it starts with making your own duck confit, a process he concludes with the immortal instruction: 'A nice touch at this point is to twist out the thighbone from the cold confit … Think of someone you hate when you do it.' That one, I think, was for you, Tony. Rest in peace, chef.

I, however, still have unfinished business on this earth, and am soon trundling south-east along the Canal du Midi towpath in the direction of Castelnaudary, and my next bowl of beans. The combination of cassoulet and sunshine means I'm grateful for the shade of the plane trees that line the route as it snakes through suburbs and industrial zones, under graffitied bridges and over vast pipes, and then the quiet that comes when I finally leave the city behind. A wave of nostalgia for 2017's summer ride hits me, for our little band of merry cyclists, with our regular punctures and even more regular chocolate stops, and I sink happily back into the tranquillity of cycling along a road it's impossible to lose, the kilometres slipping away like the sun through the sky.

Just as I'm about to go into a pleasurable trance, my phone emits a muffled, waterlogged squawk – it's my friend Alex, ringing from Oban, where it is, apparently, raining heavily. I tell her about my mobile woes, which are weighing heavy on my mind – a woman who runs a safari business in some of the remotest parts of Africa is never going to be the most sympathetic audience for complaints about Instagram being a *complete nightmare*, but she's still kind enough to offer to send an old phone of her own out to a poste restante. Given how long it takes anything to get from the West Coast to London, let alone the South of France, I regretfully decline: instead, once we've said goodbye,

I sit down by a bridge and spend 10 minutes copying down reservations and contact numbers into my notebook, just in case. With a pencil. Take that, rain, I think.

Feeling a bit better, both for having insured against total disaster and, more importantly, after 20 minutes with a friendly voice, I ride on, coming back onto the road at Le Ségala, where, just like last year, the towpath abruptly disintegrates into a mass of tree roots and potholes.

The room I've booked for my night in Castelnaudary (fresh pork, no sausage) is absurdly cheap, tucked away down a narrow terraced street that ends suddenly in the quay. There's no sign from the outside that this is a guesthouse, and no response at the door. I ring the number on the booking email: no answer. Eventually, after about 10 minutes of alternate knocking and quiet despairing, there's a noise inside. It opens very slowly to reveal a man with one leg and a thick Italian accent. I tell him I have a reservation. He tells me this isn't his place, he just lives here.

'I tried calling,' I say. 'There's no answer.'

He doesn't seem surprised. 'Well, there wouldn't be; the owner's gone to Saint-Tropez for the weekend.' Lucky him, I think. Eventually, he agrees to phone the landlord himself, and then passes the phone over – oh, I thought you'd call before this, says the unruffled and completely unapologetic man on the other end. He tells me the entrance code for the door, and that my room is at the top of the stairs ... And the code for that is ...? Oh no, you won't need one for that room.

The Italian gamely attempts to help me with my stuff, while propping the heavy door open with his stick. The space inside is small and dark, and I'd hardly dare ask if I can leave my bike inside, save for the fact there is nowhere to tether it in the street, but as soon as I do he begins to drag a heavy bench across the floor to make room for it, which makes me feel even worse about disturbing his Friday night in – I can hear a television still chatting away in the next room. Having apologised seven or eight times, I make my way shamefacedly up the narrow stairs to find my room – and realise both why it was so cheap, and why I have no need for a code. It's a windowless cupboard with a low single mattress in the middle of it, and no lock whatsoever.

I briefly think about complaining, before deciding I can't be bothered; what have I got to steal, after all? Instead, I take a shower in the spotless, if brown-tiled, communal bathroom, wedge the bedroom door shut with a pannier, and lie on the sweaty polyester sheets, trying to hatch an email plan with my editor to get an unlocked phone out to Nice next week, while attempting to stop this one sending 14 unfinished emails to one of my culinary heroes, Jonathan Meades, who I'm hoping to meet in Marseille.

I succeed, partially – he only gets three. I'll be honest, I still kind of want to die thinking about this though, so instead I throw on my glad rags/crumpled dress and go out to dinner. Castelnaudary is a pleasant little town, with one main street and not much open – something that, after two weeks in France (only two weeks! I marvel), no longer surprises me on a Friday night. Online opinion suggests the best place to eat cassoulet, apart from Le Tirou, which features in the Michelin red book and only opens for dinner on Saturdays (because why wouldn't it?), is the Hôtel du Centre et du Lauragais.

Initial signs are ominous; the decor has an Inspired-by-Laurence-Llewelyn-Bowen vibe, all monochrome floral wallpaper and massive chrome chandeliers, and my cassoulet arrives before I've even finished my blackberry kir aperitif, but I can't argue with its impressive crust, clearly formed by long, slow simmering rather than the breadcrumb-based shortcuts so frowned upon by the cassoulet cognoscenti.

Underneath, it's looser, and yes, soupier than my lunchtime version, with pork confit as well as the duck variety, and, in obedience to the rules of regional cassoulet, no sausage. I realise, as I slowly munch my way through the creamy beans, glad of the green salad it comes with, that though I've nothing against stodge, the broth element, enriched with mashed pork rinds, is a vital lubricant for all that carbohydrate – my friend in Toulouse knew whereof he spoke.

A large German party arrive as I'm contemplating my fraise Melba and begin anxiously to interrogate the waitress about vegetarian options. She looks nonplussed. I decide it's time to retire to my monastic cell, where I lie for about 10 minutes listening to the sound of Netflix and laughter from next door before falling into a fat-induced coma.

The next day feels like a holiday as I quietly let myself out of the little house, banging Eddy against everything in sight, and make my way to the railway station – for the first time in a week I'm on my way to see friends, and the prospect is ridiculously exciting. It's not that I'm lonely, but really, one's own company can get old. My *Guardian* editor, a man popularly known as Grumpy Bob, is in the Languedoc for the annual knees-up at the St John Group winery and has somehow managed to wangle me an invite to lunch. If the food and wine are half as good as their London restaurants, I'll be a happy woman, but to be honest, I'm mostly looking forward to talking at people in a language I'm fluent in.

As I wait on the platform, shedding croissant crumbs (a bronzed handsome bugger, but inside a bit dry and dull, 6/10), drinking instant coffee from a plastic cup and enjoying the singular mix of Santiago de Compostela pilgrims (one route starts in Narbonne, where my train is heading) and French Foreign Legion recruits on leave (Castelnaudary is home to the fourth foreign regiment), I feel jolly pleased with life, a feeling that quickly dissipates when I dash up to the bike carriage at the end of the train, only to be told by a man getting off with a racer that, 'You'll be lucky.' It's Saturday morning, but this local service is packed like the Tube at 8 a.m. – dismayed, I watch a youth who definitely arrived on the platform after me casually push his mountain bike into the mass of people. There seems no possible way I'll get on, yet, I think, panicking, this is the only train that will get me there in time.

All rational thought goes out of the window. In the UK, I wouldn't have even dared contemplate the thought, but this is France, and I want my lunch, so I shut my eyes and shove straight into someone's legs. Amazingly, no one so much as grumbles. In fact, people actually help, pushing and pulling us onto the carriage. Eddy spends the first 25 minutes balanced on a stranger's shoulder, and then, when even more people attempt to board at Bram, he ends up stacked on top of another bike in a strange, circus-like pyramid – yet the only note of complaint I hear during the entire ordeal is from a tall ginger man in Lycra who gets on at Carcassonne and mutters, 'Oh for fuck's sake,' in broad Glaswegian. I contemplate telling him to cheer up, but decide to channel the general vibe instead, and just smile happily as if this is indeed the best Saturday morning ever. The whole experience is like a sweaty but genial game of Twister: people even hoist my panniers over their heads to get them to me when I finally come up for air at Lézignan-Corbières, leaving a trail of apologies and pedal-shaped bruises in my wake.

The ride from the station is enough to know I'm properly in the South at last – there's a hot wind blowing from the scrubby trees (olives, I realise, with a surge of joy) and, thrillingly, vineyards, too, and the place I'm staying, run by Irene and Roger, a charming young Norwegian couple, not only has a window, but a window looking out onto pink terracotta roofs and sunflower fields! I could lie in this clean, airy room, with its white sheets and squashy cushions, forever but instead I have to go and meet Bob at the Café de la Poste. I'm sent on my way by a green chia smoothie they kindly make for me when I ask if I might steal an apple from the bowl by the door on my way out. 'Yes, they do not eat a lot of fruit and vegetables here,' Irene agrees. 'Have this.'

The only green thing at the café are people's faces – it was a late night, apparently, and hair of the dog is being taken in injudicious measures, along with short, brutal coffees. Still picking chia seeds from my teeth, I feel like a wholesome puppy unleashed on a nightclub at closing time. The crowd is a mix of wine writers, buyers, merchants and importers, and the odd artist, chef and journalist, and I quickly lose track of names and titles once we arrive at the party in the wonderfully named village of Homps, where chef Fergus Henderson is poking at a fire made of vine cuttings, while a crowd of burly local winemakers, St John friends and staff and assorted hangers-on like me are already getting stuck into the booze.

Jim Budd, an extravagantly moustachioed wine writer based in the Loire, has arrived on an electric bike with his wife, there's a German-Italian linguistics professor married to a wine merchant in Leeds who speaks seven languages and tells me it gets much easier after you've mastered four and someone who owns a gallery in Amsterdam – conversation flows as freely as the wine in the hot sun, and when we're told to sit down at the long trestle table that runs along the length of a vast barn and into the courtyard beyond, I make a beeline for the cool darkness of the very back.

The menu contains no cassoulet, to my slight relief. Instead, we kick off with bowls of long pink radishes and olives, and buttery calves' brains cut with generous quantities of capers and parsley on fire-licked toast (which, to my annoyance, the sculptor next to me, who has been busy telling me he's 'mostly vegan these days', takes two of before passing on). A big tomato and shallot salad is plonked down in the middle of the table, and a platter of gloriously garlicky barbecued quail comes round, followed, finally, by cherries on ice, rounds of local ewe's milk cheese and piles of sugary *oreillette* (little ear) pastries freshly fried by the mayor's wife, who I talk to in some detail about yoga, which I know absolutely nothing about. The sculptor looks at the electronic record of my day of hell, which I'm proudly showing off on my flickering phone, those 157.5km of utter brutality, peaks like witch's hats, and scoffs: 'We'll make a climber out of you yet.' In response, I finish his wine.

Everyone gets increasingly drunk. I'd love to tell you about the different St John wines we try – the brambly Boulevard Napoléon carignan (named after the winery's address, as Trevor Gulliver, Fergus's co-conspirator in the St John empire, takes me outside to show me on a street sign at some hazy point in the proceedings), the unknown red still foamy from the barrel and something interesting Jim has brought from the Loire – but unfortunately I don't make any notes, or if I do, I then give them to someone to mop up a spillage with. My most vivid memory (apart from one of the winemakers explaining that the secret to great wine is to poo on your vines every morning) is a trip to the public loo with Bob's partner Jac, who wisely warns me that I should go sooner rather than later. As we trek through winding streets, I spot a barn door painted a faded turquoise, with eight wild boar hooves nailed to it. Suddenly, this all feels a bit *Wicker Man* On Tour – but luckily I'm too pissed to find it anything but utterly hilarious.

Eventually we all get cabs back to Olonzac and a pizza place run by a woman who appears even more strung out than most of us, except Bob, who is now sporting a gold lamé jacket several sizes too small. I then somehow find myself at a bar, where two Italian wine importers attempt to persuade me to come back and drink rosé with them at their hotel. It strikes me suddenly and powerfully that I've done enough socialising for a bit and, making my excuses, I weave my way back to the blessed snowy embrace of an Ikea duvet.

Theatrically flinging open the shutters helps the next morning, as does a large bowl of homemade muesli ('Cyclists always order muesli,' Irene says), some Norwegian black bread, copious amounts of fresh fruit – and discovering from Victoria, the St John head of wine who's drinking coffee in the courtyard, that everyone is off to visit their winery today.

I, however, am free – once Roger has kindly pumped up my tyres for me, I'm off like a hungover rocket. Once safely out of range, I send Bob a thank-you text. Ten minutes later, as I'm bowling down the Route de Minervois, vines to the left of me, olives to the right, I get a reply: 'Get to Bar de la Poste for Fernet NOW.' This, needless to say, only makes me pedal all the harder.

The countryside is lovely: wild flowers in lilac, yellow and poppy red fringe the vines, and a great table-like hill on the horizon keeps me company almost all the way to Carcassonne. It's muggy, but not wet, and the roads are a joy with fully inflated tyres – I arrive with enough time to pitch my tent before lunch. Hotel prices being what they are in this tourist mecca, I'm staying at the same vast campsite where we stopped at last August. In fact, they give me exactly the same pitch, though this time there's a bit more grass available under the conifers for a bed.

Not much, despite all the rain, though there's more to come by the look of the clouds lowering over the old city in the distance.

Body bag assembled, tightly pegged down in case of a storm, I head into town for my third and final cassoulet – much as I'd love to leave it until dinner time, it's Sunday, and I'm not taking any chances in that department. Thankfully, I have the ravenous hunger of the newly sober on my side.

Last year, I insisted on putting away a cassoulet in the sweltering heat at the rather fancy restaurant Comte Roger in the citadel while everyone else toyed with salad. This time around, I've chosen a brasserie run by local two-star chef Franck Putelat in the (slightly more) modern bit of Carcassonne where people actually live and work. À 4 Temps is set into the city walls, with a terrace facing out onto a largely deserted, windswept park; I pick a table outside, and it immediately begins to spit with rain. Fortunately, the umbrellas are generous and, with a hot cassoulet on order (and, to the waiter's evident puzzlement – 'But you do not need anything with it, Madame!' – yet another green salad), it's not unpleasant sitting there, fuzzy-headed, watching people dash for cover.

Whatever Robuchon might claim, this particular Carcassonne cassoulet contains a generous slab of sheep as well as a piece of duck confit, and some sort of slightly tough, lean pork (possibly the cutlet he mentions), which I don't very much care for. The beans are perfect, though: creamy and plump, without being sticky or mealy, and the broth satisfyingly plain, and I manage, to the waiter's apparent astonishment, to polish off the lot. An old man who has been slowly working his way through a glass of brandy at a table nearby even tips his hat to me as he leaves, which makes me feel quite proud of my gluttony. Three in three days, and I enjoyed every single mouthful.

Cassoulet

This version is closest in consistency to the one I ate in Castelnaudary, loose and soupy, but with the Toulouse sausage and confit duck that are surely everyone's favourite bits, as well as slow-cooked pork – belly, rather than loin, which has a tendency to become rather dry with such long cooking. Call it a Greatest Hits album.

Serves 8
1kg haricot beans, soaked in cold water overnight
1 onion, peeled and halved
1 large carrot, cut into chunks
1 head of garlic, unpeeled, plus 4 cloves
2 sprigs of thyme
2 sprigs of parsley
1 bay leaf
1kg slab of pork belly, bone in
4 confit duck legs and their fat (reserve any jelly you find in the tin)
6 Toulouse sausages
300ml white wine

1 Drain the beans well and put them into a very large, ovenproof casserole dish. Pour in water until it comes about 3cm above the top of the beans, then add the onion, carrot, whole head of garlic, herbs and pork belly (if you need to spoon out some water at this point, it's okay, you can top the dish up during cooking). Bring to the boil, then cover and simmer for about 2 hours, until just tender, but not falling apart.

2 Meanwhile, fry the duck and sausages separately in plenty of the duck fat until crisp and golden.

3 Once the beans are ready, remove the onion and herbs and discard. Scoop out the pork belly and, once cool enough to handle, cut into chunks, discarding the bones.

4 Squeeze the garlic cloves from their skins and mash to a paste with 4 tablespoons of duck fat and the fresh garlic cloves. Preheat the oven to 160°C/140°C fan/gas 2.

5 Drain the beans, reserving the liquid and seasoning it well, as this will be your sauce. Grease the bottom of the casserole with a little of the duck fat mix, then tip in the beans, the rest of the duck fat and all the meat, plus any jelly from the duck confit. Mix well, then top with the wine and the bean cooking liquid to cover.

6 Bake for about 2 hours, keeping an eye on it – once a crust has formed, stir this back into the cassoulet. By the end of the cooking time, you should have a thick, golden crust.

7 Allow to cool slightly before serving with a simply dressed green salad.

Hoping to ride off at least a few mouthfuls of beans before I hit the glamorous Med, I slog up to the medieval Cité (in fact, largely rebuilt in the late 19th century after it fell into such spectacular disrepair that the French State ordered its demolition), and then immediately undo this small piece of hard work with a large ice cream.

In my defence, an ice cream was never part of the plan, but wandering the tourist-thronged alleyways, I spot the word *bulgare*, a plain but deliciously sour flavour tried once and never forgotten, and find myself powerless to resist – the name, the teenager serving tells me, is short for Bulgarian yoghurt. As I slowly lick my prize, glad to find it's as good as I remember, I watch a couple in jerkins and tights very slowly saddle up a packhorse to pull a tourist wagon. They certainly seem to have an appropriately pre-industrial mindset, methodically arranging the tack as people come, pose for selfies with them and leave, calling to each other in Spanish, Mandarin, Dutch and what sounds like Russian.

I duck onto the ramparts to get a closer look at the bright-yellow wrap that covers some of the towers in concentric circles, like neon ripples on a stone lake. A sign explains that it's an installation by the Swiss artist Felice Varini in celebration of the 20th anniversary of the Cité's inscription on the UNESCO World Heritage List, and, though I discover later that it isn't universally popular with locals, I love it – as with the giant slide on the chateau at Nantes, it's hard to imagine, say, Warwick or Edinburgh Castle daring to be so bold with their historic treasure.

Suddenly clocking the lowering clouds, I speed back downhill to the campsite, where I spend the evening holed up in the bar as the rain pours down outside, drinking red wine, stealing electricity and writing up my notes while gloomy campers watch the final of the Roland-Garros tennis tournament on the big screen, and Eddy naps in the shelter of an empty holiday lodge.

Above us, the yellow circles on the Cité have faded into the cloudy darkness. It's my final night in the Languedoc, and every time the rain wakes me up in the night, hammering onto the nylon just above my head, I thank God it's time to head east.

Km: 309.7

Croissants: 3 (average 6/10); muesli: 1

High: Getting really drunk on good wine

Low: Cycling 157km and being too low on water even to cry

STAGE 11

MARSEILLE

Provençal Fish Soup

Not to be confused with bouillabaisse, which is really a fish stew,
the traditional fish soups of the Mediterranean coast tend to be
made with fish too small or bony to be bothered with otherwise.
Most are commonly flavoured with saffron, orange peel and aniseed
liqueur, giving them a terracotta colour and a sweet, aromatic
flavour, and are often served with rouille, a spicy mayonnaise
that's hot with garlic as well as chilli.

It's so wet at dawn as I attempt to stuff my sopping tent back into its reluctant sack that I find two snails sheltering in my handlebar bag. I briefly think about binning the last of the Bayonne chocolate they're clinging to, having snobbily shunned the Milka, but then remember the old adage about beggars and choosers, and put the soggy packet back in there for whatever emergency is waiting in the wings.

After a madly splashy dash to the station, which, still in a panic after finding the campsite gates locked for the night, somehow sees me travelling for 2km along the river in the wrong direction, I arrive to discover the Marseille train is running 40 minutes late. Frankly, at this stage, this is fine by me.

Gushing water onto the polished concrete floor, I grab an execrable but scalding hot coffee from a vending machine, fail to find a single croissant and, by the time the ancient *intercité* finally creaks in, am merely wet rather than sopping, though I'm beginning to come to terms with the fact that my increasingly aromatic espadrilles are fated to never be dry again.

Such is my joy on arriving at Marseille to see the sun if not streaming, then at least trickling through the vast doors of the station that I break into a funny little jog, water squelching out of my shoes at every step, desperate to feel the South on my face. Outside is a mass of cigarette smoke and African prints and glorious warmth. Saint-Charles is set high on a hill, with the effect that the city unrolls in front of the arriving visitor like a promotional poster, a mass of tightly packed terracotta roofs as far as the church of Notre-Dame de la Garde sprouting out of the Vieux Port in the distance. The cloud hangs low, but it's not actually raining, which is good enough for me as I jauntily thread my way through the tangle of alleyways below the station feeling like I've travelled a lot further than 300km this morning (that's the same distance as London to Leeds in one little hop along the south coast).

I love Marseille: the narrow streets with their soundtrack of blaring horns and revving scooters, the air perfumed with a mixture of exhaust fumes and spices, the people sitting on plastic chairs outside their front doors, staring – they get a good eyeful today, as I battle the gradient with wholly inadequate brakes, terrified of coming smack-bang up against a speeding Vespa. My hotel, hastily booked online with cost the main factor in my decision-making, is in the hustle-bustle of Noailles, an area known (according to Wikipedia) as the stomach of Marseille, thanks to its daily market and, according to locals whom I ask for directions, as the Arab quarter.

Both suit me fine: those complaining in online reviews about not feeling safe in this 'squalid district' are also unreasonably distressed at the lack of tea-making facilities in the rooms, which makes discounting their opinions fairly easy, especially given the hotel's proximity to an excellent shop selling over 20 sizes and shapes of nail scissors alongside pocket knives, air rifles and what's advertised as the '#1 brand of dog gilet in Europe', modelled by a handsome spaniel.

While I'm here, I'm hoping, if the volley of mad emails from my failing phone hasn't put him off, to meet Jonathan Meades, *The Times*'s long-time restaurant critic before 'falling out of sympathy', as he put it, with the British scene, chucking it all in and moving to the South of France. Meades, a polymath-type figure who also writes on the built environment, has published a couple of novels and exhibited his photography, as well as winning the first episode of *Celebrity Mastermind* and the praise of Marco Pierre White (who has described him as 'the best amateur chef in the world'). He was also a regular and beloved fixture on BBC Two during my impressionable teenage years, and I've been slightly in love with him ever since – so I was most put out, after discovering they were related in some complicated way, not to meet him at my friend Anna's wedding. Needless to say, when she offered to put us in touch on this trip, I almost bit her hand off.

Not only has he kindly obliged with a list of recommendations and advice (the most important of which is the caution that bouillabaisse, the city's famous fish stew, generally served in two courses, broth followed by fish, is a 'folkloric racket' to be avoided at all costs), but he's even agreed to have dinner with me. With the 'various lumps of tired fish' I'd planned to eat apparently off the menu, Meades recommends I should try a pizza while I'm here: 'the real vernacular dish of Marseille', he explains in an email, 'much better, much lighter than in Naples'.

My hero's tentacles stretch far and wide: I quickly find a piece online by his friend, and another of my heroes, chef Rowley Leigh, singing the praises of the 'rich tomato sauce ... thickly laced with anchovies and olives' at the pizzeria Chez Vincent. Talking to Jonathan later, I discover the place they visited together has actually closed down in the intervening years, but having located somewhere of that name out near the Natural History Museum, I inadvertently find myself lunching in entirely the wrong restaurant,* just off a large traffic junction, next to a grimy-looking bar tabac.

Ignorant of this fact, however, given the imposter also offers pizza, I order a small, cold beer and study the faded photos of past customers smouldering away above my head. The owner, sometimes tanned and youthful, sometimes the middle-aged man I see behind the bar to my left squinting into a calculator, poses with a fresh-faced Arnold Schwarzenegger and numerous unidentified local celebrities behind tables strewn with faded packets of fags and long-drained bottles of wine. This Monday lunchtime crowd is a rather less glamorous collection of office workers, but Chez Vincent's pizza makes no concessions to the social niceties of the communal workplace: the smell of raw garlic arrives seconds before it does, making my heart sing after weeks of subtle flavours and restrained seasoning.

The base, thin but chewy, is, it must be admitted, nothing special, but the anchovies and olives pack a punch and I'm happy as a clam as I trek back down wide, dusty boulevards to the centre, breathing garlic on all and sundry, as I revel in the big city-ness of it all – the Senegalese cafés, the vegan street food,

---

* J. M. now recommends Chez Sauveur in the Noailles.

the Breton lobsters for sale in a tank by the tram stop; everywhere something new to look at.

After ducking back to the hotel for a glass of warm tap water, shops selling cold drinks being as rare in Marseille as everywhere else in France, I take Eddy out to feel the sunshine on his tyres, following the water beside the Vieux Port and along the coast for the thrill of seeing the Mediterranean sparkle in the fitful sun. I pause by an unusually lovely memorial to those killed in North Africa during the Great War, the sea framed in a huge arch known as the Gate to the East, jealously watching the swimmers below and wishing I'd brought my swimming costume along for the ride.

From there, I take the road up to Notre-Dame de la Garde, the church I spotted from the station this morning. The streets, fringed with palm trees, climb at first gradually and then more steeply, until I'm winding around the rock itself and then have to carry my bike up a set of marble steps to the base of the basilica. It's very hot indeed by the time I get to the top, the city suffocating under a duvet of cloud, but the view is spectacular – the pink roofs stretching out to the sea on one side, the hills on the other, and the stripy, bullet-scarred Byzantine church behind, crowned with a gold statue of the Madonna and Child, *la bonne mère*, gazing out at the watery horizon. The basilica's recapture by North-African units of the French forces in 1944, through a secret passageway from the town below, marked the start of the freeing of Marseille from Nazi control – it seems fitting that, in this most cosmopolitan of French cities, a Catholic basilica was liberated by largely Muslim forces.

On the way back down, despite such weighty socio-historical musings, it becomes increasingly hard to ignore the smell of burning rubber coming from my front wheel. I stop, worryingly slowly, and take a look: the left brake pad is worn to a sliver at one end. It must have been knocked out of place on Saturday morning's cattle train, adding an extra frisson of terror to my ride through the noisy rush-hour traffic, though I guess from the age and condition of some of the vehicles that I'm not the only person mechanically winging it in this city.

There's no time to do anything about it now, though, because I have a date with Jonathan (and, it must be admitted, his wife Colette) in one of the few Vieux Port restaurants which, according to him, 'do something approximating to *echt* [authentic] Provençal cooking', Chez Madie les Galinettes. As I stroll there, the warm evening light catches the Anish Kapoor-like mirrored canopy on the waterfront, reflecting the tourists and toddlers and dozing tramps beneath. It's quite lovely, yet I'm also glad to see, for all the glass-bottomed boats and gin palaces nearby, evidence of a working port with piles of nets and old ropes mouldering on the quay opposite the all-you-can-eat Provençal buffet.

The Meades are already installed at a table overlooking the harbour with a bottle of light red in front of them and prove to be as good company as I could have hoped, and, after a decade in Marseille, thoughtful guides too. Colette tells me the city is such a hodgepodge of cultures that it's easy to feel at home as a foreigner – not so different, her husband says, somewhat to my surprise, from his beloved Hamburg, or even Liverpool, 'not in the food, of course, but the people, and their attitude to life'. We discuss the different communities that have settled here – the Armenians, Italians, Vietnamese, North Africans: 'Because Marseille is fundamentally a load of fishing villages strung together. It's still a very local place.' (This, it seems, is one of the reasons that I haven't been able to find a big central market: everyone goes to the one in their own district.)

I stare at the menu, waiting for expert guidance, terrified of a misstep on the scale of the bouillabaisse faux-pas. Fish soup, to my relief, passes muster: Meades's objection to the 'b' word is purely conceptual – the claim that the fish that's brought out as a second course has been cooked in the broth, he says, either means it's hung around for a bit or they're lying, though his ire is certainly fanned by the existence of a 'bouillabaisse charter', which he describes in an email as basically 'a price-fixing arrangement among a cabal of restaurants, which are to be avoided'.

'I once said that bouillabaisse was the old Provençal word for "saw you coming",' he says now, 'and it's been repeated so often that I think some people believe it's true.' Chez Madie's soup gets the thumbs up, however, gently flavoured, with the merest kiss of anise sweetness, it comes with a bowl of saffron-yellow rouille, hot with garlic, a heap of grated cheese and a pile of garlic-rubbed toasts – I think I've eaten more garlic today than I have since leaving London. As I'm happily experimenting with different combinations of rouille, bread and cheese, the waiter rushes over in a great flap – 'You must put them all in together, Madame!' he scolds. I resent being told how to eat my dinner, but as it's done out of love for the dish, I meekly agree and then go on as before once he turns back round. Mad dogs and Englishmen and all that.

The other starters are wonderfully simple. *artichauts à la barigoule* – three turned artichoke hearts in a delicate broth – and stewed testicles, as soft as a finely minced meatball, and exponentially more delicious than they sound. After telling me that really offal is the thing to have here, Jonathan demurs when I consider ordering the famous Provençal *pieds et paquets* (sheep's feet and knotted tripe) to follow, murmuring that not everyone enjoys it as much as he does. 'Rowley said it was disgusting,' confirms Colette helpfully.

Instead I go for *ris de veau*, or veal sweetbreads, which turn out to be perfectly inoffensive little things, texturally more like the velveted chicken in a Cantonese restaurant than anything internal, served with two crisp strips of panisse – chickpea fries – which Colette assures me are ever so easy to make.

Conversation moves on to politics, and inevitably to Brexit, and, possibly in an effort to change the subject, Colette kindly invites me over to lunch the next day – 'You must see the view from our balcony.' This prospect, and the fact that the night porter allows me to carry Eddy up the narrow staircase to my room – 'If you can get it up there, you're welcome, lady' – sends me to sleep a very happy woman.

I'm up with the lark, or perhaps the gull, to catch the fish market in the Vieux Port, in spite of Jonathan's advice not to bother – he's right, the spectators outnumber the fish by about two to one, but I do get to look the elusive *rascasse*, or rockfish, in its spiny little face. '*C'est la poisson de bouillabaisse, Madame,*' the stallholder confirms helpfully – and the reason why it's so hard to make an authentic Provençal fish soup away from the Mediterranean. As Anne Willan notes, 'The southern coast of France is particularly rich in fish soups, partly because they suit the climate, partly because they accommodate bony local fish like "*rascasse*" (scorpion fish), which defy dissection with a knife and fork.'

Provençal fish soup

Though it will never be quite authentic without the bony little fish of the Mediterranean, you can still make an excellent Provençal soup with fish easily available here. If you're lucky, your fishmonger will be able to put together a fish soup mix for you of small fish and heads – and you will need to go to a fish-monger's for this unless you want to spend a fortune on whole sea bass and the like at the supermarket, because the bones are vital to give the soup body. I used a red gurnard carcass and flesh, some monkfish, and a hake head the fishmonger happened to have lying around, but whiting, John Dory or whatever they have in, with the exception of very oily fish like salmon, trout, mackerel, herring, etc. should do fine.

(Note that you can add a lot more oil to the rouille if you'd like to make a larger quantity, but it's pretty punchy stuff, so you might not need as much as you think.)

Serves 6

1 litre fish stock

¼ tsp saffron

2 tbsp olive oil

2 onions, peeled and finely sliced

1 bulb of fennel, finely sliced

3 plump garlic cloves, crushed

2 thick strips of unwaxed orange peel (organic oranges are unwaxed)

2 bushy sprigs of parsley, 2 sprigs of thyme, 1 bay leaf

1 x 400g tin of tomatoes

2 tbsp tomato purée

1 large fish head and 1 carcass, or 2 heads or carcasses,
    depending on what you can get hold of
About 700g fish, e.g. gunard, monkfish, hake (see above)
5 tbsp pastis

For the rouille
1 fairly mild red chilli
2–4 garlic cloves
A pinch of coarse salt
1 egg yolk
125ml olive oil (see above)

To serve
12 thin slices of baguette
1 garlic clove
200g grated Emmenthal

1 Bring the stock to a simmer, add the saffron, then turn off the heat and leave to infuse.
2 Pour the oil into a large pot, cook the onions and fennel until soft and golden, then stir in the garlic, orange peel and herbs. Fry for a minute, then add the tomatoes and purée.
3 Nestle the fish heads and carcasses in the pot, and add the stock and saffron and 1 litre of water. Bring to the boil, then turn down the heat slightly and simmer for 30 minutes.
4 Cut the fish into large chunks and add to the pot. Simmer for 20 minutes more, until falling apart.
5 Meanwhile, to make the rouille, deseed and finely chop the chilli and mash to a paste in a pestle and mortar with the garlic and a pinch of coarse salt. Beat in the egg yolk, then transfer to a large bowl and gradually whisk in the oil, a little at a time, until you have a thick mayonnaise. Season to taste.

6 Allow the fish broth to cool slightly, then remove as much of
   the carcasses as you can. Pour the liquid through a sieve into
   a large bowl, and pick through the solid matter to remove the
   peel, herbs and any bones you can see.

7 Tip the remaining solids back into the liquid and purée until
   smooth, then pass this through a sieve, pushing vigorously to
   get as much liquid out as possible; what you're left with
   should be very dry, almost fluffy.

8 Pour the soup back into the pan. Reheat. Meanwhile, toast
   the baguette slices and rub with a cut clove of garlic. Add the
   pastis to the hot soup and season to taste, then serve with the
   rouille, toasts and grated cheese.

Back in the Noailles, the traders are still laying out their produce,
tubs of olives and bottles of fermented milk, sheep's feet and
sticky pastries – though most of the hot food is not yet ready, I
come away with a big bag of blushing apricots and a chewy,
almost elastic *mhadjeb* flatbread filled with oily, slow-cooked
tomatoes and onions, which I consume, not without damage to
my clothes, outside a little bar: the Marseille equivalent,
perhaps, of my customary croissant.

The mandatory old men propping it up are delighted by my
appearance, tomato stains and all, and spend some time dispens-
ing some quite unsolicited advice on the best way to achieve an
authentic Marseille tan that will apparently be the envy of all
my friends back home. Lots of oil is the secret, they confide. I
tell them that this summer I would have gone a better shade of
bronze if I'd stayed in Britain, and they all laugh uproariously at
this absurd joke. 'What a sense of humour you Brits have!' one
says, slapping the counter uproariously.

PAUSE-CAFÉ –
Couscous

Though France invaded Algeria in 1830, and made Tunisia and Morocco 'French protectorates' in 1881 and 1912 respectively, food from the Maghreb didn't really enter the mainstream French diet until post-war labour shortages and Algerian independence brought about significant immigration from North Africa in the 1950s and 60s. By 2005 couscous was ranked fifth in a poll of France's favourite foods, though, like the British curry, the stuff sold in tins at supermarkets or offered in school canteens often bears only a passing resemblance to the real deal.

Thankfully, Algerian, Moroccan and Tunisian restaurants are easily found across France, and their liberal opening hours and often low prices make them a welcome sight for the hungry traveller in a strange town. As well as fluffy couscous and slow-cooked meat tagines, you'll find the following on many menus:

Briq – crisp triangles of deep-fried filo pastry, most commonly stuffed with egg and sometimes tuna, but also found with other fillings.

B'stilla – round filo pastry pies, often made from sweetly spiced meat like pigeon, but also available as a dessert with a filling of ground almonds and sugar.

Cornes de gazelle, baklawa and *mchawcha* – and many other sticky, sugary pastries and cakes, usually containing nuts or semolina, and often spiked with flower waters and saffron. Best enjoyed with fresh mint tea.

Harira – a rich, spicy lentil or chickpea soup, which may be made with lamb or chicken.

Harissa – a garlicky, often very fiery, chilli paste from Tunisia.

Mechouia – tomato and pepper salad, more like a dip in consistency.

Méchoui – slow-barbecued lamb.

Merguez – a spicy lamb sausage now ubiquitous at every French barbecue, kebab shop or street market – I've even had them on a pizza and in a crêpe. With a generous dollop of fiery harissa and some crunchy pickles, they're the perfect antidote to yet another gizzard and goat's cheese salad.

Zaalouk – a chunky, tomatoey aubergine dip served with flatbreads.

Pleasant as this all is, I still need to fix my brake problem if I'm going to make it home to impress anyone at all. The first bike shop, a swish place dealing mostly in electric rentals, clearly doesn't think it worth their while, but directs me to another place round the corner, full of beautiful vintage racers, where they not only swap the block but take five minutes to show me how to adjust and tighten it, ask about my route and generally restore my faith in the universal comradeship of the *rouleur*.

The day is going so well, in fact, that I'm forced to scupper it with an overly optimistic trip to Le Panier, the oldest part of Marseille. I meander around its narrow streets, eavesdropping on the daily life of the quarter, the shouts of schoolchildren (who will today be enjoying, I note from the list posted outside, organic tomato salad with a local olive oil vinaigrette, chicken fillets with chickpeas and a parsley jus, a choice of two cheeses, and a local apple and blackcurrant compôte) and a discussion in the café where I stop for an ice lolly about how hard it is to live here without papers. There's a lot to be said for travelling on your own, I think; you see more.

Unfortunately, that doesn't always include street signs – and it takes me 20 minutes of increasingly bitter wandering around decreasingly charming alleyways to locate poor old Eddy, abandoned in what I now see is a maze. I'm forced to scupper my plan to pick up Tunisian pastries in the Noailles for my hosts in favour of hotfooting it straight to Jonathan and Colette's apartment in Le Corbusier's Cité Radieuse, a 'vertical garden city' considered by many to be the pioneering modernist's great masterpiece.

Running so very late, I have no time to goggle at the architectural marvels of the exterior – though I do appreciate the great man's thoughtfulness in installing so many bike racks. Unfortunately, it takes me another 10 minutes, once inside, to find the Meades's front door: the hallways are deliberately cool and dark, and none of the illuminated red doors bear anything related to the number I've been given.

Eventually, almost gibbering with the shame of my tardiness (and this from a person who considers anything up to 15 minutes late basically on time), I practically fall into their apartment, a lovely double-height space full of light and art. The view is indeed glorious, especially from the roof terrace, where Colette takes me after a lunch of well-dressed salad, saucisson, pecorino, bread and truly excellent strawberries: small and sharply perfumed, a promise of good things to come. 'It's the produce here that's so good,' Jonathan says as we eat. 'Perhaps there's better, cleverer restaurant cooking going on in London, but these ingredients, French ingredients …' – he gestures at the fruit – 'they're just in a different league.' That's why, we agree, people still go into such rhapsodies over French restaurants: they have a head start.

Colette points out a wealth of clever detail on our post-prandial tour. The letterboxes outside each front door are actually rudimentary fridges – 'It works: we keep coffee beans in ours' – and the sun terrace on top of the building, where the heat bounces off the concrete, includes a shady paddling pool for the residents' nursery school. There's a boulangerie, a little supermarket and an extremely expensive hotel on site, though the silence suggests it's not quite the democratic family housing it was built as after the war. One original fixture remains: a very elderly lady slowly feeling her way along the corridor to the patisserie.

While we've been gone, Jonathan, who plainly thinks my endeavour quite potty but is kind enough not to say so, has looked up some recommendations for me in the various cities on my itinerary, and presents me with a restaurant guide to photograph, covers modestly folded back. 'Whose is this?' I ask, snapping away. 'Oh,' he says, and coughs. 'Mine; out of date now, of course, but it might be useful.' And suddenly I remember this narrow little paperback, which was, for some years after it ceased to be current, a beloved fixture on my parents' coffee table, and feel about 17 again.

In less of a hurry on the way out, I have more time to admire *La Maison du Fada* ('the house of the madman', as locals quickly, and apparently affectionately, christened it) – the kind of unembellished concrete Brutalism that looks starkly sexy on a sunny day in the South, but, I think, would be dreary and rotten at home in rainy Britain. Today, though, I can see why Jonathan and Colette fell for it.

Annoyingly, I now realise, looking at the map in the cool gloom of the bike park, I'm already halfway out of Marseille, but my stuff is still in the centre. Every cloud has a silver lining, however, and if I'm going back to the Noailles I may as well pick up some pastries to fortify me for the road ahead. Though it's still several hours until sunset and the breaking of the Ramadan fast, the Rose of Tunis patisserie is jam-packed with shoppers picking out huge boxes of sweetmeats – '10 of those, and 10 of those … and 10 of the white' – and I have to be bodily pulled inside the automatic doors by some large ladies squashed in at the back, though the queue itself never seems to move. After 25 minutes goggling at syrup-drenched filo, during which I gain new appreciation for the plight of those who perished in the Black Hole of Calcutta, I give up and go round the corner, where I'm rewarded within minutes with a more modest order of a sticky semolina and date roll known as *makroudh*, and something with pistachios I eat immediately without troubling to identify.

As I load up Eddy outside the hotel, I feel a pang of regret for the couscous I haven't eaten, despite staying a merguez's throw from the famous Fémina, where six generations have prepared the barley couscous of the Berbers of the Kabylie Mountains – but I've had fish soup and fried thymus glands, and eaten strawberries in Le Corbusier's kitchen, so maybe I've done right by Marseille after all. And there's always next time.

Km: 36.8

Croissants: 0; North African flatbreads: 1

High: Lunch Chez Meades

Low: Losing Eddy in Le Panier

STAGE 12

MARSEILLE TO NICE

Ratatouille

*Ratatouille is not an ancient speciality of Provence (in fact, the first
mention of this Mediterranean vegetable stew dates from the 1930s,
in the Côte d'Azur's first flush of fashionability), but it's certainly
got its feet under the table as one of the icons of local cuisine. Now
famous around the world, as Jacques Médecin, the notoriously
corrupt former mayor of Nice, wrote in* Cuisine Niçoise, *the book
that forms the untarnished portion of his legacy, 'This does not
mean that the version commonly encountered outside the Comté de
Nice bears any relation to the genuine traditional product.'*

The ride from Marseille to Cassis has been warmly recommended to me by my friend and official cycling tsar Max,
though Jonathan and Colette are distinctly more tepid in their
opinion of it – a terrifying drive, they say, all sheer cliffs and
endless hairpin bends. This gives me pause for thought: Max
works part-time as a cycle guide and, among his many other
achievements, has published a book on cycling up mountains.
He's blessed with the classic cyclist's build, and his brief packing
list for such expeditions, which he kindly shared with me before
my trip, includes twice as much gear for the bike as for his own

wiry frame. It strikes me, as I gaze from their balcony at the hills in the distance, that me and Eddy may have more in common with the Meadesmobile than Max and his sleek steed.

Nevertheless, the very name Cassis exerts a powerful pull, conjuring up images of the Riviera at its most glamorous – as the Provençal poet and 1904 Nobel Laureate Frédéric Mistral (no connection to the famous wind of the same name) observed, '*Qui a vu Paris et pas Cassis, n'a rien*' – he who's seen Paris but not Cassis, has seen nothing. I'm hoping to make it to Paris at some point, so it seems wise to at least call in to Cassis first.

Up the Avenue Prado I go for the second time that day, giving me another joyous opportunity to curse the pastis-addled designers of the cycle lane and the little old ladies that keep wandering into it, with only a brief glance at Le Corbusier's masterpiece as I head past and out of the city. The road beyond turns surprisingly quickly from a wide boulevard to a minor tributary flanked by garden-ornament yards, and then pine trees and the increasingly occasional villa as the gradient gets steeper, until suddenly the land falls away to the right-hand side and it begins to ascend in earnest.

For the first kilometre or so of the climb, I hang behind two men on fancy bikes who look an awful lot fitter and more lightly laden than me, so when they pull over I'm faced with a dilemma. Having cut my cycling teeth on the mean and aggressively competitive streets of London, I only overtake people I can leave for dust – the humiliation of being re-passed 30 seconds later is too much to bear, and as men are, in my experience, considerably more likely to up their pace once overtaken by a woman, I don't want to die up here just to prove a point. So, a mere bend behind, I also pause, have a drink, assess the sky and prod my tyres a bit. Take a photo. They're still there. In the end, I have no choice: for once, it's me issuing a cheery and ever-so-slightly patronising 'Bon courage!' as I pedal past.

The fear of being caught propels me all the way to the top – a spectacular route through a national park created to protect the region's famous *Calanques*, narrow limestone bays of azure water that look spectacular on Google, though are sadly invisible from the road. Not that it's too shabby up here either, with views back to Marseille and her shining harbour, and a kind of rocky moonscape ahead, cut with sheep tracks and decorated with only the occasional charred tree, the legacy of last summer's forest fires. The road rises, but never too steeply, and some way past the high point, the Col de la Gineste (327 metres), having stopped for the obligatory photo by the sign, I see it begin to descend and pause again, feet dangling over a stone wall into the rocky abyss, to deploy the Tunisian semolina and date cake, which proves so absurdly sticky that my hands are all but glued onto the brakes for the final 10km. No bad thing, perhaps, given how quickly I descend into Cassis.

My old cycling buddy Lu has tipped me off about a campsite she reckons is one of the best places on earth. I'm not so sure – not only do I pay €15 for a third of a cramped pitch, but said pitch is strewn with razor-sharp pebbles, the showers are freezing and, worst of all, the beer in the shop is warm and dusty. Her restaurant recommendation works out rather better. As the clouds billow ominously above the little harbour, I sit down to a huge plate of *macaronade*, a dish of huge al dente pasta tubes in a spicy, slightly sour tomato sauce, served with a fennel seed sausage and what appears to be a beef faggot studded with golden raisins. A speciality of Sète, just down the coast – a place, incidentally, also famed for its cuttlefish pies – it's not what I expected to be eating in Cassis (grilled sardines, a carafe of limpid rosé, a modernist novel tossed carelessly to one side), but it seems that, as with the pizzas in Marseille, an influx of Italian fishermen at the start of the 20th century can take the credit for some of the best food in town.

A few bites in, my waitress rushes over to warn me that the dish is *very* spicy – 'I forgot to tell you!' she says, apparently panic stricken. I have to stop myself laughing, not only because that risks spraying her with pieces of half-chewed pasta, but because the sauce is about as hot as a packet of pickled onion Monster Munch. I ponder the recipe all the way home, but shortly after midnight, the weather gives me something else to think about. It begins to rain heavily just after midnight, and continues, in a tag team with strong winds, all night, wrenching half my pegs from the gravel in the process. So much for the sunny South, I think, lying awake looking at photos of the dog hiding from the heat in baking Buckinghamshire.

PAUSE-CAFÉ – Piment d'Espelette

Though the French aren't traditionally big fans of the chilli, they do make an exception for the Espelette pepper, a variety of *Capsicum annuum*, from the area of the same name abutting the Spanish border. Though it's sometimes used fresh, you'll generally find it in the form of a vivid orange powder, which gives as much colour as heat (it only registers 2,000–4,500 on the Scoville scale, about the same as medium jalapeño), has a lovely fruity sweetness and a rich creaminess reminiscent of roasted red pepper.

Espelette the village, which is less famous as the birthplace of the first Miss France, Agnès Souret, holds an annual Fête du

Piment d'Espelette at the end of the harvest season in late autumn, featuring lots of pepper-themed merchandise, Basque music, dancing and *pelote,* an energetically violent Basque ball game much like fives or squash, and culminating in a *piment d'Espelette* feast cooked up by local restaurants – and the ceremonial procession of the Brotherhood of the Piment Pepper in their flaming red robes and Basque berets.

***

My plan for the next day is to let the train take the strain as far as Toulon, a vast commercial port with, as far as I can tell, little to detain the hungry cyclist, and start my much-anticipated tour of the south coast at the resort of Hyères, but, of course, it turns out to be another strike day in which nothing at all is running out of Cassis, and so I'm forced to cycle the whole way instead. There's a potential plus side to this, in that the route takes in the highest sea cliffs in France, which sound exciting … but that's also a potential downside, both literally and figuratively. I decide, somewhat rashly, to get them over with before breakfast, so I can use a croissant as a carrot.

Whichever way round I look at the map, however, it seems I'm going to have to go down before I go up. Having made a reluctant peace with this idea, I whizz into Cassis and crawl back out again on the Route des Crêtes, which takes no prisoners – it's almost absurdly steep from the moment I turn off the main road, culminating in a 30 per cent gradient that, together with the weight behind me trying to pull me back to sea level, makes it almost impossible to get going again after stopping for breath. The views are incredible, but it's bloody hard work – thank God for once it's neither raining, nor particularly warm, but simply sullen and grey, like my mood.

Eventually, the route resolves itself into a series of rather less strenuous hairpins, and it becomes clear why the turn-off was festooned with signs warning of danger in high winds – as I climb higher, it becomes harder to stay on the road, and one particularly angry gust blows me into the path of oncoming traffic ... at which point a Dutch campervan behind blares its horn as if I might be skidding around the tarmac for a lark. It's probably the scariest moment of the trip so far, and I'm forced to dismount, more for show than anything else, given the wind is so strong that it's equally hard to stay upright on foot. On the plus side, I can see right back down the coast to Marseille, though I don't dare venture too close to the cliff edge for a closer look at the waves crashing 300 metres below. Fortunately, the descent into the port of La Ciotat proves more sheltered, but never have a croissant and a *café crème* felt more deserved – though before I can even order the latter, the man at the bar says, delightedly, 'You're thirsty, right?' and pours me a pint of water. When I go into the loo, I realise I have mascara tear stains all the way down my cheeks, though whether caused by wind or sheer terror is hard to say. The croissant is a mere 7.5/10, a bit dry and puffy, with ends that could double as firelighters, but with an enjoyably buttery flavour and a good firm base. To be honest, it's hard to be too critical when you're just grateful to be alive.

This is to prove the scenic high point of the day. The road to Bandol, a place famed for its wines and thus its literary connections (Aldous Huxley, Katherine Mansfield and Thomas Mann holidayed here in the interwar years, though not, as far as I can tell, together), is sadly banal, running inland past building supplies stores and shuttered waterparks awaiting the start of the season. The best thing I see all afternoon is a greengrocer's hut on a roundabout with such a magnificent display of tomatoes outside that I cycle back up the hill to get to it, after realising belatedly this might be my best opportunity for lunch. The dark interior of the shed is an unexpected treasure trove of local cheeses and cured meats as well as more exotic fruit and veg, including Scottish raspberries and what looks like a basket of finger limes on the counter. With a baguette from the bakery next door, I picnic on the sun-warmed rocks of Bandol beach – bread, tomatoes, fresh goat's cheese and an entire jar of Colette's green olive tapenade, and feel almost at peace with the world at last.

Unfortunately, (you guessed it!) that feeling is not to last. Even the excitement of passing into the Var, my favourite *départment* in all France, home to so many happy rosé-tinted holidays of the past, is fleeting, as all too soon I'm heading into the ugly underbelly of its biggest city, Toulon, in the torrential rain, cold fat drops as big as blueberries bouncing off the end of my nose. This, while trying to navigate through a strange traffic system, is poor timing indeed: no chance of using my still-ailing phone, water streaming so fast from my helmet it's hard to see signs, let alone the lane markings that shimmer underneath the puddles, and in the end I pull over and join a group of other waifs and strays huddled outside a supermarket. A large dog has taken the opportunity to stretch out and go to sleep in the middle of this tiny, dry patch of concrete. I like its style.

Once the rain finally slows, and I've had time to memorise the basics of the route, I tuck my sad phone away in three layers of waterproof material and set off again in the direction of Hyères – I'm hoping to push through as far as Le Lavandou, an understated beach resort with fond memories attached, but though the skies eventually smile upon me, fortune does not. First the cycle route is abruptly barred, and then, having finally found the road, and shortly after thinking bitterly that this would be just the day to get a puncture, I feel my back tyre resign from duty. There then follows two and a half humiliating hours by the roadside, first trying to find the offending item, wedged into the inside rim (the usual tiny piece of mysterious metal wire), and then attempting to stuff the new, partially inflated inner tube into the tyre and get the wheel back on. To be fair, this is a bit of an ignominious record even for me, but for some reason, possibly because I'm so angry with Dame Fate that my hands are shaking, the task is a lot harder than on my old and, at this moment, much-missed bike.

Eventually, an old man out walking his dog takes pity on me. 'Do you know bikes?' I ask, too eagerly, oil smeared all over my face like some sort of Pictish tribal marking.

He holds up his (sparkly clean) hands: 'A little.' His wife gives me a small, conspiratorial shrug. In 30 seconds Eddy is as good as new and I reward my hero in a neatly pressed polo shirt with a wet wipe and slightly too much teary gratitude if his wife's face is anything to go by. As they potter off, I suddenly notice it has started to drizzle. It's 6.15 p.m., I'm as filthy as a chimney sweep and Le Lavandou is still 25km away. I make an executive decision.

Ten minutes later, I pull up at the most expensive hotel I could find in Hyères, the Casino des Palmiers, a gloriously grand Edwardian wedding cake of a thing with a sweep of steps crying out for a red carpet. I abandon Eddy behind a cream pillar and step through the revolving doors ... into Las Vegas. Off-strip Las Vegas at that. The glass atrium is a riot of red and plastic, the neon buzz of slot machines flickers from what once might have been a baccarat lounge or a roulette salon, and the woman behind the desk, who bears a strong resemblance to Barbara Windsor, appears to have put her lipstick on in the dark.

She's lovely, though, and if she's surprised that the high roller who's booked their junior suite is a dirty, sweaty woman in Lycra rather than a millionaire with a sudden fancy for an evening of one-armed bandit, she doesn't show it. A security guard helps me roll Eddy into a sadly neglected ballroom, full of cans of paint and old furniture, and I go up and spend 25 minutes in my huge fawn marble bathroom, scrubbing myself, and then my kit, cleanish, and then hanging it up around my palace to dry while I paint the town red.

From my vast, if rather cracked, balcony, I can see the sea in the distance, beyond a weedy terrace with a bandstand in the middle, which presumably once hosted candlelit dances in some distant and glamorous past. It's too far to walk now, though, so I duck into the first restaurant I pass, a Moroccan place, where I tuck into vegetable couscous with dollops of fiery harissa and delicious oily merguez sausages in the company of a begging cat, and several couples who don't appear to be talking to each other. Needless to say, me and my book and my carafe of rosé enjoy ourselves immensely. Still, what a bloody day, I think, as I collapse into my vast bed, taking comfort from the slow drip of laundry from next door.

The next starts early in an attempt to make up some distance, but my suite comes with a coffee machine, the sun's out on the terrace and even accidentally sitting in a pool of cold rainwater out there can't dent my spirits. The route winds along old railway lines through the woods, before moving on to the D599, which hugs the coast. I take advantage of yet another badly indicated *déviation* to stop in the village of Bormes-les-Mimosas for a fat, flaky, buttery croissant (8.5/10, a very unusual beast, crisp and rich with butter so it almost tastes deep-fried, with ends that need biting, rather than tearing off, and a sweet, slightly yeasty flavour). Sitting in the sun, catching crumbs in my helmet, I hear some passing Scousers admiring Eddy as he leans against a wall. He is fit, I think smugly, you're right.

From Bormes onwards, stunning views lurk around almost every corner: gin-clear water, stripy parasols, spiky succulents and the all-pervasive smell of hot pine and fig trees, which reminds me so powerfully of summers past that I get quite teary. Finally rolling into Le Lavandou around lunchtime, I fail to find the little beachside café opposite the presidential summer residence where we used to go for pizza and *barquettes* of crispy frites, and stop instead in the fancier resort of Sainte-Maxime for a slab of pissaladière, the classic Niçoise tart of slow-cooked onions and salty anchovies, so deliciously oily that it leaves an incriminating mark on my cycling shorts, and a box of miniature tartes Tropéziennes.

Until I ride past the first of La Tarte Tropézienne's smart roadside concessions, I must confess I've never even heard of the things, but advertising is swift to work its magic on the mildly peckish cyclist, and I rapidly roll over and allow the girl behind the counter to take the better part of €10 off me for three Borrower-sized versions of the dessert made (quite) famous by Brigitte Bardot in the film *And God Created Woman*. They turn out to be brioche rolls studded with rock sugar and filled with a sturdy, slightly cloying vanilla crème pâtissière – I eat all three at a scrubby little park by the seashore, watching a buxom old lady plough up and down in the seaweedy water, while her Jack Sprat-like companion sits, fully clothed on a deckchair, smoking.

The next 40 minutes in the saddle are spent craning my neck for the perfect spot for my own joyful immersion, which always seems to be just behind me. Once I find somewhere that fits the bill (clear water, no steps to yank poor Eddy down), it probably takes longer to decorously (who am I kidding?) exchange one set of Lycra for another than it does to swim to the other side of the cove and back, but it's still well worth the mild embarrassment of yanking my reluctant shorts back on over damp, sandy flesh as nice French families goggle in polite horror.

In fact, the whole day feels like a reward for past suffering: instead of the late-afternoon rainstorm I've come to gloomily expect, I get one of the most glorious rides of my life: the Corniche de l'Estérel between Saint-Raphaël and Cannes, a route inaugurated, as the many blue-and-white tiled plaques en route inform me, in 1903 by the Touring Club of France, following a coastal path dating back to the Romans and which, thanks to its towering masses of red rock, feels like riding through the Wild West on sea. Much of the road is completely deserted, with only the odd, highly covetable villa on the horizon, and 38km fairly flies by, despite the number of times I screech to a halt to try to capture some of it on camera.

Though traffic is light, I notice a steadily increasing number of fellow cyclists, including a few training in pelotons, too focused on the whir of their wheels to exchange the customary nod across the carriageway. I stop to let a phalanx of campervans past and consider my options for the evening. Cannes would be an easy run of it, but is unlikely to offer much in the way of reasonably priced accommodation after last-night's hilariously underwhelming blow-out, and the nearest campsite is some way from my route, as well as any possible eating options, yet still wants to charge me €20 for the privilege. It also appears likely, from its online presence, to be full of children. I decide to toss €20 more at the problem and book a room at O'Sullivan's pub in Mandelieu-la-Napoule just this side of Cannes instead, as much out of curiosity as anything else.

I have no idea what to expect from an Irish pub on the Côte

d'Azur, but it is at least on the seafront, opposite some pricey-looking yachts. I lock Eddy to the railings, ears flapping furiously at two men negotiating the sourcing of diamonds in Antwerp in heavily accented English on the terrace, and check in, amused to find that the small, spotlessly clean room comes with a free set of earplugs. No time to unpack: if the pub can offer me anything, it's surely a cold beer. I catch the eye of the girl behind the bar and ask for *'une grande pression'*. 'Sure!' she replies in a northern accent. 'A pint, yeah?' I think I actually love her. It does not touch the sides.

Showered, and disdaining the nachos on offer downstairs, I go for a wander. It strikes me it would be nice to finally have some Mediterranean fish (soup aside, I'm struggling to remember when I last had anything bigger than an anchovy), and as luck would have it, Michelin recommends the restaurant almost next door, La Palméa. As soon as I step in, I regret it – with its plump purple velvet chairs and tables of murmuring couples (and one disappointingly well-behaved bichon frise), it's a bit funereal, even when sat, as I am, within earshot of furious shouting in the kitchen. When I discover they don't do wine by the glass, I decide to go full Riviera and have 50cl of local rosé, which livens things up a bit, and happily means I'll have no need of the earplugs.

The fish soup I have on the side is very good, more savoury and less aniseedy than Sunday's version, and the staff are too busy squabbling to tell me off for eating it how I like; the sea bass with fennel and beurre blanc is spanking fresh, if not particularly exciting, and a single scoop of lemon sorbet gloriously zesty. For €33, it's the kind of solid provincial French meal I've come to expect: pleasing, without knocking my oil-stained socks off. (Which is fine, I only have two pairs.)

Tiptoeing downstairs the next morning, before the rest of the pub – last heard in an uproarious midnight chorus of 'Sweet Caroline' – opens its eyes, I'm in Cannes in time to fulfil an hour-long ambition to eat a croissant on the Croisette (7.5/10, crisp at the ends but a bit doughy in the middle, and uninteresting flavourwise, though I do get a glass of delicious fresh orange juice with it, and the people-watching is first rate). I then promptly get stuck behind a lorry emptying fresh sand onto the beach. This does at least give me ample time to admire the lion-faced little dog in front of me, perched imperiously in a wine crate strapped onto the back of an ancient bike ridden by an equally ancient man, who assures me the sand is local (*'Mais bien sûr, Madame!'*). I'd prefer to think of it being specially shipped over from the Sahara to cushion all those wealthy bronzed bottoms, I say. He looks almost offended by the suggestion.

The traffic is London rush-hour worthy as the city sets up for its annual 'international festival of creativity' (or, more prosaically, advertising, marketing and PR), and I'm glad to turn off the main road and take a little meander up the Cap d'Antibes, through Juan-les-Pins and into the territory of the super-rich, where hotels are flanked by security guards in tailored suits and shades, and everyone looks very pleased with themselves. Since I last spent any time on this coast, I notice estate-agent signs have gone Cyrillic, and at one point I'm overtaken noisily by a Russian-registered white Porsche.

One thing hasn't changed though: the view as you round the tip of the Cap – faint but unmistakable on the horizon, the snow-capped Alps. My heart thrills with a mixture of love and terror for what lies ahead; it's astonishing to be able to see both Mediterranean and mountain at the same time, and the sight keeps me going through an epic traffic jam in Antibes, a near miss with a traffic policeman on a Segway in Cagnes-sur-Mer, which strictly enforces the 20km speed limit on the cycle lane, and all the way into Nice, where the route is suddenly clogged with aimlessly wandering pedestrians and pootling hire bikes. I ride to the end of the Promenade des Anglais, just because I can, celebrate with a cold drink, and then head to my hostel near the railway station to dump my stuff.

It's been about 15 years since I last stayed in a dormitory, but Nice is an expensive place, so I'm relieved to find things have moved on: instead of a crowd of matted-haired boys rolling joints and playing the guitar to a crowd of adoring teenage girls, today's youth seems more interested in artisan coffee and free Wi-Fi, which suits middle-aged me down to the ground. The room is clean (no biro peace signs in the loo or tattered Birkenstocks in the middle of the floor), the shower hot, and I'm in, out and sitting down for lunch by 12.15. La Merenda, the place I've been highly recommended by both Rowley Leigh and recent Nice resident Max, is closed for its annual holidays (these things no longer surprise me), so I take a chance on Le Voyageur Nissart, which has been serving up local cuisine since 1908. Age is no guarantee of quality, of course, but it is just around the corner from the hostel, and in a trip that has thus far largely been characterised by inconvenience, that has to count for something.

Unfortunately, I get off to a bad start by cheerily hailing the proprietor before he's ready to acknowledge me, which leads to some rather frosty service, and a distinct unwillingness to engage in any discussion about the Niçoise salad, which in turn leads to the surprise discovery that their version contains two of my least favourite things, celery and raw onion, as well as tinned tuna in addition to my preferred anchovies. It does redeem itself slightly with some of the best olives I've ever eaten, and serves up a very good ratatouille with my red mullet, before coming up trumps with *tourte de blettes*, a true local speciality in the sense that, much like Marmite, you'd have to grow up with it to love it. Personally I'm not sold on the idea, or indeed the reality, of a sweet Swiss chard pie, two squares of floppy pastry filled with greens, dried fruit and waxy little pine nuts, and served dusted with icing sugar, but then the locals probably wouldn't fancy spotted dick made with beef suet, so horses for courses – I'm at least pleased I've tried it, just so I never have to again.

Ratatouille

Best made in the height of summer, when all the vegetables below are at their peak – though, unless you have really great tomatoes, I'd still use tinned for preference – ratatouille demands a generous hand with the olive oil, and a degree of patience; this is not a dish that can be rushed. Sautéing all the vegetables separately might sound like a pain (because it is – as the aforementioned Médecin notes, 'ratatouille, contrary to popular belief, is a particularly long dish to prepare'), but as they cook at different rates, it's the only way to ensure melt-in-the-mouth aubergines and silky peppers, and it keeps well in the fridge for several days. Trust me, it's worth a bit of work to come home to a Tupperware of this.

Serves 6–8
2 red peppers
2 green peppers
4 onions
3 aubergines
2 courgettes
Olive oil

6 garlic cloves
4 sprigs of basil, plus extra to serve
2 sprigs of parsley
2 sprigs of thyme, leaves picked
1 bay leaf
2 x 400g tins of tomatoes

1 Deseed and cut the peppers into slivers, peel and slice the onions, and cut the aubergines and courgettes into chunky dice about 2cm across.

2 Heat 2 tablespoons of oil in a frying pan over a medium-low heat and cook the onions until very soft but not brown. Scoop out into a large saucepan and season, leaving as much oil in the pan as possible.

3 Depending on how much is left in there, add another tablespoon of oil to the onion pan and fry the peppers until soft, then add to the pan and season. Repeat this process with the courgettes, then the aubergines in batches, making sure everything is very tender before tipping it into the saucepan with the rest.

4 While the vegetables are cooking, thinly slice the garlic and heat 1 tablespoon of oil in a smaller saucepan. Add the garlic and sauté for a minute, then stir in the herbs and the tomatoes. Season and bubble until it's thickened to a chunky sauce consistency.

5 Pour this over the top of the vegetables, cover and cook on a medium-low heat for about 45 minutes.

6 Remove the herbs and allow to cool slightly before serving.

Half of me feels I should spend the afternoon back in the saddle, exploring the hills that have drawn so many pro cyclists to the area, but the other half sensibly observes that while hills will be two a penny in the next couple of days, this will be my last sight of the sea for the rest of the trip – and I find that half's argument considerably more persuasive. Eschewing the wide sandy beaches of the Promenade des Anglais, I thread through the old town instead, and find a little rocky inlet just east of the port, where I can sit on the rocks and watch the Corsican ferries steam past. Beautiful, honey-coloured teenagers splash and flirt while I dunk my own rather less comely tan lines in the water. On the way back, I stop for ice cream – outrageous figgy fig, and *fleur de lait et amandes* – at the famous Fennochio's with every other tourist in town, which is so good that I can't even be angry when my swimming things fall off my bike in heavy traffic afterwards and I have to dodge a thousand angry mopeds to scoop up my bikini bottoms from the tarmac.

Seaweed washed from my hair, shorts off, dress on, I head out to meet a friend who has kindly brought me an emergency phone from London in case mine goes berserk again (though a couple of days of sun seems to have improved its mood considerably) and who listens patiently as I talk at him over several beers. Jon is here for a weekend riding the hills I rejected this afternoon, and by the time his two buddies have arrived from the airport and had a few welcome drinks of their own, and Billy, who must be six foot four, has raced Eddy round the port just for the hell of it, I, as an old French hand, am getting concerned about dinner. Jon is sure he knows somewhere just around the corner, or perhaps the next – or was it up those steps?

At 10.47 p.m., I push them all into the nearest place, and somehow persuade Madame to serve us. 'Just one course, though,' she says firmly. 'Make sure you tell them that.' I nod meekly and wonder how to break it to her that one of them is a vegetarian. The night ends with grilled octopus and more rosé, and, giggling to myself, I head back to my dorm – now occupied by invisible sleeping roommates – set my alarm for 5 a.m. and pass out.

Km: 291.3

Croissants: 3 (average score, 7.8/10)

High: Riding the Corniche de l'Estérel

**Low: Riding the highest sea cliffs in France and
nearly being blown over them**

THE COL DE JOUX PLANE

Tartiflette

*Tartiflette is an Alpine potato gratin made with copious amounts
of molten mountain cheese and local white wine, and often
seasoned with cured pork, cream and onions. It's usually served as
a stand-alone dish, with a green salad as health insurance.*

If I'm not fully awake as I slip out of the dorm, a pre-dawn argument with the hostel's Brazilian night porter, who, after taking up precious moments showing me photos of his mountain bike, won't let me leave without returning the flimsy key card ('No, you cannot pay for it, Missus, you must find'), soon gets the adrenaline flowing, as does a slipped chain on the 200-metre ride to the station. Once on the train, however, I sleep soundly through the entire Côte d'Azur – been there, done that, got the (faint) tan lines to prove it.

The vagaries of the French rail system mean that in order to travel north to the Alps, I must first spend a couple of groggy hours back in Marseille. I use it wisely, pedalling back up to the Prado to bag a bready croissant (6/10, croissant in shape alone, would have been improved by Marmite) from celebrity baker Pierre Ragot, where the queue stretches out of the door, giving me ample opportunity to admire his huge sourdough loaves and coal-black ciabatta. I eat it at a sweet little vegetarian café at the foot of the station steps, where I'd hoped to find yoghurt and muesli. Instead, I get chia seeds for the second time in a week, which seems odd given how strenuously I avoid the chewy little bastards in London. The coffee's good, though – positively reviving, in fact, after my late night and early start.

Still prising seeds from my molars, I ascend the train to Lyon, foolishly leaving my Pierre Ragot picnic (a deliciously olive-oil-sodden spinach and chèvre focaccia) in my panniers, where it spends the trip squashed behind 40 mountain bikes belonging to an excitable middle-aged French party. Ravenous with hunger by the time I get to Lyon (whatever anyone says, chia pudding does not fill you up), I eat an outrageously late lunch outside the station to stares of disapproval from everyone but the local population of small and hungry birds (whose advances give me a sudden pang of longing for the cupboard love of the dog) and then, with 40 minutes to kill before my next train, repair to the inevitable Relay newsagent for post-prandial coffee.

As I sit down at the window, I notice a uniformed man staring at Eddy, whom I've wedged carelessly against the other side. My first, and very British, thought is that he's about to report him as a security risk – please do not leave baggage unattended on this station, etc. – so I attempt to reassure him through the glass using the medium of mime. He comes over anyway – here we go, I think, typical jobsworth – and tells me that my bike is beautiful, that he longs for such a bike. This is mine, he says, pulling out his phone to show me photos of something so loaded up with panniers at all available points it's hard to tell if it's a bike or a mule: '*Je prends le tout!*' he tells me triumphantly. You really have only these bags? I'm delighted – after weeks of raised eyebrows from fellow cyclists, at last someone thinks I'm travelling light.

With a skip in my step, and a coquettish swish in Eddy's tyres, we continue our journey due east along a line flanked by turquoise lakes to Annecy in the Haute-Savoie (my second favourite *département* of France), where I have a tight connection with the Saint-Gervais train – except it's not listed on the board. Panicking, I find a man in a peaked cap (one of the great things about the heavily unionised and conservative French railway is that you're never far from an immaculately turned-out member of staff), who tells me it's been cancelled and replaced by a bus – and thus, it seems, disappeared from the official timetable. My mind races back, reluctantly, to rail replacement buses I have known and hated – 'But I have a bike!' I whimper. 'Will they take a bike?' He shrugs with the optimistic air of someone who knows this isn't his problem. 'Maybe, you'll have to ask the driver.'

First, I have to find him. In the end, it's a process of elimination: the only bus at the rank not displaying a destination or a train number that bears any relation to the cancelled service turns out to be the Saint-Gervais-bound service, and its chauffeur is a classic of the genre, complete with sharply pressed short-sleeved shirt and a sparse, nicotine-stained moustache. I humbly ask Drives if he might consider taking a bike. Unlike his British brothers-in-arms, he seems open to such a possibility, slinging Eddy carelessly into the luggage compartment as if he's no more than an oddly shaped suitcase – and frankly, after 12 hours, I'd sacrifice my loyal companion to the mountain sprites if it brought me closer to a glass of wine and a comfy bed.

My dad is waiting for me at Cluses, staring gloomily into the compact boot of his rented hatchback as the bus driver, half-smoked rollie tucked behind his ear, attempts to reverse into me on his way back to civilisation. It's now almost 14.5 hours since

I set off from Nice, from sun-baked pastels to wooden chalets, and the moment for rational thought finished around teatime, had there been any tea available. Wordlessly, I pick up poor Eddy and, before anyone can object, shove him bodily into the car, chuck the panniers in on top of his poor delicate wheels and fall into the front seat.

I'd like to say that my parents have come over especially to check up on their youngest child, to feed me and kiss my many pedal-shaped bruises better, but in fact they seized the opportunity for a cheap holiday at my sister's new flat in the Alps months before I even admitted to myself that I was going to embark on this mad adventure, so the timing is merely coincidental on their part. Me, I've based my entire itinerary on the hope of some free meals and a serviced launderette.

En route to Samoëns, after the briefest of solicitous enquiries about my trip thus far, Dad recounts every walk they've done in minute detail; it's quite soothing to be talked at for a change, and even more soothing to be met at the door with a large glass of cold wine and a demand for 'your darks'. As everything I own is filthy, I eat a hearty dinner dressed in my mum's walking tights (several sizes too small) and my brother-in-law's ski jacket (several sizes too large), enjoy a heated argument about British politics (not hard in the summer of 2018) and retire to bed in a comfortingly familiar rage.

I wake the next morning to find the rage replaced by a crushing sense of fear and a neat pile of sweet-smelling Lycra. I have my first cup of tea for three weeks (my mum travels with teabags), devour half a baguette piled with butter and Marmite and, after posing for a photo, bow to maternal pressure by stuffing my warm jacket into the pocket at the back of my jersey and take off, free of panniers, but weighed down with worry – chiefly that I'm about to make a massive tit of myself.

This is definitely the most terrified I have felt since ... well, since nearly being blown to my death on those cliffs above Cassis. I'm taking on the Col du Joux Plane, described by *Cycling Weekly* (my regular read, obviously) as 'perhaps the most picturesque and tranquil mountain pass in the French Alps' and by Lance Armstrong as 'the hardest day of my life – on a bike' ... and he wasn't running on just tea and Marmite.

I've chosen it for two reasons. Firstly, and most importantly, it starts metres from my sister's flat. Secondly, it finishes in Morzine, a place I happen to know can make a good tartiflette. Unfortunately for me, while a local bike tour company bills the Joux Plane as 'a tough climb from either side', it's apparently 'significantly harder from Samoëns', a fact that clearly did not play a part in my decision-making process.

My friend Ned, a man who has successfully completed an Alpine leg of the Étape du Tour, the amateur Tour de France stage laid on for fans each year, sends me a helpful guide to the route, which I study fretfully, unsure whether it's better to know what I'm in for or to set off in happy ignorance. Is it true that anything, including tartiflette, is achievable if you want it enough, or am I having a laugh making an attempt on what 'Dutch climbing legend' Peter Winnen apparently remembers as 'the nastiest climb in the Alps' – the point at which I stopped reading Ned's guide. I'm about to find out.

I turn off the main road and on to a side street that until now has been known to me as a place to buy cheap ski gear, but which, it appears from the bottom, could also double as a toboggan run in high season. 'It begins with a *laverie*, a laundrette. You don't see many of those these days but it's a good invitation to get into your lowest gear and start a spin cycle otherwise you'll be rinsed in no time,' the guide on my handlebars helpfully informs me. These words, along with the subsequent phrase 'the hardest part of the climb is about to begin' ring in my ears as I start to pedal in earnest – my cheeks burn with the effort and the paranoid conviction that everyone around me (three old grannies on their way to Mass) knows where I'm heading and is sucking their false teeth at my foolish hubris.

The road climbs, not very gradually, I'll be honest, through chalets and hotels, until it turns into the Col proper: a sign announces it's currently OUVERT. Bummer. The possibility that it might still be closed due to late snow hadn't thus far occurred to me, but now I'm in mourning for what could have been – there's a long way round to Morzine, after all.

Onwards and upwards the road goes, and hotels become farms and gardens become meadows, the gradient steep enough to make the idea of stopping attractive, but rarely steep enough to be actually painful – later, I read that an 18th-century regional engineer, Pierre Trésaguet, is largely responsible for the generally sensible gradients of French roads: 8 per cent, decreed to be the most a fully laden mule could cope with, is the usual limit. The Joux Plane boasts an average of 8.5 per cent, and a maximum of 11 or 12 per cent, depending on who you believe. Afterwards, I tend to favour the latter, or even American pro cyclist Chris Horner's claim that it's 'like 20 per cent all the way up', but, though that's nothing compared to some of the other stuff I've done, it seems to just go on and on.

As it does, I begin to notice small oddities: a woman in a *Mécanique* T-shirt leaning on a car by the side of the road, a small boy waving a French flag on a corner, a little knot of people sitting on the grass, one of whom shouts, '*Vive la France!*' as I labour past. I pump the air with what I hope looks like nonchalance, as if this kind of thing happens to me all the time, but as I pull level with a man in a baseball cap on the verge, who urges '*Allez! Allez!*', I stop abruptly.

He looks a bit scared, as well he might given that I can hardly muster enough breath to get the words out. Eventually I wheeze, 'Monsieur, is there a race up here today?' His face creases delightedly. '*Bien sûr!*' In fact, Mademoiselle, they're just behind you. Once again, I rue the fact that '*Putain!*' is no substitute for your average English swear word in the satisfaction stakes. Don't worry, he says kindly, it is not important! And, as I pull away, '*Courage!*'

Gradually, the serious cyclists begin to pass me, more in a trickle than a steady stream: an impossibly young-looking boy followed by a team car, or perhaps just his over-enthusiastic parents, proffering gels through the window; older, thicker men, heads down, thighs pumping like pistons. Some of them make it look easy, some appear to be finding it almost as tough as me, sweat pouring down their faces. Most are nice enough to offer some encouragement as they go past, the ones who aren't in a world of private pain, and I make it a point of pride to cheerily respond – and never to stop in view of any of them.

The world shrinks to what's immediately in front of me: the scent of warm hay, the tinkling of cowbells, the dark of the forest, the cheering gleam of Mont Blanc in the distance, and, more relevantly, the distance markers of the climb, which, as they also reveal the average gradient of the next kilometre, exert a powerful influence on my spirits.

Suddenly, as the road carves a slow curve in the mountain, which, rationally, I know isn't steep but still causes the last ounce of baguette energy to drain from my legs, I spy a little gazebo in the distance and a sign which surely must mark the top. Like Armstrong, I find there's nothing left in the tank and, unlike him, stop for a fizzy Haribo Orangina, which sits flaccid between my teeth as I push on upwards, finally dribbling to a stop by the tent, which is serving blackcurrant squash to the competitors. I take one before anyone can object and down it quickly, before wheeling Eddy back to the Col de Joux Plane sign, hoping to get a picture for posterity – or at least to remind the familial WhatsApp group that I'm still alive.

I ask a couple of men already posing by it to take my photo, as their female companion vomits into the grass. They turn out to be Brits – 'That went on a bit, innit?' one of them says conversationally as I grimace for the camera. 'Are you doing the race?' I laugh delightedly. They tell me they've come for the trail running competition in Samoëns; having run 83km the day before, they had a fancy to hire some bikes today. Having reduced me to stupefied silence, they scoop up their poor spluttering friend and shoot off at surprising speed for people whose legs 'hurt a bit', but I take some comfort from the fact that, unless they've rented all the gear as well, this is definitely not their first rodeo.

From here the road curls round a dark, glassy lake, which might be assumed, by those less well read than me, to mark the summit. Thanks to Ned, I know better. There's yet more climbing to do to the Col du Ranfolly (yet another entry ticked off on dangerousroads.org), before the D354 starts its sinuous return to the valley floor. Having sweated in the strong mountain sunshine all the way up, I find it's cold up here, and damp, too; the cloud almost touches the black water, and I'm grateful for my mum's fussing about the jacket.

Shortly after spotting my first, very gratifying piste map, and passing underneath a chairlift disgorging mountain bikers rather than snowboarders, the road begins to descend in great swooping loops and then straightens out, still at a terrifying gradient, and doesn't stop falling until I have to slam on the brakes at a roundabout in the middle of Morzine. It's proper white-knuckle stuff, and I ride it unsure whether it's better to perch racer-style, with my hands on the drops, which feels a lot more stable but leaves me unable to reach the brakes, or hold on to the brakes instead, which puts me rather too upright for comfort. Neither are entirely satisfactory, to be honest, but as I can't really stop to consider the situation, I content myself with changing every three minutes instead, mouth open in a rictus of terror, flies throwing themselves down my throat in suicidal abandon.

When I finally screech to a halt outside the Felix Ski Shop, my heart is racing like an amphetamine-addled racer from days of yore. I call my parents and discover, despite my triumphant message from the top, which I note they haven't read, that they haven't even left Samoëns yet. In theory, that gives me time to sit down with a cold and very well-deserved beer at one of Morzine's best tartiflette establishments. In reality, those all being closed (the whole town is, in fact, closed, on a sunny Sunday in mid-June), I've hardly found somewhere open and licked the foam from the top of an absurdly tiny helping of 1664 before the troops arrive and shatter the peace.

I greet them like one newly back from the face of death and manage to persuade my dad that this is the time, as the sudden sun beats down mercilessly on his bald head, to try his first tartiflette. My mum, having been put off potatoes for life by an Irish mother, instead engages in a protracted discussion with the waiter about the feasibility of swapping the chips served with her grilled perch for the risotto elsewhere on the menu, a debate that continues to rumble on long after I've intervened to offer to pay any surcharge incurred. If there's one thing that my mum, a former languages teacher, enjoys more than an argument, it's an argument in French, and the waiter, being a good upstanding Frenchman, is equally ready to roll up his sleeves in defence of the status quo. (Fish is served with chips. Surely we of all people understand that?) Eventually, a compromise is reached, and I can enjoy a glass of wine in peace.

Thankfully, given that it's the only choice in town, the tarti-flette at La Rotonde is both huge and notably good. Honestly, it's pretty hard to get a potato, cheese and bacon gratin wrong, but as I consider it my moral duty to eat at least two on every trip to the Alps, I can confirm that some are better than others. The worst examples are dry and heavy – nothing but claggy spuds and oily cheese – while superior efforts like this are lubri-cated with the same refreshingly acidic local plonk we're glug-ging with it, with gently cooked cheese that runs over the potatoes like cream.

I finish the lot, then scrape my dad's dish as well, and call for the dessert menu. Truth be told, I've only cycled 25km, but it still feels worthy of a celebratory *coupe liégeoise* sundae, complete with mound of whipped cream and sparkler, as well as the complimentary shot of génépi that, despite risotto-gate, arrives along with the bill. This Alpine herbal liqueur, in defiance of the usual order of such things, tastes disgusting in situ as well as back home, a fact that only makes me love it more, so as my dad is driving home and I'm cycling, I have his as well.

Thankfully, the way back through Les Gets (world capital of music boxes), on the thrillingly named Route des Grandes Alpes, though longer than the outward journey, is considerably gentler, and even the honking of some indignant German bikers fails to dent my triumphant spirits. As my legs spin peaceably round and round, there's time to appreciate attractions along the way, including a shop selling decommissioned cable-car cabins as garden ornaments and a display of decorated straw bales, and even, cockles warmed by génépi, to reflect on how much I love this country.

I'm having such a good time I'm almost sad to find the road runs out after Samoëns, so I go home, stick the kit in the washing

machine and walk round the lake with my parents, steering
them home via the cheese shop, where we pick up a huge slab of
nutty Beaufort (truly, this is one of the world's greatest cheeses.
If you haven't tried it, you must put this book down and go and
find some), and six plump smoky *diot* sausages for dinner.

PAUSE-CAFÉ – French Sausages, a Field Guide

The French love their charcuterie – you'll see fresh pork on the
menu far less than in the UK – and their saucisses are things of
beauty. The meat content tends to be higher than in a British
banger, which makes them a denser proposition, but a good
butcher will mix in enough fat to keep them from being dry –
just be careful when you cut in, as this can turn into a greasy
geyser on contact with heat. Here are a few sausages you might
come across on your travels:

Diots de Savoie – garlicky, spicy pork sausages from the
mountains, salty with bacon, and often smoked.

Figatellu – a Corsican pork sausage eaten fresh, dried or
smoked, it contains blood and offal, and is seasoned with
herbs, garlic and wine.

Merguez – made from beef and mutton, these North African
sausages are spiced with harissa, cumin and ras el hanout.
The name is said to come from the Berber *amrguaz*, like
man – or a certain part of a man. Wink.

Saucisse de Morteau – a large smoked sausage flavoured with
caraway, nutmeg and wine from the east of France.

Saucisse de Strasbourg – finely minced pork and beef seasoned
  with cumin, these look rather like what we think of as
  frankfurters in the UK.

Saucisse de Toulouse – sold by weight in a coil, like our own
  Cumberland sausages, these coarsely chopped sausages are
  seasoned only with salt and pepper.

Txistorra – a pork and beef sausage from the Basque country,
  which gets its distinctive red colour from piment
  d'Espelette.

To follow, there's a large and rather dry *gâteau savoyard* my mum
has somehow won in a raffle at the boulangerie after a mere
four days of custom, a jar of syrupy bilberries and a dollop of
Alpine yoghurt. I take it all on board, eating like I'm going to
spend the next day bagging yet more cols, rather than embarking on another railway marathon. I've earned it.

Following an early-morning trip to said boulangerie for a
croissant (8/10, slightly soft texture but excellent flavour – *merci*,
Tiffanie!), I ride back to Cluses station, shedding altitude with
every kilometre as the mountains recede behind me and going
so fast, in fact, that I sadly fail to stop in time to photograph the
sign for the little hamlet of Le Pissoir on the way into town.

Having missed this golden opportunity, I don't let the cheese
co-operative on the main road pass me by, and after leafing
through some rather sanitised children's picture books on the
dairy industry, I quiz the girl behind the desk on the finer details
of tartiflette. Unsurprisingly, she has particularly strong opinions on the cheese element: you can put in wine, bacon, even

cream if you want, she tells me, but without Reblochon it isn't tartiflette.

She has a point. Though based on a much older dish called a *péla*, the modern recipe was dreamt up by the Reblochon marketing board in the 1980s. It is to be hoped they were rewarded for it, because it is a work of sheer culinary genius.

We go through the various forms of this creamy, washed-rind cheese they have on offer: a soft, ripe version made with milk from a single farm, a firmer blend from the co-operative, a silver-medal-winning variety … which does she prefer, I wonder? She makes a face like I'm asking her to choose between her children, so obviously, as someone about to embark upon a long train journey on a warm day, I gamely buy one of each.

Tartiflette

A slightly looser, more wine-soaked version of my own recipe – the wine cuts through the potatoes and cheese to give the false impression of lightness. Don't blame me if you eat more in consequence.

Serves 6
1.3kg waxy potatoes, peeled
2 tbsp butter (about 35g)
1 onion, peeled and thinly sliced
150g smoked bacon lardons
250ml dry white wine
200ml whipping cream
1 Reblochon
1 garlic clove

1 Cut any large potatoes into chunks the size of the smallest, so they're all about the same, then boil in well-salted water until just tender to a fork, but not cooked right through. Drain well and leave to cool.

2 Meanwhile, melt half the butter in a frying pan and sauté the onions and bacon until the onions are soft and both are beginning to brown. Tip in the wine, then bring to a simmer and reduce by about half. Take off the heat and stir in the cream.

3 Preheat the oven to 200°C/180°C fan/gas 6. Cut the potatoes into smallish cubes (roughly 1cm). Heat the remaining butter in a frying pan and sauté them until golden. Cut the cheese in half laterally.

4 Rub an ovenproof dish with the cut clove of garlic, then cover the base with half the potatoes. Spoon over half the onion and bacon mixture and season well. Top with half the Reblochon, then repeat the layers, with the remaining Reblochon half, rind uppermost, on top.

5 Bake for 15 minutes, until browned and bubbling (stick it under the grill for 5 more minutes if you want it really crisp), then serve with a green salad and a glass of dry white wine.

Km: 93.4

Croissants: 2 (average 7/10, one celebrity, one old friend)

High: Reaching the top of the Col de Joux Plane

Low: The rail replacement bus

STAGE 14

LYON

Salade Lyonnaise

Salade lyonnaise is made from pleasantly bitter frisée lettuce, or sometimes dandelion greens, dressed with a sharp vinaigrette and topped with crisply fried bacon lardons, oily croutons and a softly poached egg. Given the relative quantities involved, it's a salad in the true French sense of the word: 70 per cent animal, 30 per cent vegetable.

I hit another strike day on my way down from the Alps – though there are only, in fact, two a week, they seem to have been carefully scheduled to cause me maximum stress. Thankfully, however, I'm now sufficiently far north for this not to mean a total shutdown of all services. Instead, I'm gifted three hours in Annecy, which proves long enough for a happy wallow in its beautiful chalky lake as a paraglider soars over the peaks above. On shore, a woman of about my age perches on a rock, fully clothed, taking selfie after selfie as her feet sink into the glacial mud. Gotta get those likes.

Afterwards, I sit, dripping but elated, on the grass and eat a cold sausage I watched my mum retrieve from the bin for my packed lunch, a slab of Beaufort cheese, and a large and very ripe tomato, and try hard to ignore the increasingly angry smell coming from the bag containing the Reblochon. So aggressive is this odour that I shamefacedly abandon the offending pannier in the bike carriage on the train to Lyon, trusting in its power to deter potential thieves.

The next stage is as close as I'll come to a peloton: my friends are, to a woman, greedy people, and Lyon, the gastronomic capital of France, has proved a popular choice. Conveniently situated on the main route between the Mediterranean and the North, the city has punched above its culinary weight for centuries, helped, in part, by a wealth of produce remarkable even in a nation known for its food. The world-famous *poulets de Bresse*, Charolais beef, the fish of the Rhône and Saône and the bountiful fruit and veg of the South all pour into Lyon's kitchens, and the wines of nearby Burgundy into its cellars.

Waiting for me there are my schoolfriend Lucy and her partner, Ned, the man who cycled the amateur stage of the Tour de France last summer, and my university friends Ali, who's four months pregnant, and Bea, who isn't. My baking- and barking-mad mate Martha has managed, completely characteristically, to book a flight for tomorrow by mistake, thus ensuring, rather tragically, that she misses out on dinner in the French capital of high-class piggery.

Like us, Lyon has a high opinion of itself in the greed stakes, the prevailing wisdom being that 'Parisians taste everything without tasting anything; the Lyonnais eat'. And by God, so do we. The city is known for its *bouchons* – sometimes, inaccurately to my mind, translated as taverns. They're rustique rather than rustic; less spit and sawdust and beer-sticky floors, more checked tablecloths and rough wine straight from the barrel, with *tablier de sapeur* or deep-fried tripe (whose name translates, somewhat mysteriously, as 'fireman's apron') in place of pork scratchings.

Ned's friend Julien, who studied in Lyon, has sent a long list of must-try foods (some of which, including the aforementioned apron, are accompanied by the pleading note 'Just do it!) and must-visit places, most of which are closed on a Monday. I spend most of the journey from Annecy frantically trying to get through to one of the few restaurants on the list that is apparently open, Le Garet – 'one of the best *bouchons* lyonnais. They do calf's head!' – and the relief when I manage to snag a table for five is such that I end up shouting, '*MERCI, MADAME, MERCI,*' down the phone after the proprietor sternly informs me she'll give our spot away if we're any more than 15 minutes late.

This warning echoes ominously around my skull a little later as I sit in rush-hour traffic with Lucy and Ned, having spent rather too long gossiping in the apartment near the railway station that the three of us are renting for the night. I text Ali, who is staying nearer the restaurant, to beg her to go and secure the table. There follows a long and extremely stressful silence, during which I try to pretend everything's fine when it really isn't, then, finally, a picture of her posing gleefully next to a large porcelain pig. 'WE'RE HERE!' the accompanying message reads. 'It just made me laugh to think how cross you'd be. Were you worried?' If it wasn't for the innocent within, I'd cheerfully strangle her on arrival, but instead I kiss Bea pointedly and sit down. Ali is delighted with herself.

For once, the stars align; not only are the womb-like wood-panelled surroundings of Le Garet, with its pendant lights and innumerable knick-knacks, very soothing, but its menu contains almost everything on Julien's hitlist – and, pregnant lady aside, I've somehow managed to assemble the perfect crack team of adventurous eaters, allowing us to go completely mad over two courses that feel like ten.

The first spread comprises the inevitable salade lyonnaise, with its soft poached egg and oily croutons, rich, sticky goose rillettes, a plate of squidgy smoked herring served with cool, waxy potatoes and a salade de cochonnailles, a dish that we only realise belatedly is priced per person for a reason. The table fills with vast bowls of pressed pig snout, soft pink sausage and the best tripe I've ever tasted – which, frankly, is a low bar this particular bovine stomach clears with ease, given it tastes of neither bleach nor shit, allowing us to appreciate its intriguingly bouncy, frilly texture without any such unpleasant distractions – plus some lentil vinaigrette as a token nod to fibre.

Even us gluttons struggle to make a dent in it before the next load arrives: the aforementioned *tablier de sapeur*, which is simultaneously crunchy and squidgy and surprisingly moreish; some of Julien's favourite creamily bland boiled calf's head (rich in 'suspicious white matter', as it's dubbed at the other end of the table), served with a spiky, vinegary sauce ravigote studded with chopped egg and pickle, and the two safe options, an intense navarin of lamb and a ragoût of seasonal ceps ... plus the thing I've been talking up all evening, the andouillette, which is anything but.

PAUSE-CAFÉ –
Andouillette

Attentive readers may recall the similarly named pressed chitterling sausage I almost enjoyed back in Brittany. This is the full-throttle version, beloved all over France, though claimed by a number of regions as their own special creation.

Let me give you a sample of the top English-language Google results for this peculiarly French treasure. 'Andouillette: One of the things you must never try eating in France' comes in at number two; 'Andouillette ... or the Dish of Death' at four, closely followed by 'The offal truth', 'Andouillette: French pig-colon sausage' and my personal favourite, the somewhat mixed message of 'Where to eat andouillette: France's stinky, urine-smelling sausage'.

Studied objectively, preferably with a clothes peg over your nose, the andouillette has a strange and terrible beauty, made up as it is of lengths of pig intestine in various degrees of cleanliness, folded into a colon, or another piece of intestine, much in the manner of a Twirl, but ideally, and for obvious reasons, with less of the chocolate colour.

They're a bit of a cult thing in France, and though the most famous examples come from Troyes, in the Grand Est, the official *Code des usages de la charcuterie, de la salaison et des conserves de viande (chapitre 10.4, Andouillette supérieure)*, a document put out by the Institut de Porc (I swear I'm not making this up), lists seven regional versions, including an andouillette provençale, and an andouillette lyonnaise made from veal, rather than, or as well as, pig.

The AAAAA, or Association amicale des amateurs d'andouillette authentique (the Amicable Association of Authentic Andouillette Appreciators), whose 5A logo denotes a truly 'authentic' (a troubling word in this context) product, is currently revising its guidelines on this Lyonnaise sausage, which has only recently reappeared on the market in the wake of BSE, so 'Watch this space!' as the website promises intestine fans. Don't say you weren't warned.

In his memoir, *Under a Mackerel Sky*, Rick Stein, a man no stranger to blood and guts, recalls being warned off the andouillette by a typically dour Parisian waiter: 'I think maybe you don't like these … it's French speciality. No for English.' For the sake of national pride, however, he ploughed his way through an entire plate of 'stumpy sausages, which I can only describe as honking, in the sense of a strong blaring smell. They were very powerful – the same order of unsettling aroma as ripe Camembert but also sharp tasting in their intestinal taint'.

Like Rick, I feel bound to finish the plate, though in fact, for once, this doesn't prove a problem. I'm not sure whether it's because veal is less pungent than pig, or because the sharp, mustardy sauce smothers any lingering 'farmyard' aromas, or simply because I've been in France too long, but, as with the tripe, here the texture, all tubes and fronds, is allowed to shine. And, I find, having looked the realities of textural interest in the face, it's quite possible to make peace with them, and even enjoy them. As Ned puts it, 'On the scale of farmyard to actual shit, this is quite mild.'

I make sure that dish is finished, even if we hardly make a dent in the overall spread. They're clearing up around us as we finally finish the last of the 'rustic' red, make a final trip to the loos to appreciate a display of vintage bloomers and arse-themed art (featuring several sculptures of women playing pétanque with their skirts mysteriously tucked around their waists, having unfortunately forgotten to put on their knickers), and roll home in an offal-induced fug.

Salade Lyonnaise

Though tripe, andouillette and calves' heads may be hard to come by in Britain these days, the ingredients for this bistro classic are not, though you might have to go to a greengrocer's for a frisée lettuce. (Other bitter leaves like chicory, or indeed the traditional dandelion greens, would also work well, or at a pinch, crunchy mixed salad.) Leave out the lardons if you'd prefer to keep it vegetarian, frying a finely chopped shallot in step 2 instead to flavour the vinaigrette.

Serves 4
½ a slim baguette (ficelle for preference, if you can get it)
Olive oil, to drizzle
1 garlic clove, cut in half
150g smoked bacon lardons
1 tbsp Dijon mustard
2 tbsp red wine vinegar
4 eggs
2 heads of curly endive/frisée lettuce (see above), washed and
   dried well

1 Preheat the oven to 200°C/180°C fan/gas 6, and cut the bread into thin slices. Drizzle with oil and arrange on a baking sheet. Bake for about 12–15 minutes, until crisp, then rub with the garlic and set aside.
2 Fry the lardons in a dash of oil over a medium high heat until bronzed and crisp. Stir in the mustard and then the vinegar, scraping the pan, and set aside.
3 Bring a large pan of water to the boil. Crack the eggs into ramekins, then slide them into the water and reduce to a

simmer. Cook for 3 minutes, then scoop out and drain on kitchen paper.

4   Rub a salad bowl with garlic and tear in the salad leaves. Add the contents of the pan and toss together. Divide between four bowls and top each with a poached egg.

I get up early for the sole purpose of hunting down a decent croissant – only to discover there's a baker a couple of streets away sporting the red, white and blue of the Meilleurs Ouvriers de France, a prestigious trade association for 'craftsmen' encompassing everyone from barmen to locksmiths, dog groomers and, of course, pâtissiers. Membership is decided by means of a high-stakes competition; if this whets your appetite, I highly recommend the documentary, *Kings of Pastry – When Bake Off Goes Bad* (and if the filmmakers ever re-release it, they can have that subtitle for free).

Having passed the test, Philippe Hiriart has earnt the right to sport patriotic stripes on his baker's whites, and, trusting in their power, I purchase, somewhat against my better judgement, a slab of clementine clafoutis as well as the pastries I've come in for – and which I promptly drop face-down on the pavement outside. It doesn't seem too dirty, so I brush it off and serve it to Lucy and Ned for breakfast. It's much better than his croissant (4/10, dry, crumbly, dull), all custardy and wobbly, with a vanilla-flecked skin on top and a delicate puff-pastry crust. Quite different from the firm flan that captured my heart in Limoges, but equally enjoyable, especially with its sprinkling of authentic Lyon filth.

We meet Ali and Bea at the world-famous Halles de Lyon indoor market, renamed after this greedy city's most famous gastronomic son, the late Paul Bocuse, back in 2006. Now, six months after his death, large posters of the great man with the legend '*Merci Monsieur Paul*' line the walls, and a five-storey mural of him glares from the side of an apartment building opposite. The plan is to assemble a train picnic, but it quickly becomes apparent that this is rather like going to Fortnum & Mason to buy a sandwich – Les Halles Paul Bocuse are more of a temple to the pleasures of the stomach than anything so base as a mere market.

Jaws open in wonderment, we pass a stall selling nothing but queues of perfect quenelles, black olive and green spinach alongside the traditional pallid pike versions, and another gaudy with Lyon's sugary pink almond praline. There are magnificent displays of whole crystallised fruit, a greengrocer offering punnets of strawberries for €10 and even an épicerie with shelves full of Colman's mustard, Tiptree jam and Waitrose hoi sin sauce.

Tempting as it is to stock up, I tick off another item from Julien's list instead: a *saucisson brioché*, a disconcertingly fleshy, softly textured salami studded with pistachio and baked into a fluffy brioche loaf. Ned and Lucy contribute a mini-Jésus, a pear-shaped saucisson originally prepared in the run-up to Christmas (mini because large versions weigh over 6kg, the same as a small dog). Bea buys some *persillade de jambon*, vivid green and jellied, and Ali bucks the porcine trend with tabbouleh and olives. Along with a baguette, the by-now powerfully odiferous Reblochon and Martha's contribution – two EAT sandwiches from Gatwick ('I wasn't sure if I'd get hungry,' she says when we finally track her down at the railway station) – we're ready to pig out all the way to Chalon-sur-Saône, where we start our Burgundy pilgrimage.

Km: 0

**Croissant: 1 (4/10, eclipsed by a clementine
clafoutis from the same bakery)**

High: Dinner, obviously

**Low: Hyperventilating in a cab because I thought
we were going to miss dinner**

CHALON-SUR-SAÔNE TO DIJON

Boeuf Bourguignon

Despite the name, this wine-rich stew actually seems to be a Parisian invention. According to food historian James Chevallier, though boeuf bourguignon does not appear on lists of Burgundian specialities until well into the 20th century, it pops up in an 1878 guide to the capital, which lasciviously describes the plump waitresses at one restaurant as good enough to even make 'boeuf bourguignon acceptable'. This suggests the dish had a bad reputation and was perhaps, as one early recipe recommends, commonly prepared with leftover meat. These days, it's the region's star culinary turn, and deservedly so.

The pig-nic, which gets laid out across two tables as soon as we board the train, does not make us the most popular people in the carriage – not only are we loud with excitement and sausage jokes, but the Reblochon has reached peak maturity in the morning sunshine, and, with my antennae now finely tuned to the exact pitch of Gallic disapproval, I notice lips being pursed all around us. My companions are happily oblivious, garrulous in their holiday freedom, busy discovering they went to the same Leeds club nights at the same time, merrily reminding each other of favourite happy hardcore tracks, and no way, you must work with my brother?

After so long on my own, give or take a few brief encounters of the parental variety, it takes me a while to get used to the volume, too, and I find myself perplexed by the rapid back and forth across my bows: what is this novel thing called conversation, and how do I do it?

The deluge of chatter is still flowing freely as we disembark in Chalon to meet the bike hire man, who allows me to use his stand pump to jolly up the tyre I so laboriously changed in Hyères, now looking ominously flabby. After a few false starts, and an impromptu raid on a startled-looking halal butcher for sweets and nuts and God knows what else, we finally make it, in wobbly convoy, onto the canal towpath. A sedate pace is enforced, along with regular stops to consume more of our booty; a monstrous pink praline bun the colour of Mr Greedy appears from Ali's basket this time, and Bea produces some ham and truffle madeleines, which we all decide are an abomination, as we finish the packet.

Peeling off from the water, the route to Beaune takes us into the vineyards, where we pedal through famous names like Puligny-Montrachet, Volnay and, thrillingly, Meursault, home of my favourite wine on earth, a rich, buttery Chardonnay with a racy hint of steel. We're too late to do any tasting, but I'm tempted to cram a handful of sacred soil into my jersey pocket, before someone points out that I'll have to carry this romantic mud around for another fortnight.

Ali, who in deference to her delicate condition has hired an electric bike, is more concerned with whether we're going to go up any more hills like the one in Chassagne-Montrachet. 'I forgot it was electric,' she tells me happily as we cruise through the well-heeled suburbs of Beaune, 'so for a bit I just thought I was much fitter than the rest of you. It was *amazing*.'

Ned, Lucy, Martha and I are sharing another little apartment in the rafters tonight, while high-rollers Ali and Bea are sprawling out in the comfort of a provincial hotel. We regroup for dinner, and immediately I curse my stupidity in not booking anywhere. Being a party of one has made me complacent: even on a Tuesday night, there's not much room at the inn for six in busy little Beaune.

We try four or five places with increasing desperation, eventually splitting up in order to comb the town's cobbled streets more efficiently. A series of panicky texts criss-cross the evening air until at last someone finds succour at the Brasserie le Carnot, a place with a laminated English-language menu and the impatient service that tends to behove a French professional reduced to waiting on barbarians, all of which pales into insignificance beside the fact that there's a table free at the front of the restaurant. We celebrate with a splurge: a bottle of Meursault to start, the ripe peach fruit barely held in by its corset of Burgundian minerality ... and if you think that's florid, you should have been there. Relief begets some very enthusiastic wine tasting, it turns out.

As we're in Burgundy, I chase up the Meursault with six plump snails in their obligatory warm bath of garlic butter (the snails, as usual, are quite beside the point, but these are at least tender, which is about all you can expect of them) and my first helping of boeuf bourguignon, which arrives with the kind of oily top that suggests repeated reheating. The meat is dry and the sauce as rich and sticky as beefy treacle – the kind of thing you'd be delighted to pull out of the fridge the day after a boozy dinner party, but surely not the best that Burgundy has to offer.

I actually find myself wondering whether the microwave meal Matt hoofed down on the ferry all those weeks ago might have been superior. As we troop out, the previously taciturn waiter nudges Ned, gestures at the rest of us and winks. Some things, apparently, are universal.

We reconvene nearby for breakfast; I've never seen a crowd of locusts in action, but I imagine it would look much like us lot in a bakery. Lucy empties them of mille-feuilles, Martha steals the last croissant from under an old man's angry nose, and all of us crowd round, cooing at the snail butter gougères on the counter ('Snail butter, not snail flavour,' Madame says firmly, trying to hurry us along). I decide, on a whim, to buy a Paris– Brest pastry, simply because, oozing cream and caramelised nuts, it looks so outrageously decadent.

PAUSE-CAFÉ – Confession Time

Until recently I laboured under the terrible misapprehension that I didn't like French patisserie. I've always been a fan of their desserts – creme brûlée and tarte Tatin in particular – but, possibly due to an overdose of soggy profiteroles at a formative school Speech Day, for a long time their pastries didn't really appeal.

Believe it or not, I didn't even like croissants until 2 April 2011, when I bought one for a friend I was surprising with breakfast, and one for myself just to keep her company, and there, at her kitchen table, the fog cleared, angels sang and I suddenly real- ised that everything I thought I knew about them was wrong. (I remember the date so precisely because that evening we went to a party and I snogged her housemate, so all in all, it was a pretty good day.)

Anyway, all this is to explain why, up until now, I've never had a Paris–Brest, one of the high priests of the patisserie pantheon, yet having read on the train that they have a cycling connection, this suddenly feels like a dereliction of duty. According to Graham Robb, these plump little choux-pastry rings, sandwiched with swirls of praline cream and topped with a sprinkle of crunchy almonds, were created to celebrate a 1,200km endurance race between the two cities, with a calorie count appropriate to 50-odd hours in the saddle.

Early competitors in the Paris–Brest–Paris race fuelled themselves on snuff and champagne, however: the winner of the inaugural 1891 event, Charles Terront, who made it back to the capital in 71 hours, 37 minutes, then ate four meals, slept for 26 hours, got up and attended 18 consecutive banquets in his own honour. What a hero. The event is still run every four years, but not, in theory at least, as a race. The Paris–Brest, however, lives on.

Needless to say, though I only intended to take a delicate bite of the commemorative pastry after my croissant (8/10, very crisp and buttery, but a touch dry) to confirm my worst suspicions, I end up begging Martha to take it off me: it's utterly delicious, the pastry crunchy on top, damp and soft within, the cream rich and sweet – and well worth the queasiness I feel, having wrested it back from her and polished off the lot. Oblivious to the fact that we've already angered the entire shop, Martha takes one bite of my Brest and goes in to get her own, and Lucy follows.

As we scoff, I impart the glad tidings that we have a mere 44.4km to ride into Dijon; this time I've deliberately kept the distances short after repeatedly reassuring my companions that no previous cycling experience was necessary. Ali, however, has decided to take the train instead, not, it seems, because of the blistering pace we've set, but because the lure of a day on her own has proved too strong for someone with two small children and a full-time job, and frankly, I don't blame her; the peloton never stops talking.

We set off in a cloud of crumbs, leaving Ali basking contentedly on a wall. The morning sun is strong as we pass triumphantly under Beaune's 18th-century stone Porte Saint-Nicolas, marvelling at the jaunty roofs in shades of mustard and Pinot Noir we missed in last night's panic, and through the flat and surprisingly unremarkable countryside to the north-east of town, the viticultural valuable high ground always on the horizon. It's not too long before a sign for Nuits-Saint-Georges thrills my half-pickled heart; if white Burgundy is my favourite wine of all time, elegant Pinot Noir is certainly up there among my favourite grapes. Tom Kevill-Davies, a Brit who, after cycling from New York to Rio, moved to Burgundy, where he runs a cycle holiday business and wine export gig, is too busy with clients today to join us for lunch, but has recommended somewhere here as a likely spot for a decent boeuf bourguignon.

The Café du Centre is accurately named, but on a Wednesday lunchtime, the almost-deserted pedestrian street at the throbbing heart of one of the world's best-known wine regions feels more like Hitchin, the quietly pleasant Home Counties town that got lucky in the twinning department. Of course, we can sit wherever we like, Madame smiles. Quite honestly, as I settle into the welcoming shade of a parasol and down a refreshing beer (not even the location can persuade me to start with red wine), the last thing I want is stew – it must be at least 30°C – but needs must.

To my relief, the beef is excellent, with a lighter, more savoury gravy that knocks the socks off last night's version, studded with generous hunks of carrot, and thanks to a laughably good-value €14.70 *menu du jour*, I can at least sandwich it with a *salade composée* and a biscuity little raspberry tart, though Bea's dessert of icy-cold curd served with a side of crème fraîche – because nothing goes better with high-fat dairy than more of the same – has me more than a little envious.

The heat and the bottle of basic Côte de Nuits we've put away makes us slow to get going afterwards ... I wander into the Tourist Office to find out about vineyards to visit between here and Dijon ('All of them,' the woman behind the desk says unhelpfully) and come out with a Meursault fridge magnet filled with dubious neon yellow liquid as a souvenir of last night's aperitif.

Eventually wagons roll, albeit at the pace of a particularly indolent snail – laziness I pay dearly for when we end up on the kind of Google Maps Special Itinerary familiar to me from the first week of the trip: a road that turns into a farmer's track, and then peters out altogether in the middle of some very scenic vineyards. The view proves of scant comfort when the land suddenly drops off a terrace.

By the time we finally make it to Morey Saint Denis, no communication is necessary. As one, we fling our bikes outside the Cave des Vignerons and march in, moaning appreciatively as the air-conditioning hits us. Unfortunately, this little shop, run by the local winemaker's co-operative, is both small and already overfilled with expensively dressed Australians in the middle of a tasting. They give our pink and sweaty faces a look of fleeting alarm, while Madame, to my surprise, excuses herself and comes over – and instead of quietly telling us to leave immediately before we scare off the serious customers, pours us all a large glass of something cold and white 'while we wait'.

After 15 minutes of milling awkwardly around in the limited space, we realise that we may have come as light relief. The Australians, not satisfied with living somewhere that produces excellent Chardonnay and Pinot Noir, are it seems buying up the entire Burgundian stock, too, and arranging shipping with agonising slowness. At one point I hear one of them say in a world-weary tone, 'I'm just worried I've got too much of the '04, you know?' as he sends Madame off on yet another stock check.

The troops, hot and cross, having dispensed with the wine in short order, are beginning to look mutinous when the big spenders finally depart and we're handed more glasses, Gevrey-Chambertin, Aligoté ... I'm beginning to wonder whether they've driven Madame crazy, such are the measures. When the freebies finally stop arriving, I ask her to recommend something light, and perhaps a little fruity, suitable for an aperitif this evening. 'This evening! But it's so hot!' she says. 'White, you must have a white.'

I sadly explain we have nowhere to chill it, being on bikes. 'You're on bikes?' she says. 'Stopping at every village? Oh la la!' I swear she does actually utter these words, whatever anyone claims about no French person ever saying that in real life. In the end, I buy a bottle of something light and red, and Martha does too, and then Ned and Lucy buy some crème de cassis as gifts, and then everyone wants Madame to refill their bidons, and just as she's losing patience with us as well, an enormous Chinese group come in, and we make a swift exit.

The road to Dijon is thronged with viticultural traffic. All along the Côte de Nuits workers are busy driving huge pieces of machinery through the vineyards, every lay-by dotted with the obligatory white vans, men in caps bent double, pruning with the delicacy of a florist putting the final touches to a wedding bouquet. It's a beautiful sight, the serried ranks of vines, the solid stone walls bearing the name of the plot, the occasional shiny Mercedes parked up to inspect the fruits of their labour – though it feels a long way from the slightly scruffier wine scene down in the Languedoc. I can't see any of these guys pooing on their vines.

It's still so hot that, even this late in the afternoon, I spot someone driving a tractor with one hand and holding a stripy beach parasol over his head with the other, and we arrive in Dijon sleepy with sun and wine. Thank goodness, this time I've booked ahead for dinner, so by the time we scoop up a relaxed-looking Ali and roll into little Chez Léon, two bottles of wine and a fair few snail butter gougères down after some very civilised pre-loading at the apartment, I'm more chilled than a glass of Chablis.

Powerless in the face of hot garlic butter, I start with yet more snails, and then, inevitably, another boeuf bourguignon. Let no one ever say I don't suffer for my art. Not that my third beef stew in almost as many meals is too traumatic. Indeed, happily this proves the best of the three, with a richly-savoury sauce and great hunks of gelatinous meat, served with not one, but two types of heavily garlicked carbs – a sourdough crouton, and a dish of pommes purée. Throw in an outrageously boozy rum baba to finish, and I couldn't feel more French if you stuck a beret on me and a Gauloises in me – though, truth be told, with the amount of alcohol we've consumed, this may well constitute a fire hazard.

Happily, unsteadily, after bidding an emotional farewell to Bea and Ali, who are leaving early the next morning, we wend our way back in the shadow of the great cathedral, and then, determined to test their friendship to the absolute limits, I force Lucy, Ned and Martha to sit round the table in our little flat and help me drink my wine so that I'm not obliged to carry it to Strasbourg tomorrow. In fact, we drink so much that I feel quite teary at the idea of having to say goodbye to them all. After all, I've only just got used to the noise.

Boeuf Bourguignon

The fruits of my stew marathon: ridiculously rich, with just a hint of sweet spice. Try to get the cheeks and oxtail if possible; they'll make the results far stickier and more delicious than ordinary stewing beef. The garlicky croutons are optional but delicious.

Serves 6

1 bottle of fruity, relatively light dry red wine

1 onion, peeled and quartered

1 large carrot, scrubbed and cut into 2cm chunks

2 garlic cloves, peeled and squashed with the back of a knife

A small bunch of parsley, plus a handful for garnish

2 sprigs of thyme

1 bay leaf

1 tsp ground nutmeg

1 tsp ground ginger

2 cloves

5 peppercorns

2 tbsp olive oil

35g butter

200g unsmoked bacon lardons, or a thick piece of unsmoked bacon cut into 2cm cubes

18 baby carrots
200g button mushrooms
24 pearl onions, or 12 small shallots, peeled
2 tbsp flour
1kg beef cheeks, cut into 3cm chunks
400g oxtail
60ml brandy
300ml good beef stock

For the toasts
½ a thin baguette
1 garlic clove
Olive oil, to drizzle

1 Put the wine into a pan with the onion, carrot, garlic, herbs and spices and bring to the boil. Simmer for 30 minutes, until reduced by about half. Preheat the oven to 170°C/150°C fan/ gas 3.

2 Heat the oil and butter in a large ovenproof casserole dish over a medium-high heat, and when the foam has died down, add the bacon. Fry until golden, then scoop out with a slotted spoon and set aside.

3 Add the baby carrots and mushrooms to the casserole dish and sauté until lightly golden, then scoop into a fresh bowl. Add the pearl onions or shallots, turn down the heat slightly, and fry until just beginning to brown.

4 Meanwhile, put the flour on a plate, season, then roll the chunks of cheek and pieces of oxtail in it. Tip the pearl onions or shallots in with the other vegetables and turn up the heat slightly in the pan.

5 Fry the beef in batches until crusted and deeply browned, being careful not to overcrowd the pan or it will boil in its

own juices (add a little more oil if it feels like it's burning rather than browning). Scoop out and set aside in a bowl. Turn up the heat.

6 Add the brandy to the pan and scrape to dislodge any caramelised bits on the bottom. Strain in the reduced wine (discarding the vegetables), followed by the stock. Return the cheeks and oxtail to the pan and bring to a simmer.

7 Cover and bake for 2½ hours, then tip in the pearl onions or shallots, mushrooms and carrots and bake for another half an hour. Meanwhile, make the toasts by cutting the bread very thinly, toasting it under the grill, then rubbing with cut garlic and drizzling with oil. (If you don't have a separate grill, do this once the stew is out of the oven.)

8 Scoop out the oxtail and strip the meat from the bones, fishing out the original herbs if you can find them. Stir back into the pan with the lardons and season to taste. Chop and add the remaining parsley, scatter the toasts on top, and serve with mashed potatoes and steamed greens.

Km: 84.2

Croissants: 1 (8/10); beef stews: 3

High: Falling in love with the Paris–Brest

Low: The disbanding of the merry men

STRASBOURG TO MEISTRATZHEIM

Choucroute Garnie

Choucroute garnie, better known outside France by its German name, sauerkraut, is a dish of warm fermented cabbage with a light 'garnish' of pork and boiled potatoes. It's heavy, Teutonic comfort food, utterly delicious on a cold day with a glass of Riesling or a pint of golden Pilsner.

Only one of my new band of brothers is up early enough to see me off: having missed out on the offal feast first time round, Martha is absolutely determined to make it back to Lyon by lunchtime, so we slip out together, while Lucy and Ned are still sleeping, and share an emotional croissant (8.5/10, very voluminous and flaky, but still with that all-important central squidge, and a restrained but quietly satisfying flavour) on the steps of a Dijon boutique. This tender moment is brought to an abrupt end by the rather chic and very disapproving girl who comes to open it up for the day and we go our separate ways, Martha south by bike, me north-east on my final railway odyssey of the trip, heading for Strasbourg on the German border.

Sadly, the Maille mustard emporium is still shuttered as I pass, denying me the chance to 'savour summer' with the limited-edition seasonal mustard multipack advertised in the window. It's a shame, because I think the next four days are going to feature a lot of sausages.

PAUSE-CAFÉ – 'French Mustard' n'Existe Pas

Perhaps fortunately, the French are ignorant of the sweet, muddy so-called 'French mustard' accredited to them by the British in an ancient act of culinary aggression – though sadly for them you won't find any fiery English stuff across the Channel either.

Mustard has been cultivated in the Mediterranean since ancient times, and the plant was much-valued in the Middle Ages for its medicinal qualities – French commercial production began in the mid-14th century in Dijon (the Dukes of Burgundy apparently sent mustard out by the barrel to curry favour in the courts of Europe) and it's still big business in the city today.

Since the mid-19th century, Dijon mustard has been made with verjuice (the acidic juice of unripe grapes) rather than the wine vinegar used elsewhere, though these days it's often replaced by a cheaper combination of wine and vinegar.

Though it accounts for the vast majority of French production, Dijon does have its rivals: Bordeaux mustard is sweeter and milder, and often includes herbs like tarragon, while Meaux makes a punchy wholegrain variety.

Flavoured mustards, often in delightfully lurid greens, oranges or pinks, are far more common than in the UK – but then France is apparently Europe's largest producer and consumer of the stuff. Interestingly, though mustard is still grown in France, most seed now comes from the Canadian prairies.

Disappointed, Eddy and I push on with only the briefest of glimpses at the tiled riot taking place on top of the cathedral; like its mustard, Dijon's architecture will just have to wait. I have trains to catch, connections to make: Dijon to Mulhouse, where the station offers no more tempting lunch options than a packet of salted almonds and a black coffee, but does offer me the welcome chance to slide down another set of steps on my bum, and then finally on to Strasbourg, where everything looks different again: pointier, slate-ier and generally more Germanic.

The all-pervasive smell of hops that hangs over the city this afternoon, however, might be as much down to France's match in the group stages of the World Cup as Strasbourg's proximity to the border. My interest in the competition extends about as far as a fromagerie sign I spot urging '*Allez les Bleus! Bleu d'Auvergne, Bleu des Causses, Bleu de Chèvre, Bleu de Bresse*', but I have a feeling that my next travelling companion, Gemma, currently en route from Paris, is going to want to watch the match, and as she's had to hire a car to drive her bike here, thanks to the vagaries of the French train system, I feel it would be churlish to deny her this small pleasure.

Meanwhile, I'm excited just to be in Alsace, a region described by Waverley Root as 'the most foreign in France', a place whose culinary wealth, according to Joël Robuchon, 'stems from the union of French and German traditions' in the form of Parisian chefs and local produce. (German chefs are not mentioned, naturally. Perhaps Robuchon didn't believe they existed.)

High on the promise of beer and the smell of sausages, I fairly skip up the stairs to our Airbnb for the night, a hippy treasure trove stuffed with everything a traveller could ever want, from a pink velvet skull to a fridge full of vegan cheese, and am cordially introduced to a massive furry cat, which doesn't seem overly impressed by my overtures. I don't waste too much time worrying about it, though. Having finally exhausted my mum's laundry legacy, I have exciting jobs to do before Gemma's arrival; jobs of the sort that remind me I'm not actually on holiday – washing, getting Eddy's recurring brake problems sorted at a canal-side bike shop and, finally, a visit to the Tourist Information Centre in search of local colour, where I pick up a promising-looking leaflet in the shape of a cabbage. Le Pic – La Maison de la Choucroute, a family choucroute business that has 'worked the cabbage for five generations' proposes a guided tour that sounds right up my strasse – but only with a reservation, and depending on availability.

I take the leaflet up to the desk and make the mistake of kicking off in French. Madame peers at the cabbage as if she's never seen it before, as if guided tours of the fermented cabbage factory aren't big business in these parts, though that surely cannot be, and agrees that yes, it seems they do tours but no, she doesn't know when; I should probably call them and ask. It seems she's not going to do the legwork for me, so back in the laundrette, watching my Lycra spin – a sight that never fails to gladden my heart – I phone and am 60 per cent sure I've managed to arrange a tour for tomorrow, though the machine's on a spin cycle and the lady on the phone speaks so rapidly that I might just have agreed to buy a metric ton of choucroute instead. Let's cross that bridge when we come to it, I think, tucking the cabbage away for safekeeping.

Practical matters almost sorted, I have time to pop into the

Museum of Alsatian Life, a fascinating rabbit warren spread over three tottering old townhouses arranged around spacious cobbled courtyards. Cutting to the chase, I ask the lady on the desk whether the museum has any artefacts pertaining to chou-croute. It's the second time I've surprised someone with a cabbage-related question in as many hours, and she has to think for a while. There might be a cabbage grater in the kitchen displays, she says finally, and maybe an old jar.

Such rare treasures seem to more than justify the price of admission, and I set off at speed, startling a guard who's propped his phone on an antique butter churn to watch the football, and locate something unlabelled which may or may not be a grater. Either way, it's got nothing on the lobster cake tin in the next room, or the Christmas cookie cutters in the shape of pigs, and definitely pales into insignificance next to a carved stone lintel decoration featuring two lions fighting over a pretzel. On the strength of my 20-minute whip round, I think I'm going to like Alsace.

With a final surge of Germanic efficiency, I even manage to purchase some special-edition World Cup cans of 1664, which, we discover, once Gemma has stopped weeping with gratitude at my generosity, fit perfectly in the bottle cages on her bike. With them safely wedged in place for later, we repair to the nearest bar to watch the second half of France versus Peru, but even she admits the match is a bit dull (I mean, obviously it is, it's football), and we quickly abandon it in favour of videos of Wilf spreadeagled on his back on her dad's favourite chair, snor-ing loudly. In fact, so entertaining is this footage of His Majesty that I almost forget our dinner reservation at Chez Yvonne, a *winstub traditionelle* that comes recommended by J. Meades – 'years since I've been there, of course, it's probably awful now'.

PAUSE-CAFÉ – The Wine-Snugs of Alsace

Winstubs – a word that literally translates to 'wine-snug', 'the tub' or 'living room', being the place in Alsatian houses that was heated throughout the winter – are, as wikipedia.fr so winningly describes them, '*coquettement rustique*' establishments, often low-beamed and cosy, usually patronised, *Cheers*-style, by regulars. Some French claim that the *winstub* is a purely Alsatian institution, as opposed to the *biertubs* favoured by the area's new German masters after the annexation of the region in 1870, but in fact, such bars are common in grape-growing regions on the other side of the border, too.

The food is always hearty, old-fashioned stuff: quenelles of freshwater fish, cheese tarts, piggy stews, braised tripe, marrow bone salads and sausages, all served with piles of sautéed potatoes, with cakes and pastries made with local fruit to follow. As *Travel + Leisure* magazine puts it, 'A restaurant with the trappings of a *winstub* but that serves roasted langoustines with vanilla butter is not a *winstub*. Just as, sorry, choucroute garnie … served in a place with valet parking and crystal chandeliers will never be a *plat de winstub*.'

Chez Yvonne, which has been going since 1956, when the eponymous Yvonne Haller bought and rebranded the less catchily named S'Burjerstuewel, is the most famous *winstub* of the lot. Jonathan's right that it's no longer in her hands (she sold it in 2001 after 47 years at the helm, and died in 2014), but it remains a favourite with French celebs, designated *'une belle addresse'* for solid, authentic cooking by the famous red guide. In his memoirs, the late president Jacques Chirac recalls dinners there with his German counterpart Helmut Kohl: on the menu after his election in 1995, 'as well as confirmation that France would join the single currency', were snails, brawn, sausage, calf's head and plum tart, washed down with beer, white wine and Pinot Noir.

No choucroute, apparently, though Chirac was a fan, once telling a journalist who asked him if he was leftist, 'But of course, I eat choucroute, and drink beer,' as if that was proof beyond doubt of his socialist credentials. In fact, after tasting the wines put on for a Franco-German summit in Chez Yvonne's upstairs room in 2004, Chirac pronounced them excellent, and then demanded a beer. Corona was the *'plus gourmand de tous les présidents de la Ve République's'* favourite, apparently

Yvonne has also played host to more recent dignitaries, including Nicolas Sarkozy (impatient to eat and get on the road), Ségolène Royal (took the time to eat three courses and even have a chat), Jean-Luc Mélenchon and Alain Juppé – it's basically politico central, though not on this particular Thursday evening when the whole city is out watching football and celebrating a peculiarly French affair known as the Fête de la Musique. We trip over several small children marking this national festival of public music-making by playing the recorder in the street as their proud parents look on, and one middle-aged couple awkwardly dancing to hip-hop in an otherwise empty street.

Behind the red-and-white chequered curtains, Chez Yvonne, with its dark wood settles and tasselled sconces, is a place where it is forever November – an excellent time of year to load up on lard, washed down with a bottle of Pinot Blanc, served in goblets with fat green stems like spun caterpillars.

Gemma kicks off with my favourite Alsatian onion tart, so I take one for the team by ordering a foie gras crème brûlée for the simple reason that it sounds completely revolting, though the reality proves disappointingly innocuous – the kind of thing that Chirac, that man of the people who once claimed 15,000 francs in expenses for foie gras, probably ate for breakfast during Lent.

The main event, of course, is the choucroute garnie, which features a liver faggot, a piece of pork knuckle, a slab of bacon and three types of sausage – smoked, Strasbourg (which looks a bit like a frankfurter) and black pudding – on top of a pile of surprisingly mild fermented cabbage. It's oddly comforting – instead of the sharpness that I was expecting, the cabbage has a mushy vegetal sweetness, which sounds disgusting but somehow isn't. In fact, it's the perfect foil for the pigfest on top.

Like the poule au pot down in Pau, or the cassoulet, I'm beginning to understand that provincial French cuisine is a subtle, if rarely delicate, beast, and it's taken some time to realign my palate to its hidden depths. What can appear old-fashioned, even bland, actually has quiet charm in spades.

We finish with two scoops of a delightfully floral granita made with late-harvest Gewürztraminer wine served in the same little metal dishes we used to get arctic roll in at school, and waddle into the night, pausing only to embarrass ourselves on the way home by throwing some authentically inelegant Anglo-Saxon moves to 'Rhythm Is a Dancer' in a square packed with more restrained revellers.

Choucroute (based on the Chez Yvonne recipe)

Choucroute is surprisingly simple to make yourself (see below) but is also widely available online – avoid the pickled or pasteurised stuff sold in jars in supermarkets, as this is often very sour indeed (and you lose the health benefits too); look for 'live' and 'raw' sauerkraut or choucroute instead. Note that if you're making it yourself, you'll need to leave it at least 3 weeks before use.

You don't have to use Riesling in the recipe below, though you will have enough wine left over for a couple of glasses as you cook: any dry, fairly fruity white will do if the only stuff you can find is prohibitively expensive. The black pudding is likewise optional. Replace it with another sausage if you prefer (or leave them out altogether; there will still be plenty of meat to go around if you aren't Alsatian).

Serves 4–6 depending on greed

2 tbsp goose fat

1 large onion, peeled and finely chopped

4 cloves

4 juniper berries

¼ tsp black peppercorns

2 garlic cloves, crushed

1 bay leaf

500g pork belly

1kg smoked gammon (soaked if recommended)

550ml Riesling (or any dry white wine will do)

4 small black puddings (or enough of a larger one for 4)

4 German-style sausages

12 small waxy potatoes

For the choucroute (or use 1kg ready-made)
1 large white cabbage, c. 1.5kg
1–2 tbsp salt
1 tsp juniper berries, lightly crushed

1 If you're making the choucroute yourself, core and finely shed the cabbage and put it into a large bowl. Sprinkle with 1 tablespoon of salt and begin to massage the cabbage vigorously between your fingers, almost as if you're rubbing fat into flour, until it begins to weep liquid. Continue until when you press down there's a significant amount of liquid in the bowl. If it's not releasing much, try adding a little more salt, but be careful not to overdo it (taste it to check).

2 Pack the cabbage and liquid down into a large, clean fermenting jar, add the juniper berries and weight down. Leave in a cool place for at least 3 weeks, then begin to check it; once it's done to your liking (it should be mildly tangy, a flavour that will only become more pronounced the longer you leave it, so this is very much up to your personal taste), it's ready to use. (For more practical information about different fermenting vessels, I'd suggest going online.)

3 Once you're ready to cook, heat the fat in a large ovenproof casserole dish over a medium-low heat, and cook the onion until soft and golden. Meanwhile, lightly crush the spices and drain the choucroute. Taste the choucroute – depending on how long you've left it (or the brand you've bought), you may wish to rinse it first if it's very sour and you don't like that.

4 Stir the garlic, bay leaf and spices into the onion and fry for another minute or so, then add the choucroute and stir well to coat with fat.

5 Push the pork belly and gammon down into the cabbage, then pour over the wine. It should cover, or almost cover, the cabbage – if not, top up with water.

6 Bring to a simmer, then cover, leaving the lid slightly ajar. Turn down the heat, and simmer very gently for 2 hours 10 minutes, turning the meat after an hour. If you have enough room, at this point, you can add both types of sausage and cook for another 20 minutes – if not, cook them separately. I generally bring a large pan of water up to the boil, add the sausages, then cover, turn off the heat and leave for 25 minutes. In that case, cook the choucroute for 2½ hours in total, then test the meat: it should be tender.

7 While the sausages are cooking, peel the potatoes and cook them in salted, boiling water. Once the choucroute is ready, push them and the sausages in, take off the heat, cover and leave to sit for 5 minutes before serving with plenty of Dijon mustard.

The following morning, Gemma watches me hoick myself into my Lycra with an expression I translate as 'Jesus, what have I let myself in for?' The cat is less coy, turning tail and meowing angrily as I attempt to charm it into joining us for the breakfast our host has left of wholesome seeded bread, fruit and green tea. Either my Marmite has put it off, or it's noticed the tiny willy one of us has added to the already rather lewd blackboard in the kitchen,* along with our grateful thanks for the hospitality.

I collect Eddy from the bike hospital, laughing merrily with the mechanic at the bizarre configuration of British brakes (like

---

* Not me.

I have any idea which lever operates which brake, and would know what to do with that information even I did), and skip town. I haven't told Gemma exactly where we're headed; I want to be well out of range of the Europcar depot first, but as we leave Strasbourg behind, passing obvious attractions like the Abattoir Café without stopping, she begins to ask awkward questions about where we're going. West, I say vaguely, waving at some hills in the far distance.

We pick up a picnic in a supermarket in Duttlenheim well stocked with spätzle (a type of Germanic pasta), beer and heavy black breads, and wind on increasingly narrow roads through pretty villages with high, stepped gables and floral window-boxes, until we get to Krautergersheim, and I can contain my excitement no longer – a sign proudly declares this tiny place (population 1,751) to be the CAPITALE DE LA CHOUCROTE. 'Ah,' says Gemma, not sounding terribly surprised at this turn of events. 'Would you like a photo?'

After a quick picnic, and just as a sulphurous wind begins to whip up from the cabbage fields, we ride to our rendezvous with destiny in nearby Meistratzheim. Le Pic turns out to be a collection of large sheds up a bumpy farm track, and despite their fancy advertising material, the place is all but deserted. I have a very bad feeling as I wait for the lady in the office to finish her phone call. Gemma, meanwhile, is examining miniature bottles of local whisky in the little shop, which means at least it won't be a wasted trip if I have got the wrong end of the stick, but no, by some miracle she's expecting us. There might be some more people, she says, but they weren't sure if they'd make it in time, so let's start without them.

Let me tell you, if you want to give your French an intensive workout, I'd highly recommend a one-on-one tour of a chou-croute factory: we spend an hour and a half in conversation about

cabbage. I can thus inform you that 70 per cent of French choucroute comes from Alsace, and Le Pic alone produces 5,000 tonnes
a year, an amount that calls for twice that weight in cabbage.

Not any old cabbage either: white cabbage, both for taste and
appearance, finely sliced into 15cm filaments, and then salted
and left to ferment in storage tanks outside – how long depends
very much on the season. An August cabbage, she tells us, is a
very different beast from a November one, and of course (of
course!) as the temperature drops in the storage tanks, the
fermentation slows down, too. Once it's judged ready, it may
then be cooked for sale or packed raw, either to be eaten as a
salad or prepared at home. 'Here in Alsace, we sell more raw,
because we all have our own recipes. In the rest of France, it's
the opposite.' There's a brief, pitying pause, possibly as she
prays for their enlightenment in the ways of the cabbage.

As we set off on a tour of the processing plant, I spy a poster
featuring two small pink children wearing nothing but cabbage
leaf hats, celebrating the start of the new choucroute season
with the tagline *'C'est trop chou!'* (It's too sweet!) Is the arrival of
Choucroute Nouvelle as eagerly anticipated as, say, Beaujolais
Nouveau in Burgundy? I ask our guide. Madame considers the
question surprisingly seriously. Yes. Yes, it is.

There's not much going on in the factory at the moment, she
says apologetically, as we stand watching a young man in a
hairnet stuff tub after tub with fermented cabbage. Between
seasons, you know. In a few months' time, all this will be
go-go-go. (I imagine cabbages being mercilessly dispatched
under bright lights to the rhythm of thumping teutonic dance
music.) We wander back to the shop, where she excuses herself
to prepare the *dégustation*, included in the price of the tour.

Gemma, who has manfully been holding the conversational
fort while I've been scribbling down notes, lets out a long and

mournful sigh. I try not to catch her eye as the first sample arrives: a generous dollop of sauerkraut cooked in Riesling, as yellow as straw and very much like the stuff I had for dinner last night. This is followed by the paler, crunchier raw kind, which is apparently great rinsed and mixed with crème fraîche and horseradish, and then, the pièce de résistance, a choucroute pasta bake packed with salty bacon and stringy cheese that I could very definitely get used to on the basis that everything tastes good with melted cheese on top.

At this point, right at the end of the tour, when we've absorbed over an hour's worth of cabbage chat, the other group bursts in, all apologies and excuses about traffic – here, in the middle of nowhere. I can almost smell the long lunch coming off them.

Madame, after reassuring them that she can repeat the tour for them, no problem – HA! TAKE THAT, SUCKERS! I think – says the pasta, which I'm trying hard to finish before the interlopers get to it, is her kids' favourite, too. Personally, she likes to sandwich the choucroute in layers with slices of cured pig fat, and then bake it in a torte with a lard pastry. 'Oh yes, lard pastry is the best with choucroute,' someone pipes up from the back. There's a general murmur of agreement. 'God, I love France,' I sigh, slightly more loudly than I mean to, and everyone except Gemma claps delightedly.

Sadly (for me at least), Le Pic's choucroute only comes in Alsatian family-sized packs, so we have to content ourselves with a jar of spiced choucroute jam (ideal apparently with foie gras or game, should we find any of that in our picnics over the next few days) and a whisky miniature for the road, before taking our leave of our new friends, who wave us off with many expressions of good luck as they embark upon their tour.

To be fair, we are heading straight for the last mountains between here and the Americas, but they don't look too bad from here. And if they are, well, we've always got the whisky.

Km: 71.3

Croissants: 1 (8.5/10), plus a 10/10 banana and Marmite sandwich in the Strasbourg apartment

High: The choucroute factory, obviously

Low: Being dissed by a cat

MEISTRATZHEIM TO NANCY

Quiche Lorraine

You think you know quiche. You don't know quiche Lorraine. This much-abused Grand Est speciality, generally served warm as part of a proper meal, rather than cold from a picnic hamper, contains no onions and definitely no cheese and should never see the inside of a chiller cabinet; won't somebody think of the pastry!

Stocking up on strong liquor rather than fermented cabbage proves to have been a wise move: having covered a mere 27.6km en route to the choucroute factory in Meistratzheim, there's still a fair way to go on Gemma's first day in the saddle, and shadowy mountains loom on the horizon. Having looked at the map, it's clear (to slightly bastardise the well-known children's story) that we can't go over them, we can't go under them, so we'll have to go through them.

On any other day Obernai, a charmingly Germanic market town with a cobbled square of brightly painted houses corseted in timber, would merit a cake stop, but even with the Alps (okay, a single col) under my belt, the Vosges range looks like it means business – and almost as soon as we wobble through the turreted 14th-century gatehouse in nearby Boersch, the road begins to climb.

Having passed from cabbage fields to vineyards, we now exchange farmland for forest, deep shade and dappled sunshine, lush ferns and mountain meadows. It's some of the most beautiful countryside I've come across thus far, and, despite the heat, Gemma's always on my back wheel, meaning that my considerable pride allows no slowing down, even in the picturesque little villages huddled in rare areas of flat ground. The fact that we don't yet have a bed for the night pushes my legs round all the faster, and after a grand descent into Schirmeck, I decide to ring the nearest campsite in neighbouring Rothau. Yes, they have space. No rush, no problem!

We do rush, though, mainly because we're both pretty thirsty – and once Gemma has assembled her laughably flimsy sleeping arrangement, which boasts pegs like a gerbil's toothpick and is apparently designed for mountain climbers (apt), she disappears and comes back with two bottles of beer and some saucisson, which is kind of her, given that I've just made her spend the day at a cabbage-fermenting factory. We sit on the damp grass, fielding curious glances from passers-by (mostly elderly Dutch and German couples who seem to have moved in for the summer if their elaborate set-ups, complete with dustbins, hanging baskets and washing lines are anything to go by), and glug contentedly until – 'I hate to be the bearer of bad news,' I say finally, shrugging on the now familiar mantle of Prophet of Doom, 'but we should probably go and find something to eat.'

The village, curiously enough, is not badly supplied with options – ever the classy ladies, we choose the bar with several leathery men smoking outside, a no-nonsense hybrid of a pub and a caff, with bright lighting and not even the smallest attempt at what is known as decor. Nevertheless it serves up a zinger of an Alsatian dinner: *flammekueche*, or tarte flambée, a kind of thin, flaky pizza topped with crème fraîche, slow-cooked onions and (of course) lardons, and an ice-cream kugelhopf, which has definitely come from the same catering catalogue as those sorbet-filled orange shells beloved of old-school Indian restaurants and is just as delicious. Jumpers on against the sudden mountain chill that's descended along with the sun, we retire to our tiny tents happy.

The next morning, I find Gemma in the shower block, taking a picture of an endearing little laminated poster reassuring English-speakers about the nearby Strasbourg–Saint-Dié line: 'Don't be afraid,' it soothes, 'it's a small railway, just for small train passenger'. The cleaner is watching her suspiciously. I yank her away, just in time for us both to enjoy a five-minute interaction with a very genial old German who seems to share the British view that anyone can understand any language if one speaks it slowly enough. Try as I might, I'm unable to shoehorn my only words of German, *Schwarzwälder kirschtorte*, into his monologue, though frankly the relevance of Black Forest gâteau is anyone's guess.

He has another go while we're packing up, and this time through the art of mime manages to convey the information that our tents are very small, which, after almost a month spent squeezing in and out of it, is reassuring to have independently confirmed.

When I come back from filling our bottles, I find Gemma touchingly engaged in duct-taping a small figurine of Wonder Woman onto my handlebars as a mascot. She quickly proves her worth, too: our route this morning rapidly climbs 300 metres, after which it's downhill all day – but the way up to the Col du Hantz (363 metres) is a sweaty one. The thick forests stifle any breeze, and, anxious not to show myself up in front of Gemma, a woman who's sailed most of the way around the world and once ran six marathons in almost as many months, I push the pace, figuring she has one pannier and a tent the size of a sausage roll, so it's only fair, even if her bike probably weighs as much as she does. I catch Wonder Woman's beady blue eye as I rise out of the saddle to accelerate. She looks disapproving.

Again, the countryside is a treat, hills and all – the villages surrounded by meadows with mesmerisingly neat tessellated stacks of firewood in every well-tended garden. After a strong and sugary coffee in a beer garden in Belval, the road winds on, flatter now, through villages in varying degrees of picturesque, landing us around French lunchtime in Moyenmoutier, which seems to be home to a vast abbey, yet very little in the way of sustenance. With the clock pushing half-past twelve, however, time is of the essence, and we do a smash and grab in a middling boulangerie: my first quiche Lorraine, and a pretzel the colour of a competition-ready bodybuilder, which we eat by the side of the road in a picnic area plagued by wasps. The quiche is fine, the pretzel so saline I have to down the accompanying Orangina slightly more quickly than is ideal for my digestion.

Somewhere around the Forêt de Mondon, we pass the first thrilling sign for homemade 'Eau de Vie: Mirabelle, Poire, Kirsch', which allows me to spend the next 50 or so kilometres boring Gemma with stories about some old neighbours who hailed from just this part of the world, and would ceremonially present my parents with a bottle of homemade plum brandy each Christmas, usually in an old Perrier bottle labelled 'Mirabelle de Lorraine 1984' or similar in place of the skull and crossbones which would have been more apt. She listens with commendable patience, before cutting to the chase: 'Do you or do you not have these people's address?' I regret I do not, I say, and fall silent.

Skirting the great forests to the north, we pass from Meurthe-et-Moselle to the Vosges and back again as the land flattens out into the wide agrarian plains that are to accompany me all the way into Paris. Notable points of interest include a place called the Auberge of the Hard-Boiled Eggs, named, apparently, because these were all Napoléon's aide-de-camp could find when he ransacked the kitchen for supplies (or 'went in in search of nourishment' as the Tourist Office glosses it), and which also served as a command post for the future Maréchal Foch, Supreme Allied Commander during the early months of the Great War. There is no sign of any eggs as we pass through, just a group of men in vests standing around a barbecue, on which lies a lamb so small it prompts philosophical consideration of the point at which a foetus becomes fair game for dinner.

We also smash through Baccarat, a town which has given its name to a thousand gaudy chandeliers, and then along straight roads fringed with corn and sunflowers finally out! I note with pleasure – to Lunéville, possessed of a firmly shuttered factory daubed with angry graffiti proclaiming it a workers' graveyard. There's apparently a rather fine chateau here, too, if the signs are to be believed, but we don't see it.

Mid-afternoon, we roll into Dombasle-sur-Meurthe, an even more unremarkable town, were it not the home of the Confrérie de la Quiche Lorraine, which hosts a regular festival devoted to the world's best custard tart (and yes, I mean that – Portugal can come fight me if it wants) though sadly the next such gathering isn't scheduled until June 2019. I've had no luck contacting the Brotherhood's grand master either, but, after our success with the choucroute, I'm assuming Dombasle will boast a museum to baking tins or, at the very least, a quiche-shaped sign I can get a photo next to – yet the place is mysteriously shy about its culinary heritage.

Indeed, everyone I find seems to be more interested in the continuing national Fête de la Musique (like Black Friday, it seems to spread over the entire weekend) at the Salle des Sports, and the only bakery in the centre is still firmly shuttered at 4 p.m., so we repair to the charmingly ill-named Bar le Moderne for a whistle-wetter.

In the dim interior, while Madame pours our beers, a man propped up by the bar is thrilled by my accent. 'AMERICAN!' he says joyfully. Reluctantly I admit the less exciting truth, before seizing the opportunity to find out if Dombasle is indeed the capital of quiche Lorraine. The assembled company agree it is, though not with a great deal of conviction, but my new friend shakes his head into his red wine: 'No, no, you won't find it here.' I wait expectantly as he pauses, whether to collect his thoughts or simply remind himself to keep breathing is unclear.

'It's a winter thing,' he says with some finality. 'Now, is that your husband out there?' (As I say to Gemma later, it really is impossible to see her clearly through the door – even sober.) Of course, he's delighted when I say that no, *she's* not – 'ALORS, VOTRE FEMME?!'

'I'll bring your drinks out,' says Madame quickly. 'You'll be able to find a quiche in Nancy, I promise you.' (It is true, it seems, from further quizzing, that quiche Lorraine is seen as a cold-weather dish, rather than a picnic classic, served as a family dinner rather than on a rug on the grass. Who knew?)

We're only halfway down our pints (proper measures in this part of the world at least) when my new friend appears again to smoke a Winston over us, tell us the British are mad, absolutely mad to leave the EU, say some politically incorrect stuff, and then invite me to come and have dinner with him – don't worry, my wife will cook! We have seven children, there's always lots of food. Then we'll go and watch some fireworks for the feast of St John!

I try to imagine his wife's reaction as he stumbles in dragging two nonplussed British women and their bikes. We have to be in Nancy this evening, I say, it's very kind, but we really can't. He stops, thinks again, hard, before responding – 'Are you American?'

As he staggers off, he calls back over his shoulder, 'Be careful, drinking and cycling, the police will get you.'

'Is that a set of car keys in his hand?' murmurs Gemma.

Despite an initial lack of quiche, Nancy proves a lovely place, with steep cobbled streets and a vast pedestrianised central square lined with elegant 18th-century buildings in shades of creamy stone. In the middle stands a statue of Stanislas, King of Poland, Grand Duke of Lithuania, count of the Holy Roman Empire and, pertinently, Duke of Lorraine. Though we don't pay much attention to him at first, keen as we are to sit down and have a drink, having scrubbed ourselves clean of bike oil in the first blissful hotel power shower I've had for days, old Stanislas is to follow us across eastern France. I discover later that the chateau we couldn't find in Lunéville belonged to him, after he was chased out of Eastern Europe by a rival monarch and had to content himself with this relatively minor dukedom instead, which, after his death in 1766, was subsumed into the Kingdom of France.

The *place* that bears his name, celebrating the scientific and philanthropic work he threw himself into in later life, is filled in midsummer with cafés serving drinks at extortionate prices that are only somewhat mitigated by the miserly portions of free pretzels. Nevertheless, it proves a very civilised start and end to an evening low on quiche but rich in free-poured Mirabelle – 'But of course we have it, Madame, we are in Lorraine' – cured meat and yet more veal sweetbreads. They really are remarkably popular for a cut that tastes of so very little. Seriously, if you want a low-risk way to show off how adventurous an eater you are, order *ris de veau*, and take your own chilli sauce.

PAUSE-CAFÉ – The French Menu/Carte

Though I sometimes struggle to remember basic 'this', 'that' and 'the other', thanks to years of greed, I'd modestly say my menu* French was a solid 9/10. But even I learnt some stuff on this trip. Here are five things which popped up again and again until I'd got the hang of them:

Ris de veau/d'agneau – not a dish of rice and veal or lamb, as I first assumed, but the thymus glands, or pancreas, of said animals. If you haven't had sweetbreads before, they're pretty innocuous little things, I promise: soft and without much flavour of their own, they're what I'd class as starter offal.
Steak à cheval – a (beef) steak with a fried egg on top. *Steak de cheval*, or *chevaline*, is the real equine deal, though I only saw

---

* Note that 'menu' in France only refers to a set menu or *formule* of a certain number of courses for a fixed price, *'le menu à €15'* for example. The actual list is called *la carte*, so don't be surprised if a request for *'le menu des vins'* is met with blank incomprehension.

it in the supermarket on my travels, as, apart from in the North, it's the kind of thing one's granny would cook at home rather than something you'd go out for. That said, if you see it, and can put Thelwell out of your mind, try it. It's a quite inoffensive lean meat with a slight iron-tinged sweetness.

Cervelle de canut – a Lyonnaise speciality that translates terrifyingly as 'silk-weaver's brain', it's actually a creamy cheese spread seasoned with chopped herbs, shallots, oil and vinegar.

Sauce chien – often served with *accras de morue* salt cod fritters from the French Caribbean, dog sauce, to my relief, turns out to be a mildly spiced onion, pepper and herb salsa.

Topinambours – okay, I only came across these once, but I loved saying the word so much I've included it here so you can enjoy it, too. It means Jerusalem artichoke. You're welcome.

Stanislas's square has a curious air of expectation as we pass back through at 10.30 p.m., with people sitting on the ground in front of the Hôtel de Ville, which is in utter darkness. I ask a group of teenagers placidly smoking weed under the Duke's disapproving bronze nose what's going on. '*Son et lumière,*' they reply. Ah, the sound and light shows beloved of French municipal authorities: always worth waiting for. We lower ourselves onto the floor expectantly.

It's a corker of the genre: kicked off by Stanislas himself with the lines, 'From childhood I have always been afraid of the dark … So, all my life I have never ceased to search for light … All the lights,' it's a riot of trippy strobes and crazy projections of the

Age of Enlightenment. ('Descartes!' shouts Gemma joyously at one point, in the manner of someone who's spotted Mr Punch approaching with his stick.) The buildings shimmer with colour, the square fills with rousing music, and by the time we're done, I feel like we've all been smoking dope.

Having failed to find a restaurant serving quiche the night before, much rests on breakfast – though, it being Sunday, the winner of the Best Quiche Award in the last bi-annual competition is firmly shuttered. Nevertheless, I get a nice little deep-filled number, bronzed nutmeg brown on top, creamy soft within, at the sweet little Maison Cadici bakery in the old town, as well as a torte Lorraine, a flaky disc filled with pork marinated in Riesling, and a tiny almond flour sponge known as a *visitandine*, which Madame is insistent I also try – '*Ça c'est typiquement Nancy*'. (Gemma gives me a hard look as I stagger out laden with bags – what can I say? A French patisserie is to me what the Harrods shoe department was to Imelda Marcos.)

Having packed Eddy with baked goods, we creak out of town on a road that rapidly warms up to 7 per cent. Strangely heavy Sunday traffic and a full complement of traffic lights don't make progress any easier – though, somewhat surprisingly, an old man at a bus stop shaking his stick and bellowing '*ALLEZ, LES FILLES!*' does.

Once we've hauled ourselves out of Nancy, with its ski-slope roads and kindly pensioners, our route runs alongside the A31 motorway, and is consequently rather gruesomely rich in road-kill; I swear to God I see a beaver at one point or, at least, an ex-beaver. It's fast but bumpy, as if the authorities have decided to abandon it to rustics on tractors – if you can't run with the big boys on the autoroute, then you'd better at least have big tyres.

Coming fast down a hill, I see Wonder Woman's torso vault off towards the clouds and manage to stop in time to tenderly wedge her back on – Kinder clearly doesn't test its toys in high-speed situations. During this delicate operation I come face to face with two grim-looking, heavily stubbled men trudging up the side of the road. They look exactly like murderers, possibly of wildlife, possibly of women in Lycra, but as they fail to return my squeaked '*Bonjour!*' we're not sticking around long enough to find out – after a month in France, such egregious rudeness is enough to convince me they must be up to no good.

We leave the thunder of the autoroute behind at Gondreville, where we cross the wide, placid Moselle on a bridge decorated with two teenagers snogging in the drizzle, and find ourselves on a low road lined with poplars and then a grassy dyke on one side, separating us from La Moselle Canalisée. It almost feels like I'm back in the polders of Normandy, the only thing on the horizon a long, low, flat-topped hill – yet suddenly, we're pedalling into Toul, a quiet place with a startlingly grand medieval cathedral. The church springs from nowhere – no brown tourist signs, no handsome surrounding square, just a municipal car park, a deserted *office du tourisme* ... and a café advertising quiche Lorraine, *fait maison*. It seems God has just guided us in using an enormous pointy Gothic church as bait.

In the circumstances, it feels rude not to at least go into His House to say thank you. The empty nave offers lots of soaring perpendiculars unencumbered by humans for scale, and a desiccated velvet-bound foot of surprising length in a glitzy glass case, which is claimed to be that of Saint Mansuy, the first bishop of Toul in the 4th century, who, judging by his bunions, walked all the way here from his native Ireland. The lovely cloistered gardens are similarly, almost sinisterly quiet. In fact, it all feels exactly like we've wandered into an M. R. James spinechiller.

Across the road, and back in the 21st century, the café at least boasts one occupant: the proprietor, a youngish man reading the paper, who leaps up to prepare our orders, breathing heavily with concentration as he does so. My quiche is served blisteringly hot, possibly straight from the microwave, but it's definitely homemade, and there's even a postcard for sale with the recipe on the front. It's not quite as good as the quiche fridge magnet I'd hoped for, but I buy one anyway.

Quiche Lorraine

Several weeks later, I get a response from Evelyne, the Grand Maistre de la Confrérie de la Quiche Lorraine, who has been, of all places, in London, thanking me for my interest in her native quiche and wondering whether I managed to find one, and where. She's kind enough to share the Official One and Only Approved Recipe, which seems to hang on one vital point: 'the authentic quiche Lorraine contains only three ingredients: bacon, eggs and thick crème fraîche' – and never, ever cheese.

That bacon must be good-quality smoked stuff (ideally from the charcuterie, Evelyne says somewhat optimistically), and the eggs and cream would, in a perfect world, come from local producers. Black pepper is encouraged, nutmeg permitted and the pastry must be shortcrust. (Originally, I learn, it would have been housed in bread dough, but times have changed.)

I'm interested that Evelyne does not blind bake the pastry; indeed, the authentic versions do appear to sport a rather doughy bottom – a bit of squidge, is, apparently, desirable. Personally, I'd still let it cool before eating, though.

Butter and flour, to line the tin
200g good smoked streaky bacon, thick cut
4 medium eggs
120g full-fat crème fraîche
Nutmeg, to grate

For the pastry (or 300g bought shortcrust, if you don't fear Evelyne's wrath)
200g plain flour
100g cold butter
A pinch of salt

1 Put the flour for the pastry into a large bowl and grate in the butter. Add a pinch of salt, then rub in the butter until well coated with flour. Sprinkle 1½ tablespoons of cold water over the top, then bring together into a dough, adding a little more water if necessary. Alternatively, put the flour, grated butter and salt into a food processor and whiz until you have rough crumbs, then add cold water as above.

2 Grease a deep 22cm tin with butter and coat with flour (add a spoonful to the tin, then tilt it to coat the inside, tipping away any excess). Roll out the pastry on a lightly floured surface to about 5mm thick and use to line the tin. Prick the base all over with a fork, then put in the fridge to rest for at least 30 minutes.

3 Preheat the oven to 220°C/200°C fan/gas 7, putting a baking sheet in there to warm up. Cut the bacon into chunky strips. Beat together the eggs in a large jug, then whisk in the crème fraîche and season lightly with salt, pepper and a little nutmeg.

4 Trim the sides of the pastry, then scatter the bacon over the
   base. Pour in the egg and crème fraîche mixture, and push
   down any floating bacon. Put on the hot baking sheet and
   bake for 25 minutes. Allow to cool a little before serving.

Km: 127.9

**Croissants: 0 (Proper Planning and Preparation
Prevents Piss Poor Performance, as they say in
the Army)**

High: The *son et lumière* in Nancy

**Low: Dombasle-sur-Meurthe, a culinary capital
crying out for a quiche museum**

STAGE 18
TOUL TO BAR-LE-DUC

Madeleines

Briefly mentioned by French novelist Marcel Proust in his magnum opus À la recherche du temps perdu, these rather plain little shell-shaped sponges have since become an international shorthand for the power of memory, even among those of us who have never even been tempted to tackle the books themselves. Whether you agree that it's the greatest work in literary history or not, however, the cakes are indisputably delicious.

We're firmly in big-sky country now: sprawling farms, villages strung out along the road rather than huddled round a church and everywhere shining green, thanks to the last six weeks of rain. For a while there are just a few distant hills on the horizon, and then, startlingly, as we turn towards Troussey, I spot what appear to be the White Cliffs of Dover looming to the north, which eventually resolve themselves into a somewhat anticlimactic gigantic quarry: a sign we've now left the Vosges mountains behind and are entering the chalky plains of Champagne, home to some of the world's most expensive grapes.

Gemma's getting twitchy: England are playing Panama this afternoon, and as we pull into Commercy, AKA madeleine central, she slows to a crawl to peer into a bar screening the match – to, it must be said, a distinct lack of interest from the drinkers within. Twenty-five minutes into the game, it's already 2–0 to England, so I nobly give Gemma dispensation to go and watch while I brave the madeleine-themed tourist trap of a bakery on the other side of the square, packed like a sardine tin on a Sunday afternoon. Perhaps they're all fleeing the football.

The shelves of *À la Cloche Lorraine* are laden with prettily packaged boxes of cakes, tied with red string, alongside tins of butter biscuits – it seems La Cloche is owned by the St Michel group whose biscuit factory I passed on my way to Mont-Saint-Michel almost exactly a month ago. While I have nothing against big business, the queue is huge, so I drag Gemma away from her match and we head to the rather less picturesque La Boîte à Madeleines instead, which, despite being located in a light industrial estate on the outskirts of town, proves a much more satisfying experience. A window into the kitchen offers a view of workers beavering busily away; they produce 10,000 cakes every single day, and every so often, someone pops out with a tray warm from the oven for the punters to try.

A screen suspended from the ceiling flashes the ingredients that go into every thousand: 10kg flour, 7kg butter, 5kg sugar, 700g honey, 520g baking powder, 200g lemon juice, 160g Breton sea salt – and somewhat less obviously, 1kg of sorbitol, a sugar substitute often used by diabetics, and 800g trimoline, an inverted sugar syrup that creates a softer, longer-lasting final product, something I will have cause to be thankful for in a few days' time. (Eggs aren't listed for some reason, though I see some go in on the video.) The woman in charge of explaining the process stresses the importance of a blisteringly hot oven in achieving the correct degree of browning; take them slightly darker than you might think is desirable, she says, and then eat them up quick. It's true, even theirs don't taste as good once they've been packaged up for sale as they do hot from the tray in the gift shop.

Brown Butter Madeleines

Here's my recipe, with browned butter and granulated sugar to give it a little extra crunch. Chilling the mixture will help give the cakes that characteristic bump: and don't worry if you only have one madeleine tin (metal ones are best); you can bake them in consecutive batches. Try to make them as soon as possible before eating, though; they lose that lovely crisp edge pretty quickly.

Makes about 20
140g butter, plus a little extra
125g plain flour, plus a little extra
1 tsp baking powder
¼ tsp fine salt
2 medium eggs
90g granulated sugar
2 tsp runny honey
40ml milk

1 Melt the butter in a light-coloured pan (so you can see it changing colour more clearly) and simmer until golden brown. Pour into a heatproof bowl and leave to cool to room temperature.
2 Whisk together the flour, baking powder and salt. In a separate, larger bowl, whisk together the eggs, sugar and

honey until voluminous, then gradually whisk in the dry ingredients, followed by the melted butter and the milk. Cover and chill for at least 2 hours for best results, though you can bake immediately if necessary.

3 Grease your madeleine mould well, then lightly dust with flour, tipping out any excess. Put this in the fridge too.

4 Preheat the oven to 220°C/200°C fan/gas 7. Put a scant teaspoon of batter into each mould (it will be thick – don't worry too much about this, as it will spread as it bakes) and bake for about 8–10 minutes until dark golden; you'll need to keep an eye on them towards the end. Cool on a wire rack.

Retiring to a corner to discreetly stuff my mouth with free samples, I find myself staring into the handsome face of our old friend Duke Stanislas, who, according to a rather romantic cartoon on the wall, is responsible for the madeleine's success. When his pastry chef fell ill before a grand party, it claims, a buxom maid stepped in to save the day, and the Duke, depicted as a d'Artagnan-like figure with a rakish feather in his extravagantly floppy hat, was so impressed by her cakes, or perhaps by Madeleine herself, with her low-cut dress and big blue eyes, that he named them after her – and a legend was born.

Legend or fable, they're best known in connection with 'the episode of the madeleine' in Marcel Proust's epic novel sequence, published between 1913 and 1927, and apparently inspired by the flood of memories prompted by one of these 'squat, plump little cakes'. 'No sooner had the warm liquid mixed with the crumbs touched my palate,' he writes in the first volume, 'than a shudder ran through me.' A recently discovered early draft suggests that the original trigger was actually honey on toast. Fortunately for Commercy, if not for bees, Marcel changed it.

Having eaten our fill of the freebies (it's not like they don't have enough to go round) and shuddered obediently with delight, we retire to the café for a shandy but are quickly driven out by a table of pensioners, one of whom has irresponsibly been given a microphone, singing hymns as a lone child in their care cringes with shame. I'd like to help you, I think, but instead I'm just going to make a swift exit via the gift shop.

It looks like being a hot run up to the town of Bar-le-Duc, a mere 45km away, so we buy a bottle of Mirabelle eau de vie as well as a big bag of madeleines pimped with booze-soaked plums on the way out. How pleased I am to be carrying the extra weight when we run, almost immediately, into the first real climb since the Vosges: a leg trembler that isn't improved by a group of gormless ramblers who, on seeing us grind slowly into view, stand bewildered in the middle of the road, before deliberately moving into my path as I swerve to avoid them. I can only hope my 'BONJOUR *messieurs-dames*', delivered with all the menace of an aggressive British 'sorry', proves sufficiently galling to make up for the little speed they've robbed me of.

At the top, the road dwindles to little more than a single lane through the trees, dropping and climbing with gay abandon, and it's bloody good fun, despite bidding a sad and final farewell to the top half of Wonder Woman on one particularly thrilling descent. Leaving the woods behind, we ascend a long, slow hill up to what looks like a shady copse, but turns out to be an enormous pile of manure buzzing with flies, one of which manages to bite me through my jersey, only to be slain by a helpful hand almost knocking me off my bike from behind: Gemma proving her worth yet again.

Bar-le-Duc, picked solely for its campsite, feels surprisingly large – we approach through an industrial estate pitted with potholes, overlooked by some grim-looking tower blocks straight out of a Mike Leigh film, making the campsite even more of a welcome surprise, located as it is in the garden of what can only be described as an urban chateau or, at the very least, a turreted townhouse. Obviously the view of its lovely pointy towers is completely blocked by Dutch campervans, but it's still a grand spot to enjoy some torte Lorraine once I've spoken to Madame by phone ('I'm on the lake at the moment,' she says airily, as I imagine a stately galleon – 'You can pay me tomorrow morning').

Bar-le-Duc's sole gastronomic claim to fame appears to be as the home of what the *Telegraph* describes as a 'highly regarded preparation of jelly originally composed of select whole seeded currants', whose USP is that the seeds are removed, one by one, with a goose quill. Gemma is fairly beside herself with excitement on learning that the paper has designated this jelly as one of the 50 foods one should try 'before you die', but sadly, it'll have to go on the retirement bucket list, as our 16 hours here prove an entirely currant-free zone.

The best restaurants don't look far away, if one doesn't take gradient into account; they're all in the older *ville haute*, which hangs, rather beautifully, over the new bit we've just ridden through, much like Edinburgh's Old Town, but with added sun. Having sweated our way up there, admiring the way the honey-coloured stone houses perch above the valley like a Tuscan hill village, it transpires that none of them are open on a Sunday, so we pedal morosely along the handsome main street, grudgingly admiring the Renaissance facades, each waiting for the other one to crack and suggest doubling back to the McDonald's we passed earlier.

Fortunately, just before I give in, Gemma spots some promising-looking parasols, which turn out to belong to an Italian restaurant of the French school: melon and clammy cured ham with bouncy, bland olives and spaghetti carbonara that comes with more cheese and bacon than noodles. Having resigned myself to *un grand veggie burger et frites*, I'm delighted.

We drink a bottle of wine from the South, admiring the spectacular sunset over streets that look more Mediterranean than I've seen in a week, and finish with some powerfully alcoholic 'sundaes' so liquid with booze that they're served with straws. I wake up the next morning to find I've inadvertently used the bag of madeleines as a pillow.

Km: 78

Croissants: 0 (must try harder)

High: Those 'sundaes'

**Low: The horse-fly bite, still going strong
in Paris**

STAGE 19
BAR-LE-DUC TO REIMS

Soupe à l'Oignon Gratinée

*The French may not have invented onion soup, but they certainly
perfected it – there's little more comforting than a bowl of intensely
savoury broth, thick with sweetly caramelised onions and topped
with a bubbling raft of cheesy croutons. Often credited to the bars
and cafés clustered around Paris's old Les Halles market, where it
was served as a pick-me-up for traders up early and revellers out
late, or to the bouchons of Lyon, Champagne also has a good claim
to have popularised the dish, even if it doesn't shout quite so loudly
about it. Interestingly, onion soup has a reputation in France as
being an excellent way of masking the smell of booze, and is
thus frequently cited as a good thing to have the morning after
the night before – the idea of which, much as I love it,
makes me feel a bit queasy.*

While I'm engaged in chatting to yet another bronzed
couple of retirees at the campsite, Brits riding to Lake
Constance in no particular hurry ('The only place we wouldn't
cycle again is Texas – the guard dogs are *something else*'), Gemma
trots off to the boulangerie and returns with four croissants
whose various flavourings (almond, chocolate, butter and

margarine) fail to disguise the fact that they're all rubbish (4/10 generously, very bready and bland).

Never mind, Bar-le-Duc has been good to us, and we even fit in a brief visit to the McDonald's we spurned last night on the way out for a cup of coffee and some free Wi-Fi.

PAUSE-CAFÉ – Coffee Break

If you're still not quite sure what a flat white is, France is the land for you. Coffee culture here doesn't seem to have moved on in the last 50 years, which makes ordering the stuff far less of a palaver – and believe me, if you're on two wheels, you will be ordering a lot of it.

Coffee and cycling go together like hillwalking and Kendal Mint Cake – while I wouldn't recommend it, six double espressos a day are not uncommon among the pro peloton, who tend to travel with their own equipment, because, in the absence of any other sustenance to get excited about, they take their coffee very seriously indeed. I think French coffee is fine – just don't expect to get take-away; it's not really a thing. If you're in a hurry, ask to have it '*au comptoir*' or at the counter.

'*Un café*' is generally taken to mean a small, black coffee – if you want a normal British measure, ask for '*un café allongé*'. '*Un déca*' is a decaf if you must.

First thing, you might prefer '*un café crème*' with your croissant, which, despite the name, may contain either milk or cream – a '*café au lait*' suggests a big homely bowl of milky coffee, which you won't get in a café – or perhaps a cappuccino if you're feeling brave. Many French like to dunk their croissants in their coffee, but personally I think that's a heresy you can only get away with if you were born into it.

The later it gets, the smaller the servings become – '*un petit café*' and '*un espresso*' are used fairly interchangeably. My favourite order is a 'noisette', literally a hazelnut, which is an espresso with a dash of milk. Actually, I lie. My favourite is a '*café gourmand*': coffee with bonus cake (usually two or three tiny pieces of patisserie), though, McDonald's aside, even the smallest coffee generally comes with a complimentary biscuit balanced on the saucer. Take that, Starbucks.

Once again, our route this morning rolls through a floodplain between two waterways; this time the River Ornain, on our right, and the Canal de la Marne au Rhin to our left, which connects Paris and Normandy with the mighty Rhine at Strasbourg, and to Switzerland and the North Sea beyond. The villages are gradually beginning to look less Germanically Gothic and more northern French, with as many shutters and plain facades as tall gables and half timbers, while the landscape has flattened into great plains of just-cut straw fringed with fluttering poppies. A rare hill near the village of Charmont is marked with a great wooden cross, and many of the smaller settlements, with their collections of long, low barns with sides made out of what appears to be giant sheets of wicker, have something of the Old American West about them – an impression reinforced by the white dust that hangs in the air behind every car.

I'm excited to spot, in the one-horse town of Possesse, a sign for Sainte-Menehould, which enables me to regale Gemma with a bitter anecdote about how, years ago, on the recommendation of one Hugh Fearnley-Whittingstall, I ordered the famous '*pied de cochon à la Sainte-Menehould*' in a restaurant nearby. The dreadful memory of these slow-cooked trotters, deep-fried and eaten whole, lives with me still, in particular the bones, which, I tell her several times, had the exact crumbly consistency of a mint left to rot in a damp coat pocket all summer, but sadly none of the flavour.

While I'm still wittering on about old Polos, we cross into the *département* of the Marne, and the ancient region of Champagne. The roadside trees are gone, replaced by chalky fields, on the horizon is a cluster of 10-storey grain silos, and it's hot, the morning's clouds lingering in fluffy cotton puffs above the field crops of white poppies. There's a surprisingly large amount of heavy traffic thundering along the tracks to either side of us, travelling at speed and throwing up clouds behind them. Maintaining a slightly more leisurely pace, we roll down into Le Fresne, a prosperous-looking little place, which, like many round here, appears to have been recently hit by the apocalypse. Everywhere's neat, and tidy, and entirely devoid of life; it's a far cry from the villages of the South, with old men outside every bar, and cars idling outside the bakers as people grab their lunchtime loaf. Indeed, there are no bars to be seen at all, and certainly no bakers. We follow a Google lead to La Boulangerie d'Adrien, only to find it long deserted, the only clue he was ever there a sign decorated with a faded baguette swinging gently in the warm breeze. Where on earth do all these people get their breakfast? I wonder.

I can't even berate myself for not stocking up earlier. I'm pretty sure we haven't passed anywhere for at least two hours, which is how we end up dining at the top of someone's drive on some squashed but still sticky madeleines, the last of the spicy

Bayonne chocolate so enjoyed by those snails back in Carcassonne (I knew it would come in handy eventually) and two salted almonds apiece, along with a tot of Alsatian whisky. By the time we get back on the road, we're both feeling more than a little crazed, and it's a relief as we crest a long, straight hill outside Longevas to see the towers of Châlons-en-Champagne squatting on the featureless horizon.

Not just an exciting name (changed in 1998 from Châlons-sur-Marne, ostensibly to return it to its medieval roots, although associations with the world's most famous wine surely can't have hurt): Châlons is said (by some) to have spawned one of France's best-loved culinary exports, soupe à l'onion gratinée, a bowl of molten cheese dipped in a homeopathic amount of savoury broth.

I've loved this heart attack in soup's clothing since childhood, so it's a joy to finally find myself at the (disputed) source, though Châlons itself is strangely quiet about it – far more so, in fact, than boastful rivals to the claim like Paris and Lyon. In this particular version of its creation myth, Louis XV, or perhaps Louis XIV, returned to his hunting lodge one night, ravenous with royal hunger after a hard day sticking pigs, and found nothing in the cupboard but onions, butter and champagne – and lo, in a 17th-century prequel to *Ready Steady Cook*, this cosseted monarch, who had been waited on manicured hand and foot his entire life, put them together and came up with culinary perfection.

In an alternative version, Stanislas (him again), who regularly stayed in Châlons en route from Lorraine to Versailles, was so taken by the 'so delicate and so refined' soup served at the city's Pomme d'Or Inn that he insisted on visiting the kitchen in his dressing gown to see how it was made. 'Neither the smoke nor the smell of onion, which made him weep, could distract his attention,' explains wikipedia.fr. Just when I thought I couldn't love him any more.

The quiche debacle in Lorraine has somewhat dashed my hopes of finding a steaming bowl of soup in June, but we're here now, ravenously hungry, and it's worth a try. Having checked in to tonight's apartment, we bundle all of my washing into a pannier, dump it on a laundrette and head straight to a café for refreshments.

I demand blue drinks all round – I don't feel like I'm on holiday unless I've had a cocktail the colour of a swimming pool, and though strictly speaking I'm not on holiday, Gemma is, and no one deserves to drink alone. Having watched me bamboozle bar staff from the Alps to the Balearics with a demand for 'anything as long as it's blue', she knows the drill. Even if they don't have anything containing blue curaçao on the sticky cocktail menu, there will inevitably be a dusty bottle lurking somewhere behind the bar to spoil a nice gin and tonic with. The girl behind the bar here clearly thinks we're crackers, but harmlessly so, and plays along gamely (*'Vraiment? Bien sûr, Mesdames!'*), even giving us an extra-large bowl of salted peanuts to accompany them. Perhaps she thinks we're on drugs.

Peanuts finished and laundry folded, I'm unsurprised to find that Châlons is not bubbling over with onion soup at this time of year, but dinner at the Bistrot Les Temps Changent (presided over by the wonderfully named Chef Feck) does at least gift me my first proper French Waiter Experience. The chap prepared to argue for hours over risotto in Morzine proves a mere amateur in comparison with tonight's titan of hospitality.

After a superb piece of pollock poached in champagne with local favourite white asparagus (the charm of which has always escaped me) and a wild garlic sauce, I order a sablé Breton with strawberries and a mint sorbet. I'm a little surprised when said sorbet arrives looking like vanilla ice cream – but hey ho, I love ice cream. I take a greedy spoonful ... and pause.

'What?' asks Gemma, sensing a chilly cloud coming to rest over the table.

'What does this taste of to you?' I ask, passing a teaspoon across.

Gamely she gives it a go, and nearly chokes. 'Garlic ...?'

I summon the waiter and explain the problem. His face suggests that, au contraire, *I* am the problem – instead of whisking the dish away immediately, he begins casting around for a spoon. Just as I'm wondering if he expects me to offer up mine, a minion arrives with a fresh one on a silver platter. He samples a smidgen, and, to his great professional credit, manages to keep an entirely straight face. There's not even the ghost of a gag reflex on his marble countenance.

No, Madame is mistaken.

The manager arrives, and on being brought up to speed insists on speaking to me in slow and very bad English. For sure, he will change it if I do not like it. Struggling to keep a lid on my rage, I explain, in suddenly fluent if not entirely orthodox French, that it is hardly a question of not liking it – it's not what I ordered, and, perhaps more pertinently, it's completely *vile*. He disappears with the dish. I can almost see him rolling his eyes through his back as he stamps into the kitchen.

Five minutes later, when Gemma has tried and failed to placate me with half her dessert, he returns with another scoop on the same plate – explaining that Chef has a garlic ice cream on the starter menu and maybe – perhaps! – they used the wrong spoon.

Gemma, kind as ever, tells him not to worry, it's not his fault. 'HE NEVER SAID IT WAS!' I say loudly as he stalks off. In fact, no one has shown the slightest bit of contrition. This time the sorbet (which is still an ice cream) tastes mildly of toothpaste. The crumble underneath, however, still reeks of garlic. The first waiter glides smugly over to ask how it is. I explain. He shrugs. I give up. We leave, after paying the bill in full. We do not bid them goodbye. *That* is how angry I am.

Onion Soup à la Stanislas

There are many ways to make French onion soup – red wine, beef stock and more than the odd slug of brandy – but this one, bulked out with stale bread like many old recipes, is based on a 'soupe à l'oignon à la Stanislas' from 1831, though with wine and stock rather than the original water, because apparently I have fancier tastes than the King of Poland, Grand Duke of Lithuania, Count of the Holy Roman Empire and Duke of Lorraine.

Serves 2, generously, or 4, more elegantly
2 tbsp butter
3 fat onions, peeled and finely chopped
1 stale piece of sourdough or other robust bread
Butter, to spread
300ml dry white wine
800ml good chicken stock

For the croutons, if desired (you desire them)
2 thin slices of baguette
Olive oil, to brush
50g grated Gruyère

1 Melt the butter in a frying pan over a low heat and gently, slowly, fry the onions until soft and golden.

2 Meanwhile, toast the bread, then butter and cut into small pieces. Cut the crusts off, and cut these into extra-small pieces.

3 Turn the heat up slightly, add the bread and fry, stirring almost continuously, until the onions brown.

4 Transfer the onions and bread to a saucepan over a medium heat, add the wine and stock, and leave to simmer gently for 20 minutes.

5 If you want croutons, in defiance of the Champagne recipe, brush the slices of baguette with oil and toast under a hot grill until golden, then turn over and repeat. Once the soup is ready, divide between ovenproof bowls and put one in each. Pile with cheese and grill until golden and bubbling.

I'm still cross enough the next morning to eat half a packet of butter on the brown seedy bread I buy for lunch, which looks so good I can't resist it after a disappointingly flabby 7/10 croissant from the same baker's. This leaves only a modest amount to melt into my freshly washed kit as we pedal through the dead flatness of the Marne, the villages now pale stone and red brick. Gradually a wooded ridge shows itself on the horizon and, after we come off the road and on to the Canal de la Marne, suddenly we're back in wine-making country, with vineyards sloping down almost to the luminous chalky green water.

It's a long time since I was last in this region; not just because of that unfortunate experience with the pig's trotter, but because, after spending several damp spring holidays here in search of cheap champagne, I felt like I'd had enough of winds that seemed to come straight from Siberia – there are, after all, many warmer places in the world to get drunk. These days, of course, I'm well aware that there is at least one set of mountains between Russia and Champagne, because I've just cycled over the bastards, but at the time, it seemed highly plausible that this vast flatness might stretch on for ever.

One of my fondest memories of Épernay, where we stop for lunch, concerns a little tourist train that took us round some champagne cellars one April long ago – I text my ex in the hope his memory is better than mine, and he responds immediately: 'Mercier is the one with the train. Beware of the gross trotters,' so I book us in for an afternoon tour. There is a time and place for visiting one-man-band winemakers in their garden sheds, and that place and time is not right now, on a bike, unless I want to throw out my tent to make space for the bottles I'd be all but obliged to buy having taken up an hour of their afternoon and drunk them out of house and home. (Which, I'll be honest, I kind of do.)

In the meantime, we forage for lunch. Épernay's global reputation means that it's home to any number of smart restaurants who would no doubt fall over themselves to welcome two such elegant ladies, but the sun is irresistible, and we end up in the lovely formal gardens of the town hall, which, unusually for France, seems to positively encourage picnickers (I've been chased out of them from Aix-en-Provence to the Alps before I've so much as shed a crumb). We eat *jambon beurre* sandwiches made from the leftovers from breakfast and so many cherries they threaten to give me a stomach ache, and drink warm champagne straight from the miniature bottle. In short, the kind of sophisticated pleasures no Michelin palace could have hoped to live up to.

After an hour of gentle snoozing in the shade of a plane tree (it strikes me sadly that this may well be the first impromptu snooze I've had since my early-morning train out of Nice), we head up the Avenue de Champagne, lined with the solidly prosperous-looking mansions of all the big names – cycling over, a sign informs us, 100km of storage tunnels full of fizz. Moët & Chandon's HQ looks like an art-nouveau Parisian townhouse, while across the road Martell Mumm Perrier-Jouët has the appearance of a provincial chateau and a few doors down Pol Roger boasts a vast building fortified like the Bastille. I'm amused to note that the street signs at either end are marked '*Propriété de la Ville d'Épernay*'; clearly a fair few have ended up as drinking trophies.

As befits its founding ethos as a champagne 'for the people', Mercier's sprawling modern site lies well beyond the welltended cobbles of the Avenue de Champagne proper – in fact, it's so real I can even see tower blocks from the car park. As we lock up, a large hairy mastiff emerges yawning from a Belgian saloon car, the owner pleading its case with the security guards, begging for just a few minutes of air-conditioned relief for the animal. He, and the dog, lose, and it's tethered in the shade, where I can see the doormen eyeing it warily for possible infractions of politeness.

I shoot it an apologetic glance as we enter a cool, almost hanger-like space dominated by an enormous carved wooden barrel. On the end facing us, two meaty-looking broads are fondling a bunch of grapes, apparently representing the historic friendship between Champagne and Britain (a relationship that, I'm pleased to say, remains strong to this day; for all the other political shenanigans between the two countries, the UK is the world's largest importer of champagne). The audio-guide informs us that this barrel was a gimmick (rough translation) dreamt up by the house's entrepreneurial founder, self-made man Eugène Mercier. Designed to hold 160,000 litres of champagne, it took 16 years to plan and build using 150 Hungarian oaks personally selected by his cooper, the aptly named Jolibois, and once finished was used as a giant advert at the 1889 Universal Exposition in Paris.

Getting it there was a marketing opportunity in itself. Pulled by 24 oxen and 18 horses, the barrel was so heavy that it crushed its first set of wheels after only 4km, and several buildings that threatened to impede its elephantine progress towards the capital were simply flattened to make way. An excited crowd and newspapers all over the world followed its journey for three whole weeks. Unfortunately, on arrival, even the monster barrel could not quite compete with the highlight of the fair, the Eiffel Tower, but still, having something that big with your name plastered all over it driven 140km to be seen by 32,250,297 visitors at the show itself … well, that can't have hurt.

I find myself more interested in the ethos of the Mercier house than the way it makes its champagne, which, unsurprisingly, doesn't appear to have changed much since my last visit. Mercier seems to have been quite the character. The child of a single mother, he went out to work in the vineyards of local monks at an early age, and was clearly pretty good at it given that he managed to realise his dream of starting his own business, a co-operative of small champagne producers, at just 20, when I was still drinking Snakebites.

He struck out on his own 13 years later, founding Mercier Champagne in 1871, and at the turn of the century commissioned the world's first publicity film from the Lumière brothers (which is basically like asking Tim Berners-Lee to build you a website). It was shown at the Universal Expo of 1900, the same event at which he tethered a Mercier-branded hot-air balloon to the ground and invited people to enjoy a glass of his champagne a thousand feet up in the air.

The plan was to fly the balloon back to Épernay once the fair was over, but strong winds sent it sailing northwards instead, where it crashed down into a wheat field near Belgium. The passengers were found safe and well, toasting their good fortune with champagne – and Mercier was fined for attempted smuggling, a punishment he shrugged off, calling it the cheapest advertising he ever paid for.

The 30-metre-deep cellars to which we descend in a great glass elevator with a motley collection of other visitors were designed by Mercier as yet another tourist attraction: he christened this 18km underground city, directly linked to the Paris–Strasbourg railway, by driving a four-horse calèche round its silent streets. He repeated this feat on the visit of the President of the Republic, Sadi Carnot, in 1891, when they were illuminated by 100,000 candles (though the modern-minded Mercier had in fact had his pride and joy electrified five years earlier).

They were opened to the public – another first – in 1885, and as we climb into a little train, our guide Barbara, a Brazilian, proudly tells us we'll be conducted around the cellars entirely by infra-red beams. If Eugène Mercier were 'with us today', she says, 'he would have loved the Internet'. I believe it: the man has viral stunt written all over his amazingly moustachioed face.

Mercier was determined to rock the rarefied world of champagne by focusing (one assumes, though it's never explicitly admitted) on price rather than quality, a view also apparently taken by current owners the luxury LVMH group, who brand his wine as 'an easy-going champagne for a target market of urban consumers' in contrast to some of their blingier brands like Krug and Dom Pérignon.

Though it's the biggest-selling *marque* in France, Mercier has never really targeted the export market, perhaps because – the man pouring upstairs muses – the Brits in particular view champagne in a different way. I agree wholeheartedly. No one I know really wants champagne to be 'good value' – they want to feel decadent, to splurge. Value is for the baked beans you have for dinner afterwards.

To this end, he says, they no longer produce individual vintages: 'It is not in the spirit of the house. We want to make champagne for everyone.' I feel gratifyingly of the people, though I've shelled out for the most expensive tickets, the Golden Bubbles, which get us three glasses of decent if unexciting fizz: brut, rosé and réserve – of course, champagne socialist that I am, the cheapest does me just fine. I'm sad to leave without a bottle, but having looked at the gradient profile for the afternoon, it feels unwise to splash out just to lend any further support to this democratisation of fizz. Bubbles for all, yes ... but not right now.

Something I've never noticed on previous visits by car: between Épernay, the capital of champagne-the-Wine, and Reims, Champagne-the-Region's largest city lies the Montagne de Reims. Its high point, the ambitiously named Mount Sinai, is a mere 286 metres, but as Wikipedia notes, it earns the title by the 'brutal' change in gradient between the plain (80 metres) and the slopes on which the vines grow, 200 metres above. Certainly brutal feels the right word as we push up it in the mid-afternoon sun, initially on the gloriously quiet D251, which snakes languidly through the immaculately manicured corduroy of Champillon's vines, and then on the much-busier D951, which right now seems to be carrying the entire workforce of Épernay home for dinner. At the top of the hill, we stop for some water and a photo, and a closer look at what I've decided after gazing at it all the way up is a strong contender for the region's ugliest building, the super-fancy Royal Champagne Hotel & Spa, though it presumably looks rather better from its outdoor infinity pool with a glass of Krug in hand.

That said, had I known how awful the road to Reims would be, I might have been tempted to pop in and enquire about rates. Though the D951 passes through a nature reserve, in reality it's no scenic route at rush hour, the carriageway so narrow, despite the generous margins of protected green to each side, that we're hooted at several times for daring to take up any space on it at all. One ancient BMW with purple tail lights even roars abuse at us as it passes – I stick my finger up at them as they slowly retreat into the heavy traffic and pedal furiously. Later, when it's all over and we're enjoying a compensatory ice cream, Gemma confides that she was seriously worried lest I catch him up. I point out that he started it, but nevertheless, it's probably a good thing that we're finally separated by a set of lights as the road descends into Reims.

The outskirts boast the usual complement of impenetrable ring roads and incomprehensible cycle directions, and once we finally make it into the centre, a bus turns left into me, necessitating a very noisy emergency stop. By the time we find our hotel, I'm feeling about ready for another drink. And then we go in.

The Monopole (One Star), with its bay-windowed frontage and Edwardian lettering, has the air of a hotel that was once fairly grand, though back in the UK I find it in the 1935 Michelin guide to France listed as 'simple, offering only partial comforts'. Now, with its ground floor occupied by a punky-looking hairdresser's and a kebab shop, it has very much ceded even this pre-war lustre. A neon sign flickers 'Open' all day long above a dim staircase – we lock our bikes to the balustrade, and then to each other for comfort, and advance upwards, squeezing past a man sitting despondently on a large zippered tartan plastic bag, the universal symbol of hard times.

There's no reception desk, just a young man leaning against the wall on the first floor, who is very keen to confirm we've booked a double room. I tell him twin or double, it doesn't matter, which seems to please him inordinately. A sign tacked on to a closed door behind his head informs us that breakfast is sadly unavailable due to building works. I'll be honest, this does not make me very sad.

Our room is a cupboard in the eaves, furnished with a small double bed covered with a furry blanket decorated with a leering pink rose. Above, a framed poster instructs us to 'Live Well, Love Much, Laugh Often'. It also boasts the world's smallest bathroom (easily wresting the crown from the previous title holder in Avranches; thank God Gemma is five foot two to Matt's six foot three), and handily doubles as a steam room, as the window appears to have been painted shut sometime in the last century.

I'm anxious about bedbugs, Gemma's worried about football, but one thing that makes us both feel better is an Americano, of the cocktail variety, and a bowl of salty pretzels before our last supper – tomorrow Gemma's driving back to Paris, and I'm setting off in the same direction under my own steam, so this feels particularly poignant. The next time I see a familiar face will be under the Arc de Triomphe in five days' time.

L'Alambic is a fitting venue for such an emotional occasion: an atmospherically lit, brick-lined former wine cellar, it would be the perfect spot for a romantic tête-à-tête. Unfortunately, Gemma has to put up with my face across the table, rather than some handsome French man who actually knows what goal difference is, but funnily enough, this little restaurant, picked without too much thought from the guide, offers some of the best food I've eaten so far: a pressed cuboid of pink *jambon de Reims*, which looks disconcertingly like Spam but tastes wonderful, some perfectly cooked turbot and a very generous local cheese plate to finish.

The sweet teenage waiter insists on taking a photo of us grinning awkwardly at the camera (I think he's hoping one of us might propose), Madame insists on giving us a glass of Marc de Champagne brandy when we go upstairs to pay, and it's a high-spirited duo who stagger back into the Monopole, where the man on the stairs has gone, to be replaced by some very strange noises from the shuttered breakfast room. Fortunately, we've sunk enough booze to fall asleep almost immediately beneath the nylon fur. Not in each other's arms, though. Sorry, Monsieur Reception.

Km: 140.5

Croissants: 5 (average score: 4.6/10)

High: Snoozing in the sun in the gardens of Épernay's Hotel de Ville

Low: Garlic Ice-Cream Gate

REIMS TO BONDY

Croque Monsieur

*The croque monsieur (or 'crispy mister') ham and cheese
toastie is a relatively modern invention, credited to a
Parisian café that ran out of baguettes and had to use soft
white bread instead, or workmen who accidentally left their
packed lunches on a radiator. The truth is probably more
prosaic: salty ham, warm cheese and fried bread is such a
delicious combination that perhaps the croque was always
inevitable. Found all over France, it's at its very best in
cheese-producing regions.*

I feel quite emotional as I cycle with Gemma to the car hire
place the next morning to wave her off. While she's standing
up in court tomorrow, I'll be cross-examining a round of Brie.
And believe me, I'll be thorough.

Before she goes, I insist on buying her a croissant to say a very
modest thank-you for my early birthday dinner the night before
– tellingly, she goes for curly *nature* (margarine) and I for straight
pur-beurre (8/10, excellent elastic texture, nice crisp outer,
slightly lacking in flavour) and I think again that she is the yin to
my yang, the cherry to my cake, the faithful *domestique* to my

world-class Chris Froome, and it's going to be a lonely few days without her.

As if to underline my sad plight, the way out of Reims is a horror-show; a dual-carriageway so terrifyingly fast and busy I stop twice to check I'm on the right road before being finally funnelled off, limp from nerves, onto the rather less stressful D27. It heads straight and flat for some low wooded hills and what looks like a small factory plonked by the side of the carriageway, but in fact turns out to be a concrete grandstand with a commentary box painted with the old BP green-and-gold shield. The sheds either side bear brightly painted advertisements for Pneu Englebert, Phares Marchal and other such antique brands. It's like cycling round Le Mans: surreal, oddly thrilling and deeply puzzling. Finally, I find a plaque explaining that this little road served as a Grand Prix course between 1926 and 1952, and was the site of the Reims–Gueux 12-hour race in the 1950s and 60s, the first of which was won by Stirling Moss. A group of volunteers is now in the process of restoring it to its full glory, hence the fresh paint.

Gueux itself proves to be a wealthy-looking small town with a fairy-tale church set on a lake, and no fewer than two golf clubs on its fringes – clearly this is Reims's stockbroker belt. Heading due west, the route is surprisingly hilly after the last couple of days of gently rolling plains, and I find myself climbing through vines again; where once a sign for a champagne producer would have been exciting, now they act as depressing proof of how far I still have to go – each one is surely the last, and then 20 minutes later, another pops up out of nowhere. Actually, the official Champagne grape-growing region stretches as far west as Charly-sur-Marne, about 75km from Reims, which is almost three-quarters of my total for the day.

Nevertheless, it's dispiriting, and after five days of company, the longest since Matt saw me off in the north-west, strangely lonely on the open road. The scenery is a welcome distraction; the hills supply some lovely views and all this wine wealth makes for exceptionally pretty little villages. On one perfectly empty big dipper of a road, I see a mass of crows on the tarmac ahead. Disturbed by the sudden appearance of a post van from the other direction, they rise as one black cloud, chattering to each other, before settling down again to their well-squashed breakfast, apparently oblivious to my approach. I don't know whether to be gratified that I make so little environmental impact or offended by what this says about my speed.

I stop for some water in Lagery, which boasts of its 12th-century church, 17th-century market and 'vestiges du château', though the only sign of life is a call-and-response choir of barking dogs from behind a dozen closed doors as I stretch my legs on an old cattle trough. From there, I seem to be inadvertently following signs for the Abbaye d'Igny. My first sight of this 12th-century Cistercian community is a high stone wall that peeps through the trees, and then suddenly, there it is, still cloistered, still home to an order of Trappist nuns drawn from throughout France, who make some very fine-sounding chocolates. Sadly, the shop is closed for lunch, so I have to fondly imagine what a chocolate champagne cork filled with Marc de Champagne brandy might taste like while tucking into a supermarket apple in the car park instead.

It strikes me that, while I've passed lots of places this morning that would be only too happy to supply me with a case or two of champagne, it's been a while since I saw anywhere that might throw in a ham sandwich to go with it. The closest I've come, the wonderfully named Café Lard in Faverolles-et-Coëmy, despite the bravely fluttering tricolore at an upstairs window, looks like it called last orders in 1945. Further on is an immaculate American cemetery, neat white crosses standing to attention in grass mown more sharply than a parade-day buzzcut, but still no shop.

I think the relief of finally finding somewhere open may have sent me a bit mad. That's the only plausible explanation for emerging from the Super U in Fère-en-Tardenois with a tin of Mediterranean sardines in Tunisian harissa, a faintly Germanic cucumber chive and fromage blanc salad and a huge baguette.

Twenty minutes later, I'm eating the world's weirdest sandwich perched on a rock in a beauty spot called the Devil's Basket, while children scramble around me and bright red, fishy-smelling oil drips all over my clean shorts. On the plus side, this does keep the children away.

Hunger sated, I have a brief look at the signboards, and discover the scattered rocks take their curious name from the story of a local man commissioned to build a monastery. Unfortunately, the stone he required was so far away that the client got impatient, medieval-style – which is when the devil turned up and offered to finish it overnight in exchange for the desperate builder's soul. Sadly, Satan is a poor timekeeper ('You wouldn't believe the traffic, squire') and dawn broke before he'd even got all the rocks in place – forcing him to drop them willy-nilly where they lie to this day. Totally plausible. More interestingly, apparently one of them looks like a giant tortoise, but my stupid shoes are no hooves to be clambering around on, and once I've cleaned as much fish juice from myself as possible, I leave the kids to it.

The sun is now so hot that the roads have begun to melt, covering my tyres with a sticky slick, which quickly becomes coated with the tiny pebbles that seem to have been laid down to counter the problem. The noise of them grinding against the mudguards is painful, so I hate to think what effect they're having on poor Eddy, and the pleasant countryside offers little in the way of shade, just the odd fat pheasant and numerous villages that should offer cold drinks, but don't. (Not for the first or even the twenty-first time, I wonder where French kids buy their ice lollies and penny sweets.)

A more pressing problem presents itself as the afternoon wears on: I've determined to make it as far as Meaux this evening, and indeed pass into the region of the Île-de-France just before 3 p.m., which is like entering the Home Counties en route to London, so synonymous is it with the capital at its centre. Unfortunately, I've forgotten all about Disneyland Paris, which means that, though campsites are plentiful, they're also bloody expensive, and most make no mention of tents among the glossy pictures of chalets for rent, kids' clubs and heated swimming pools – plus the minimum stay is three nights. In three nights, I'll be almost home.

In the end, I pin all my hopes on the Camping le Pont in Trilport, just across the river from Meaux proper, which I find briefly mentioned on one online camping directory. There's no answer on the phone number it gives, and Google doesn't seem to know exactly where it is, but I figure the name should be clue enough; find the bridge and the campsite will be obvious.

Unfortunately, this does not prove the case. With apologies to its residents (I'm sure there must be a nice part somewhere), Trilport has the sad distinction of being one of the least pleasant places I visit in the entire country – one long traffic jam in the direction of Paris. The Camping Municipal signposted down a steep side street is nowhere to be found. I go back up to the bridge, where lorries are queueing bumper to bumper, and peer down to the shore. No sign of life on either side. I try my luck on the other bank, tetchily weaving through the stationary vehicles in pursuit of a sign for an alternative campsite, which proves to lead to some overgrown sheds that look very much like a crime scene.

After 20 minutes of increasingly furious circling, during which time I curse France and all who sail in her in several different accents, I finally discover the entrance down an unmarked track cunningly concealed behind a huge pile of gravel. I ride in, wobbling around the potholes, and find that, though the site is full of caravans, the shed daubed 'reception' is shut up. I quickly check my phone for alternatives, regardless of price – but too late. Madame appears from nowhere, smiling and wiping her hands on an apron, and instead of the Campanile in Meaux, I'm stuck here for the night. Sometimes, British politeness feels like a distinct handicap.

On the plus side, the site is right by the river (though a row of dilapidated vehicles block any view) and seems to be home to several small free-range dogs. Negatives include the large number of workmen drinking beer while watching me put my tent up, and the worst *bloc sanitaire* I have ever seen – festooned with thick cobwebs, and so dirty I'm loath to take my shoes off in the shower, which lasts exactly three seconds and veers between icy and scalding with cunning unpredictability. The loo floor is covered with grass clippings, which makes more sense when a fat topless man begins mowing the site at 7.35 the next morning.

Having made the best of a bad job, I go out in search of dinner … and instead of a restaurant devoted to the delights of runny cheese, I find a truckers' stop full of lone men, which looks like it might do good couscous with a side order of unnecessary stress, two pizza takeaways and a late-night shop of the kind so rare in France that I walk past it twice without realising the door is open. The nice man inside is either so bored or anxious about thieves that he insists on following me round, helping me find things I'm not sure I want – and then politely puts back the melon I've selected in favour of a better one. I stick the new, approved version and a piece of cheese on the counter and look around vaguely. 'You want a drink?' he asks solicitously, gesturing in the vicinity of a fridge. I take out a can of Perrier. There's a pause.

Screw it. I'm not French and I don't care. 'Do you have any beer?' I ask. He's delighted at my uncouthness. Yes! Yes, he does! So, after being guided through the modest selection on offer, I end up dining tentside, to the music of six or seven blaring televisions, on a can of 1664 and a packet of Pringles (with which I try and fail to entice a miniature Yorkshire terrier to sit with me for a while), followed by a melon and cheese sandwich, all seasoned by the unmistakable aroma of high-strength insect repellent. To add to its other attractions, turns out Camping le Pont has mozzies, too.

As I lie in my chemical-scented tomb trying to sleep, but feeling very vulnerable all of a sudden in this unusually unfriendly environment, where the only other woman I've seen for hours seems to have gone home for the night, it strikes me that this will be my last campsite of the trip. I can't say I'm sorry – though I've felt perfectly safe elsewhere and have laughed off comments online about how lonely my little tent looks, now Gemma's gone, it does feel a bit weird sleeping alone, with only the flimsiest of nylon layers between me and the world.

The next morning demands a positive mental attitude, however. Not only is it my final full day on the road, but more importantly, it's my birthday. Friends and family have worried about me being on my own – though not, I note, to the point of coming out to surprise me with champagne – but actually, though it would obviously be a delight to wake up to a friendly face, furry or not, it feels like an excellent excuse for complete self-indulgence. Possibly I'll even have two croissants for breakfast if they're good enough to merit it.

Packing up as quickly as possible, while the temperature is still a few degrees shy of actually boiling, I collect a croissant and a scalding coffee from the bakery on the main road and wobble my way over to the town hall car park, where I sit on a wall in the sunshine and open my three cards: one shoved in my bag by my parents back in the Alps and two given to me in Reims by Gemma: one from her, one from her parents and Wilf. One bike themed (my parents), one dog themed (Gemma's parents) and one just plain rude (guess who). The croissant, meanwhile, proves a mere 7.5/10: crisp in parts, a bit sweet for my liking, and there's not even a Paris–Brest on offer to make up for it. Time to skip town, I think happily. Surely Meaux has more to offer on my big day?

Most immediately, along a bloody big road, it offers a thrilling, generously air-gun-pelleted sign reading 'PARIS 46', which I stop to photograph – the end is so near I almost feel sad about it – and then, in the centre, a standard-issue Gothic cathedral and a patisserie opposite selling plump strawberry tarts. After I've demolished one with a coffee and spread crème pâtissière all over my face like a proper grown-up, I respectfully zip up my jersey and go into the church. There's an exhibition on to mark the centenary of the end of the Great War – Meaux, I learn, was the site of the Battle of the Marne, in which two million fought, almost a quarter of whom were wounded or killed – and a strangely affecting memorial, tucked away in a side chapel, to the memory of the one million dead of the British Empire, 'of whom the greater part rest in France'. When you've been away from home for a while, you cry quite easily, it seems.

Meaux boasts Europe's largest museum to the conflict, built on the site of the battle on the outskirts of town, but I've come here on the strength of its world-famous Brie, the '*roi des fromages, et fromage des rois*', so delicious that Louis XVI, stopping for dinner while fleeing the murderous forces of the Revolution, couldn't bear to leave before he'd finished his cheese course – and ended up captured. Meaux itself doesn't boast any particular recipes using its most famous creation, but I'm happy enough to stuff it into a sandwich to go (if only Louis had thought of that).

I pedal over to La Halle aux Fromages in search of the good stuff, but, today at least, the marketplace is full of cars rather than cheese. Not to be defeated so easily on my birthday, I decide to go straight to the horse's mouth: the Fromagerie de Meaux Saint Faron, picturesquely situated on an industrial estate some way out of town.

It seems I'm just in the nick of time: though Madame is closing for lunch, she generously opens up again for me, and gives me a brief overview of the process. 'Come back tomorrow!' she urges, bringing back depressingly damp memories of another failure of timing in another city on the other side of France – 'I'll give you a whole tour!' The walls are covered in certificates, the shelves with trophies, many of them cow-shaped, and in pride of place is a team photo of a group of men in white robes wearing curious cylindrical white hats, who'd look remarkably like a far-right cult if it weren't for the pennant above their heads declaring them to be the Confrerie des Compagnons du Brie de Meaux.

I tell my new friend, once we've discussed how far I've come to taste her cheese, that I'm after some Brie to eat RIGHT NOW. She carefully assesses the selection in front of her, and I point at the least promising looking, which has the ashy complexion of something recently dug up from a plague pit. 'Ah, the Brie Noir!' she says. 'You've never tried it?' As she cuts me a sliver, she explains that this cheese is aged for up to two years, during which time it loses almost a third of its weight. It's the colour of mushroom soup, and tastes strongly, but not altogether unpleasantly, of ammonia; more reminiscent of a blue than a Brie. Interesting, certainly, but I go for a younger cheese for my lunch, because it's my birthday: the one day of the year I'm not obliged to try the weirdest thing on the menu.

Suddenly oddly embarrassed to admit I'll be lunching alone, I buy enough for two, take several recipe cards in a vain attempt to pretend I'm not just going to eat it straight from the paper ('Try the croque monsieur!' she urges. 'It's really good!'), and then follow her directions to a roadside fruit stall, where I get a huge punnet of cherries. Along with a baguette from a boulangerie voted the best in France (four years ago) and a bottle of local cider, it feels like a decent celebratory lunch, especially after a birthday dip in the River Marne, the water a vivid chalk-brightened turquoise. Watching children shriek as they run into the water and lovers canoodle by the rowing boats, I wonder why more British riverside towns don't open something similar. It's quite delightful, despite the odd dog poo on the beach.

I'm sitting on a clean patch of grass, working my way through both portions of the cheese, which has melted to the delicious consistency of Laughing Cow in the afternoon sun, almost like a croque if I shut my eyes and imagine the ham, when a policeman on a bike pauses on the other side of the fence. '*Madame, c'est du vin ou du cidre?*' he asks, pointing at the bottle.

Suddenly, I feel about 13 again, my heart in my throat. '*Cidre, monsieur?*' I say hopefully, showing him the label. Thank God it seems to be the right answer.

'*Bonne après-midi!*' he calls over his shoulder, before I have a chance to explain that it's my birthday, and I don't make a habit of it and honestly please don't tell my mum.

In an ideal world, I'd then be on my way – I have a restaurant reservation on the outskirts of Paris, and I'd really like to look nice for it. (Hell, I've even brought some new nail varnish for the big day.) First though, I have an appointment at the Maison du Brie de Meaux, which offers a daily tutored tasting between 3.15 and 3.30 p.m. When I get there, however, the young man behind the desk apologises: they have a special party in today, so the tasting will be private. My face falls. My lip may even have quivered. If you're quick, he says as I turn to leave, I can let you see the film before they start, and then you can go round the museum afterwards?

Beggars, I think, can't be choosers, and really, I have eaten quite a lot of Brie already, so I agree.

Minutes later, I'm left alone in an auditorium with three large platters of the stuff, watching a video about cheese production. I learn that it takes 25 litres of milk to make one cheese, and that the best season for it is the summer, when the cheese made using the rich spring milk is finally ready to eat – I nod in agreement; my lunch was indeed very good.

Suddenly, the door creaks open and a couple of men appear wearing – I am thrilled to note – the same faintly sinister white robes I'd seen in the photo at the cheesemaker's; the crushed cream velvet hats, it's now obvious, are supposed to represent rounds of Brie. They look at me, surprised, and then ask if the sound is loud enough. Am I sure I'm getting it all? I say yes, yes, it's fine, at which point one of them springs forward! 'But you are German!' My hair has gone quite Saxon-flaxen by this point, which may well have helped with this not uncommon assumption. 'We have the film in German.' No, I say, I'm British, but French is fine (if you stop talking over it).

They confer quietly in the corner, watching the film atten-
tively, and then when it's over, introduce themselves to me as
Monsieur Troublé (with a jaunty moustache to match his name),
Grand Chamberlain of the Confrerie du Brie de Meaux, and one
of his lieutenants, whose name I don't catch, but who probably
rejoices in a title like Grand Cutting Officer, or Grand Minstrel.
(These are all actual positions in the hierarchy of the
Brotherhood.) Another one of them appears, the *'Grand Ministre'*.
I make a whistling noise intended to convey my great honour. *'Ah
oui, on est tous des grands,'* Monsieur Troublé concedes modestly.

I tell them I am on a Brie pilgrimage, which pleases them no
end, and we discuss the availability of decent Brie du Meaux in
the UK (good) and the novelty of the Brie Noir, and then the
difference between Brie de Meaux and its many poor relations,
with particular pitying reference to British lookalikes. It's not
about the cows, they tell me, no, no, you can use almost any
breed of cow, though here we like Prim'Holsteins. It's the grazing land, the terroir, that makes the milk special. The inferiority
of our terroir is implied but tactfully left unsaid.

Instead, they insist (I don't put up much of a struggle) on
giving me my own private tasting of the cheeses intended for
the poor old delegates, whom I can already hear gathering
outside the door – they sound like they've also had a boozy
lunch, so perhaps they won't notice a few bits missing. We
spend several minutes pondering the particular qualities of each
age of cheese, a process which stretches my vocabulary to its
limit (what *is* the French for slurry pile?) and then, still cooing
appreciatively about what an honour it's been to make their
acquaintance, I bid farewell to their Highnesses and slip away
past the throng and into the museum. Here, after admiring the
fabulous display of Brie packaging through the ages, I discover
that in 1992 the Brotherhood entered into a 'symbolic' (as

opposed to actual) marriage with the Brotherhood of the Vines of Henri IV, a dynastic alliance intended to defend the big names of Burgundy and Brie against, one assumes, the massing forces of barbarism. The party afterwards looks like the best wedding reception EVER.

Somewhat reluctantly I tear myself away. Paris may be within my sights, but I'm keen not to rush this last afternoon in the saddle; I want to savour every lazy minute.

Croque Monsieur de Meaux

A croque monsieur using Brie instead of béchamel, as recommended by Madame at the cheese factory, because you can never have too much cheese in a toasted sandwich. Traditionally it's made with soft white bread, crusts removed, but, rebel that I am, I prefer this version with sturdier bread, crusts and all. Probably best served with a green salad for the sake of your conscience.

Serves 2
2 tbsp melted butter
4 slices of white bread
2 tbsp Dijon mustard
2 slices of good ham
60g Gruyère, grated
About 160g Brie, thinly sliced

1 Preheat the grill to medium-high, line the tray with tin foil and brush one side of each slice of bread liberally with melted butter. Put under the grill, butter side uppermost, until golden and crisp.

2 Spread the untoasted sides of half of the bread with mustard, then put the ham on top, followed by the Gruyère, and pop under the grill for a couple of minutes until the cheese has melted.

3 Top with the remaining bread, with the toasted side upper-most, and push down, then top with the sliced Brie. Grill for about 5 minutes, until bubbling and golden, and serve immediately.

Four hours and 70km later, I arrive snivelling with self-pity, having survived a pitched battle between my two direction-finding apps, Komoot, which wants to take me on the terrifying N3, a road so chocka with huge lorries that I lose all sensation in my fingers from gripping the brakes so tightly, and Google, which firmly recommends the Canal de l'Ourcq towpath, paved with huge spiky rocks. I zig-zag pointlessly between the two, always convinced the grass is greener on the other, lose all phone signal and see my longed-for dinner disappearing from my grasp in the Parc Forestier de la Poudrerie, which I'm sure is lovely for an afternoon wander, but will forever represent, for me, a forested hellhole with no 4G. Stopping in some nameless village for a lurid blue ice pop, I find the supermarket under police surveillance – I'm almost surprised not to be arrested myself, the way this afternoon is going.

On and on I pedal, yet Bondy, where I've snagged a cheap room for the night (excitingly described on TripAdvisor as 'an especially unappealing and inconvenient suburb') never seems to get any closer. Finally, I find myself bumping along a busy dual carriageway, and, after executing a terrifying U-turn by a vast IKEA, I arrive at where the hotel should be to … nothing.

Nothing at all to suggest that there ever was a hotel here; in fact, 90 Avenue Gallieni is just a shed. I cycle round the block. *Rien du tout*. This is the point where I feel like hyperventilating. Dismissing Google, I click on the map on the booking app, which shows the same address about 1km to the east back along the unpleasant main road.

Sure enough, there, through my tears, I see the hotel in all its magnificently ugly budget glory. By this point, it's 8 p.m. – the exact time of my dinner reservation, 20 minutes ride up the road in Aulnay-sous-Bois, a name known to me only from the 2005 Paris riots. I check in, shoving Eddy by the lifts without so much as asking permission (the security guard looks like he's considering saying something, then sees my face and turns on his heel), and passively aggressively 'inform' the check-in clerk as he dawdles over my booking that the address on the app is wrong – 'Just thought you ought to know.'

He's interested, in the way a sloth or an elderly tortoise might be interested – let me see, he says. He slowly scrutinises my phone. No, that's right. I show him their location on Google. Yes, that's us, he agrees happily, though the two are clearly entirely different places.

Eventually, rather more slowly than I would like, the truth dawns on him: 'Ah, you were in Avenue Gallieni in Noisy-le-Sec,' he explains happily. 'That's another town.' I literally cannot believe my ears. There are two identically named roads five minutes away from each other, relying on a town limit invisible to the naked eye? I'd laugh if I wasn't quite so furious.

Instead, barging through the lift queue, I run up the stairs, push into the room, tear off my clothes and ring the restaurant. No answer. I leave an answerphone message apologising for my lateness through breathy sobs, wash my hair briefly with hand soap, throw on a very crumpled dress and, with sopping hair, pink cheeks and tragically unpainted toes, dash downstairs and pick up Eddy.

It takes me 25 minutes to get to the restaurant, thanks to more roadworks and the efforts of some kind drunkards outside a bar to redirect me, and all the way I'm trying very, very hard not to cry on the basis that this will only make me look worse. I think the technique is called (barely) controlled breathing.

The Auberge des Saint Pères, is in an unassuming suburban backstreet. Two Americans are outside phoning round other restaurants, having been turned away. Morale at an all-time low, I creep in looking like a terrier that's been caught in a rain shower – and Madame behind the desk actually beams. 'No problem!' she says. 'We got your message.'

If they've been laughing at it ever since, she hides it well. She shows me to a table and asks me if I'd like an aperitif. Yes, I say, I'd very much like a glass of champagne, and a large bottle of Badoit *toute de suite*. The other diners, mostly couples, and a few glum groups that look like they're out for a business dinner, watch me curiously, but, hiding my ragged toes beneath the starched tablecloth as I alternate between my two glasses of fizz, I literally could not be happier.

PAUSE-CAFÉ – The Restorative Restaurant

The first mention of a 'restaurant' occurs in 1767 – the name suggests a place which serves reviving foodstuffs such as broths and tonics to restore one's health, though records show these establishments quickly branched out into solid foods like roast meat and desserts, much to the anger of the professional *trait-eurs*, or cooks, who had been granted a virtual monopoly on high-class catering by King Henri IV the century before.

The Revolution not only marked the end of such powerful trade corporations, but left an awful lot of aristocratic cooks looking for work, and many found it by opening their own restaurants: by the turn of the 19th century, writer Louis-Sébastien Mercier claimed there was 'one on every street corner'.

One of the most successful of the early names was Beauvilliers, who had previously been employed by the Count of Provence. His menu is described as 'the size of an English newspaper' and included, among other things, 13 soups, 11 different dressings of beef, 32 choices of poultry and game, 23 varieties of fish, 39 desserts and 'wines, including the liqueur kind, of 52 denominations'.

Brasseries, meanwhile (the word literally means brewery), usually served food and beer from Alsace – choucroute, sausages, pickled herring and onion or cheese soup (though not, crucially, onion and cheese soup, or not as far as I've found). The origins of the more casual bistrot are unknown, but possibly the word comes from the slang term *bistouille*, or bad booze, suggesting they started life as dive bars.

Even during the Prussian siege of Paris from September 1870 to January 1871, many restaurants continued trading. That year's festive menus included novelties such as wolf cutlets chasseur and elephant filet with Madeira sauce. A month after the siege was lifted, one commentator observed that there was not so much as a poodle left on the streets of Paris. Yum!

I proceed to eat my way through the most ridiculous frills of the menu with a half-bottle of white Burgundy for old times' sake: foie gras meringues, which I prefer to the foie gras crème brûlée I had in Strasbourg, but which doesn't quite compare to the foie gras toasts I was presented with on that rainy evening in Pau what feels like months ago; my old fishy friend from Marseille, the *jolie-laide rascasse*, here served with mango and fennel, and best of all, a Michelin take on my newest love, the Paris–Brest – three exquisite little buns all for me, which come complete with a huge flaming birthday sparkler. I should feel self-conscious about this, but after all today has thrown at me, I just feel pure happiness at having made it this far. As I leave, I explain to Madame that this was my birthday treat to myself, because I'm on my own this evening. 'No!' she says kindly. 'You weren't alone. You were with us.' And she comes round the counter to give me a birthday kiss.

For the third or fourth time today, I'm close to tears as I ride off, but by the time I get back to my hotel, I'm feeling merry enough to exchange some of Gemma's World Cup predictions with the security guard as I casually wheel Eddy into the lift. Okay, it hasn't been the best birthday ever, but I probably won't forget it in a hurry – and it seems to me as I lie in my little bed, listening to the roar of traffic outside, that today, my last in the saddle, in many ways sums up the trip as a whole. There were some tough and very thirsty times on the road, but there was good food, beauty, even in the suburbs of Paris, and most of all, many small kindnesses from strangers. France, *je t'aime*, I think, dropping off.

Km: 184.1

Croissants: 2 (average score: 7.7/10)

High: The sparkler in my birthday Brests

Low: Where do I start?

BONDY TO PARIS

Croissant 101

*The croissant needs no introduction. A flaky, buttery pastry the
shape of a new moon (though not always, as we shall see), they're
an international shorthand for all things French, though in truth,
they're only good freshly baked, and even France is not immune
to the crappy croissant. Warm from the oven, however,
they are pure bliss.*

I wake up feeling weird. Not a glass of champagne and half a
bottle of Burgundy weird, and not post-birthday blues either.
No, it's the *tristesse* of my last proper ride; once I hit Paris, it will
all just be commuting. I lie in bed already nostalgic for all those
desperate lunch hunts and the dark kilometres at the end of the
day, when your feet have lost all feeling and each pedal stroke
feels like pushing through treacle.

Perhaps fortunately, I have a deadline to get me out of the
best bed I've slept in since the Alps: the prospect of a good
lunch, booked weeks ago as a celebratory full stop. I'm
determined to make this reservation without tears, so it's back
on with the Lycra for almost the final time, and out into
the traffic.

Thanks to the British couple we met at the campsite in Bar-le-Duc, cycling in the other direction, I won't be doing battle with the Parisian equivalent of the M1 for long; their tip-off about a well-paved cycle path along the Canal de l'Ourcq, which runs right into the centre of the capital, proves the saviour of my sanity. Initially lined with factories and sprawling, occasionally beautiful graffiti, as I pedal into Paris proper it starts to feel more like East London: towpath cafés, floating bookshops and the shiny mirrorball of the Parc de la Villette across the water, beaming the morning sun back at me.

I peel off at the Villette basin and head for the Gare de l'Est, where I take several triumphant selfies, get changed in the world's smallest loo and then dump my stuff in the left luggage for the day. Dressed only slightly more appropriately for the (alleged) fashion capital of the Western world, and with time to spare, I head over to the 12th arrondissement for a late-morning croissant at Blé Sucré, a tiny patisserie run by the former pastry chef at the very grand Hotel Bristol. Their viennoiserie comes highly recommended by local resident Harry, of tarte Tatin fame, who annoyingly, and not a little inconsiderately, happens to be in London while I'm in her hometown.

I take a table outside, next to an elegant woman eating salad, and to the happy screams of children in the playground opposite, tear into what is comfortably the best croissant of the trip so far: absurdly crisp on the outside, so damply elastic within it's like pulling apart string cheese. A clear 9/10, right off the bat. I didn't want Paris to be the cut above it clearly thinks it is (as surely all capitals think they are), but if this is the standard, it's going to be hard to beat.

After this 12.30 breakfast, it's straight on to lunch at Chez Georges in the financial district of the Bourse, a place chosen partly because the only fault Jay Rayner can find with it is that the floor could do with a bit of a clean – 'When people wax unendurable about the joys of the classic Parisian bistro, Chez Georges is exactly what they are describing: a battered and weary wooden facade, lightly grubby net curtains in the windows, and inside a tiled mosaic floor with decades of grime in the cracks' – and partly because Michelin also rate it. Rayner is not a man shy in his opinion that the famous guide is 'a complete irrelevance', so if it's pleasing both of them, it's probably worth a try.

Jay clearly has stricter hygiene standards than me: to my eyes, the place looks more like a set from *'Allo 'Allo*, the pleasantly womb-like interior shaded from the uncouth sunlight by some (fairly clean-looking) nets, and just the faintest glow of ancient nicotine above the red leather banquettes. From my table next to the dessert trolley (best seat in the house), I can see a broom, two mops and a broken chair only half concealed behind a nylon curtain. It feels like what it is: an old-school Parisian bistro, with an overpriced wine list and a curious mixture of city workers (it's just round the corner from the stock exchange) and tourists – the American couple next to me are, I think, on their honeymoon, and talk wistfully of bologna sandwiches as they eat steak and salad. 'Go on, have a glass of wine,' he says to her hopefully. 'Oh no!' she says. 'Not at lunchtime!'

Feeling sorry for him drinking on his own, I have a tiny cold beer with my dish of radishes and butter as I consult the menu. Truly, I have never eaten so many radishes in one go in my life, and I still think they're nicer with mayonnaise, however lovely the idea sounds of smushing them with cold, creamy beurre and the merest sprinkle of salt. I still manage to put away the entire pat, though, to the slight surprise of the black-uniformed waitress who, with her stout, sensible shoes and frilly white pinny, looks like she's stepped out of central casting.

Jay's description of the entrecôte, served with 'so much bone marrow my Irish-born companion at first thinks it's potatoes', makes choosing a doddle. I haven't had a steak since those faintly disappointing versions in Limoges, but this is enough to banish any ideas that the French produce great beef and cook it badly (unlike Americans, who tend to do just the opposite). Deeply branded on the outside, rare and juicy within, it arrives attended by a huge platter of golden, rustling frites and two wobbly cylinders of blushing marrow that make my arteries contract on sight. A glass of house red feels in order to help tackle this lot, and it takes me a very pleasant half an hour to make a decent fist of it, while the Americans sweetly share a dessert and the Parisians peel back to the office. As I'm mopping the plate with a piece of bread, the curtain in front of me is drawn back for the retrieval of some utensil or other and I spy a defibrillator concealed behind its folds.

I decline pudding.

The rest of the afternoon is spent wandering in the way that Paris seems designed so perfectly for, peering in the windows of patisseries, watching the human traffic pass by – a tattoo artist and his canvas stepping out for a smoke in the Marais, a crocodile of immaculately dressed children in the Jardin du Luxembourg and enjoying a little scene in the famous Une Glace à Paris when a small boy is told by the counter staff that he can't have an EU flag in his ice cream like his brother, 'because it's only for vanilla'. What particular political point they're trying to make is unclear, but however much I want one too, there's no freedom of movement here, and not even a flag will persuade me to order vanilla instead of Provençal lavender ice cream and ewe's milk sorbet.

As I'm passing (sort of) and it's been recommended by almost everyone I've spoken to, I also pop into Du Pain et des Idées, where the baker is so good he doesn't need to work weekends. The queue, even mid-afternoon, is staggering: Dutch, Singaporeans, Americans – and that's just the people I sit down with outside. Customers jostle to photograph the counter, with its magnificent displays of flaky 'escargot' with pistachio swirls and perfect triangles of yolk-yellow flans, but the croissant itself is a bit of a let-down: crunchy and flaky, it's more a skinny curl of puff-pastry, with little but air in the centre, a mere 7/10. Not my style.

Full as I am, I'm delighted to have a dinner date for my first night in Paris: Harry may be on the other side of the Channel, but I get the next best thing in the form of her sister Georgie (the very same who will, some months later, cycle a very merry Harry and Caroline round Paris on the front of her bike when they should be preparing for operation tarte Tatin) and husband Max, who've just moved into the 3rd arrondissement after several years in Beijing. Despite not even having had a chance to unpack, they are kind enough to invite me over for an aperitif beforehand. I know I've got the right door when I hear shrieks of childish glee and the rapid-fire of Chinese from within.

Perhaps I'm getting soft in my old age, but it's delicious to sit and listen to their nanny read a bedtime story with a warm pyjama-clad toddler nestled carelessly against my knee. Clearly, my Mandarin being considerably worse than my French, I understand nothing of what the family of ducks concerned is up to (I'll be honest, it sounds anything but soothing), but I'm still a bit sad when the kids are all chased off to bed so we can have a glass of fizz and go out.

Harry's restaurant recommendation, Les Philosophes in the 4th, has a queue out of the door – as Parisians are not known for their patience, this feels both promising and very ominous. 'Go in and mention your sister,' Max suggests to Georgie, and lo and behold, a table appears like magic. Clearly, Harry's a good customer at this local institution, bustling to the point of downright loud, with bright lights, red banquettes and barely room to swing a *chat*.

The menu begins with a stern letter on the importance of provenance. Owner Xavier Denamur is a fierce critic of the French food system and its weaselly regulations, and has launched legal action against TripAdvisor, which he accuses of falsely linking his restaurant to inferior establishments. Thankfully his food is less angry. Though they've already run out of their famous tomato tarte Tatin, I finally get my steaming tureen of wine-soaked onion soup, and the chocolate mousse that follows, served completely unadorned in a plain white ramekin with a careless, cocoa-coloured drip down the side, is a thing of simple beauty, perhaps the best pudding I've had all trip.

Our talk flows like the lightly chilled Burgundy, and on hearing my tale of birthday woe, Georgie and Max very generously insist on buying me dinner, a kindness that makes my heart sing with pleasure. As I ride over to my bed at Harry's neighbours' apartment in the 10th, through the beautiful Place des Vosges and round the Bastille for what feels like the twentieth time that day, I feel quite at home suddenly, in a strange city perhaps, but among friends.

The fact that I am not, however, at home is reinforced by my abject failure to actually gain entry into the apartment. Like almost all Parisian buildings, this one boasts a complicated system of keys and codes, and I have to haul Eddy as quietly as possible through a high wicket gate set into a vast outer door, through a second, more ordinary-sized door across the courtyard and up a narrow spiral staircase (bikes, apparently, being *interdit* in communal areas) before I can even begin to tackle the two locks on the apartment itself.

Once I'm finally in, I discover that the flat, whose tenants are on honeymoon, has the tall Parisian windows I've always craved, yet having never had them, I have no idea how to work the shutters to avoid giving the people opposite a live strip show. Giving up and wriggling out of my clothes on the floor instead, I fall into bed like a dead woman and don't wake up until my alarm shrills at 7.30 a.m. to tell me it's time to get on the croissant trail.

The Official Finish is scheduled for noon under the Arc de Triomphe, which doesn't leave me much time, so I've decided to hit as many of the patisserie power-list as possible in one fell swoop, starting with La Maison d'Isabelle on the Boulevard Saint Germain, which, though it seems to fly somewhat under the radar of all of those 'Top 10 pastries in Paris' lists, has recently been named as producing the best croissant made with AOP butter in the Paris Île-de-France area.* There's a huge banner proclaiming the fact on the outside of the shop, and as I hurriedly lock my bike to the Metro railings, I can already see a crowd forming outside.

Thank God I got up early, I think, fumbling with the keys – this line looks serious. As someone who once stood in the snow for an hour and three-quarters for a cheeseburger, I'm resigned to the fact that people are inherently ridiculous, but thankfully, as I found with those famous moules marinières back in Normandy, queuing for food doesn't seem to be a French hobby

---

* AOP (*Appellation d'origine protégée*) is the fancy EU Protected Designation of Origin label signifying produce of exceptional quality from a specific region. AOC (*Appellation d'origine contrôlée*) is the older French equivalent.

– getting closer, I realise the people outside are just standing around drinking coffee and smoking as they wait for the little market out front to get going. Embarrassed, I drop my pace and try to look casual as I duck inside and join the three people who are waiting. Later, Harry explains to me that there are so many good bakeries in Paris that the lucky buggers who live there don't generally deign to travel outside their arrondissement – you find your favourite local place and stick to it. Unlike in the UK, the difference between them is never big enough to be worth the price of a Metro ticket.

I seize my prize, which at only €1 feels like a laughable bargain, and pause only to read the essay posted out front lovingly detailing their vital statistics (organic bread flour of the highest quality, the finest French butter and a sourdough starter fed daily with milk are credited for the dough's aromatic bouquet and lingering flavour), before taking it back to Eddy, patiently waiting in his by-now familiar role as pastry stand.

It's a good'un, a firm 9/10. I know it as soon as I break the ends off. Extremely crisp, but still moist inside, it has the pleasingly bulbous shape of every good croissant I've had – mostly middle, tapering to crunchy ends, with minimal puffy no man's land in between. The layers may not be perfect (too much squidge), but that's what makes it so delicious. Hard though it is to stop eating, I carefully tuck the second half in my handlebar bag, sensing that finishing even the second-best croissant in Paris (Blé Sucré still ahead by a nose) may be an error this morning, and set off for my next destination.

PAUSE-CAFÉ – The Croissant, Une Petite Histoire

Like many national emblems, a cursory glance into the history of the croissant reveals it to be a symbol of cultural appropriation of the most outrageous kind – the French take on the Austrian kipferl, brought west not by Marie Antoinette, as is often claimed, but by an enterprising Viennese baker, Auguste Zang, in the middle of the 19th century.

The first references to croissants occur in France in about 1850, classed, like English muffins, as a 'fancy bread', yet until the start of the 20th century, the term seems to have been used for almost any crescent-shaped bread or cake, and it's not until 1906 that a recipe for the modern flaky version appears in print. According to Jim Chevallier, author of a book on the history of the croissant, Zang is also responsible for starting a trend for the glitzy, mirror-lined French patisserie we know and love today – before this time, the boulangerie was a distinctly rustic affair. Why he isn't honoured with, at the very least, a statue underneath the Eiffel Tower I don't know.

Though margarine was invented in France in the 19th century, the *nature* croissant has fallen out of favour in recent years, and you're more likely to find straight croissant *au beurre* in boulangeries, though many still sell both – the margarine version is cheaper after all. Croissants are best enjoyed warm, before their crispness turns stale; any unsold stock will be stuffed with ham and cheese or drenched in sugar syrup and rebaked.

Next stop is the Boulangerie Anthony Bosson in the 5th; en route, I catch a brief glimpse of the Panthéon, which is about all I have time for in the way of sightseeing. This place is definitely fancier, with flavoured coffees and an orange juicing machine, and the croissant is a thing of beauty, the layers on the outside curled like a seashell, but it's bready, almost fluffy, rather than elastic, though the flavour, which has a subtle but complex, almost winey sweetness, is more pleasing. At an ambitious €1.10, however, it's not getting any more than 8/10 from me, and two-thirds of it joins Isabelle's scantier remains in the bag.

After this (very slight) disappointment, I don't have high hopes for my next port of call, Des Gâteaux et du Pain in the swanky 15th, for the sole reason that it feels like a high-end jeweller rather than a bakery – even the canopy, in light-sucking thick black canvas, feels beyond my means. Inside, it's all black paint and marble, with the cakes spot-lit on the deep, glass-covered counter, and black-clad staff presiding over it all like security guards at the Louvre. Having parted with an eye-watering €1.50 (a record, though frankly I'm relieved not to be relieved of much more in there), I sneak off with it to the scrubby gardens opposite, where a man sleeps on a bench and mangy-looking pigeons gather at my feet. This one is more elegantly slender than the last two, with handsome tiger stripes. It screams dryness, but in fact, beneath the shatteringly brittle shell, almost deep-fried in its buttery crunch, it's perfectly flaky, with the all-important core of damp dough that unfurls like a spiral in my teeth. Another 9/10, drawing with Blé Sucré as my favourite croissant of the trip so far (Isabelle's is ever so slightly too doughy in the middle to approach perfection).

La Maison Pichard and Cyril Lignac have already sold out, so after a slightly flabby but tasty croissant at Maison Landemaine (8/10), last up for this morning, to my regret, is Laurent

Duchêne, also in the 15th, whose window also puzzlingly proclaims the first prize for the AOC butter croissant in the Paris Île de France region. Duchêne's cakes are things of precise beauty, but his croissant is a let-down. Again, the flavour is excellent, but the ends are dry, almost stale rather than crisp, and the middle fluffy rather than soft and moist; in this tough crowd, it's a 7.5/10, though I suspect it would have scored a little higher earlier in the trip. Into the coffin it goes with all the others, and I heave myself heavily back into the saddle.

Butter Croissants

This is not a project to be undertaken lightly – you'll need both time and patience with a rolling pin – but the results are very good indeed, as crisp and light on the outside as the Des Gâteaux et du Pain croissant, and as deliciously squidgy as the Blé Sucré version. Consume warm, preferably on a wall in the sun after an early-morning bike ride along with a plastic cup of terrible coffee.

Makes about 15
500g strong white flour, plus extra to dust
10g fast-action yeast
1 tsp salt
50g caster sugar
100g unsalted butter, softened and cut into small pieces
330g unsalted butter, cold
1 egg, beaten with a little water

For the starter
100g strong white flour
A pinch of fast-action yeast

1 To make the starter, put the 100g of strong white flour into a medium bowl with the pinch of yeast, then stir in 100ml of tepid water until you have a smooth mixture. Cover with a tea towel and leave at room temperature overnight until very bubbly.

2 Tip the remaining 500g of flour into the bowl of a food mixer, along with the remaining yeast, salt and sugar. Whisk briefly to combine, then tip in the starter, and add the 100g of softened butter and 150ml of tepid water. Mix on low speed for about 20 minutes, scraping down the bowl as required in order to incorporate all the flour; it's quite a firm dough, so depending on the strength of your food mixer you may need to take it out and do the last bit by hand to stop it overheating.

3 Tip the dough on to a clean work surface. Take the left side and bring it into the middle, then do the same with the right side, as if you're folding a letter. Repeat with the bottom and the top. Grease a large bowl and put the dough in it, fold side down. Cover with a tea towel and leave for 1 hour.

4 Meanwhile, roll out the 330g of cold butter between two large pieces of baking parchment or strong clingfilm to a rectangle about 17 x 19cm. (Start by whacking it with a rolling pin to help flatten it.) Refrigerate this, and line a smallish baking tin (I use one 30 x 21cm) with baking paper. Ensure you have enough space in the freezer for this with a square of dough on top.

5 Lightly flour a work surface and tip the dough out on to it. Pat it out to a rectangle about 25 x 19cm (I find it easier to have it landscape, rather than portrait), then put it into the

lined tin. Cover with clingfilm and put into the freezer for 20 minutes.

6 Tip the dough back on to the lightly floured surface, and dust the top with flour. Roll out to a 40 x 20cm rectangle, about 1.5cm thick. Put the butter in the middle, short sides parallel to the short sides of the dough, then fold the two ends of the dough over the top to cover the butter, and press together to seal.

7 Turn the dough if necessary so that a short side is facing you, and roll out to approximately 55 x 22cm and 1cm thick, trying to keep the edges as straight as possible, and tucking in any butter that threatens to spill from the ends. Fold the bottom third up into the centre, and the top third down to cover it, again like a letter. Put it back into the tin, cover and freeze for 20 minutes.

8 Put the dough back on the work surface, with the exposed folds on the right (think of it as a book you're about to open: the spine will be on your left, the pages on your right). Repeat the previous stages of rolling and folding and freeze for another 20 minutes, then repeat a third time, always starting with the folded sides on the right, and freeze for another 20 minutes.

9 Dust the top with flour, and roll out on a lightly floured surface to about 60 x 22cm. Cut in half horizontally, then cover and freeze for 20 minutes.

10 Line two baking sheets with parchment. Lightly flour a work surface and put one of the rectangles of dough on it, putting the other into the fridge. Roll it out to about 45 x 22cm, then trim one of the long edges until straight. Measure 10cm along this straight edge, then cut up to the left corner of the dough to make a triangle. To make the second triangle, measure 10cm along the top of the dough, and cut down to the bottom. Repeat.

11 One at a time, roll each triangle out to about 30cm long, then roll up the dough from the base to the top; once you get about halfway, stop pressing down with your hand and hold it by the little ears that will begin to poke out from the sides instead, using them almost like the spindles on a rolling pin. Put on a baking sheet, brush with egg, and leave to prove for 2 hours, until, when lightly prodded with a finger, they don't spring back. Repeat with the other rectangle of dough.

12 Preheat the oven to 200°C/180°C fan/gas 6. Turn the heat down to 190°C/170°C fan/gas 5 and bake for approximately 25 (fan) to 35 (conventional) minutes until deep golden, swapping the sheets halfway through so they cook evenly. Cool on a wire rack – hot from the oven they will be very doughy. Eat as soon as possible, or wrap individually and freeze. When ready to eat, defrost, then reheat in a 180°C/160°C fan/gas 3 oven for 5 minutes.

13 Alternatively, freeze the shaped croissants on their sheets, and decant into a bag once frozen. Defrost, then allow to prove and cook as above.

Running late as usual, even for my own grand finale, I race back across town, collect my stuff from the apartment and hotfoot it to the Élysées, an area I have so far avoided, thanks to its apparent lack of attractions in the food department. Just like the Tour itself, I'll be finishing my journey on the Champs-Élysées, though instead of a crowd of thousands, I'm going to be met by my friend Lucinda, whom wild horses wouldn't persuade onto a bicycle, but who has kindly agreed to be the official wielder of the chequered flag instead.

Having agreed before my departure to meet at 12 noon on 30 June under the Arc de Triomphe, we've had no further contact because she's the kind of person who makes a plan and sticks to it, lending an extra frisson to proceedings. As usual, the moment is somewhat spoilt by my poor timekeeping: at 12.10, as I swerve through a West African street market that has spilled onto the bike lane, I get a message demanding to know if I'm on my way.

Something that hasn't struck either of us, of course, but does hit me with some force now, on the bone-shaking cobbles of the grand boulevards, is that if the Place de l'Étoile is absolutely terrifying in a car, it's practically suicidal on a heavily laden bicycle, but the romance of dying there is undeniable, so I just pull out and make for the Arc in the centre, ignoring the hooting, and hope for the best. It works, though I'm sorry Lucinda is too busy checking her emails to have filmed my final death-dash.

I haul Eddy over some very stout chains and wheel him up to her, feeling justifiably pleased with myself. She squeals, oh so gratifyingly, and breaks out the champagne, dipping a dodgy-looking St Pancras croissant into a plastic orange cup liberated from some bar and shoving the whole thing in my mouth to celebrate my achievement.

Having discreetly removed this, my sixth croissant of the day (4/10), we toast Eddy. It's been a hell of a trip. Miserable at times, scraping against the limits of my endurance in endless rain and relentless sun, battling strikes, diversions and seasonal closures, yet all of these pale into as much significance as that pesky horsefly bite when I think of the places I've seen, the food I've enjoyed, the people I've met. Not every meal has been a gastronomic odyssey, but I've learnt something important about the subtler pleasures of French food, and about the virtues of patience and courtesy, too. Okay, I've not lost weight, but I have got thigh muscles the size of Bayonne hams – and I'm deeply, profoundly happy. And I couldn't have done it without this poor, long-suffering bike, with his headless Wonder Woman charm and dodgy brakes.

As I splash a little of the warm liquid over his handlebars, feeling a bit teary myself, an angry-looking official marches over and points at my noble steed, finger wagging in an international symbol of disapproval. 'No allowed, *vélo*. You must go!' she barks. It does occur to me at this point, belatedly perhaps, that drinking at a war memorial is in somewhat bad taste, so I nod meekly and obediently begin to drain my glass.

As she beetles off to harass some unfortunates with a buggy, two policemen slide over to take her place. Blimey, I think, these people really mean business. '*Nous partons!*' I tell them slightly impatiently, lifting the bike up by his sticky top tube to show willing as Lucinda hurriedly shoves the cups back in her bag.

But wait – they say, not so fast! First, they want to know what I'm doing, where I've been. Brittany? Marseille? The Joux Plane? Really? And with all this stuff? And then they congratulate me with real sincerity and tell us to relax, we can stay as long as we like. The quiet one even briefly, thrillingly lifts his cap: '*Chapeau, Madame.*'

And suddenly, I can't stop smiling.

VITAL STATISTICS

Total Distance: 2,334.3km

Total Ascent: 23,157 metres

Number of croissants eaten: 35 (poor)

Average score: 6.9 (brought down by 4 stinkers from the same boulangerie in Bar-le-Duc)

Best croissant: 9.5/10, Blé Sucré and Des Gateaux et du Pain, Paris

Worst croissant: 3/10, Vic-en-Bigorre, Hautes-Pyrénées

Number of punctures: 1 (balanced by sets of brake pads gone through: 3)

Maximum speed: 50km/h, on a wide, swooping, empty road near Châlons-en-Champagne

Average speed: 15.4km/h

Interest shown by the dog on my return, in seconds: 27 before going to hide under my friend Elaine's coffee table and having to be dragged out. I think he missed me.

ACKNOWLEDGEMENTS

Innumerable people on both sides of the Channel made this book what it is – and I only regret I don't know all of their names (but do go to Camping Le Chemin Vert in St Lys if you're ever near Toulouse). Of those I do, huge thanks to my agent Sarah Ballard and Eli Keren, who persuaded me to turn my passion into my work and write something about cycling in the first place, and to my fabulous editor Katya Shipster whose humour, enthusiasm for tartiflette and stash of unlocked iPhones were invaluable en route, and who has been an absolute pleasure to work with throughout this book's journey – thanks for allowing me to do the trip of a lifetime and tell everyone 'it's not a holiday actually'. Everyone at HarperCollins who has put so much enthusiasm into making it what it is: Sarah and Holly for making my words beautiful, Holly for making them look beautiful, Isabel, Julie and Dawn for making them sound beautiful, and Tom, Anna, Dom, Eleanor, Isabel, Charlotte, and Damon for persuading the world they're beautiful. The wonderful Annie, as ever, for her sterling work on the recipe front, Sarah Lacurie for her generous French corrections and to Café du Cycliste for making me look good most of the time, despite my best efforts.

Thanks to Trevor, Fergus and the St John crew for allowing me to crash your party with such enthusiasm and Bob for suggesting it, to Jonathan and Colette Meades for being such good hosts in Marseille, and to Anna for making that happen. Jon for being a phone mule and rosé enabler, my parents for looking after me in the Alps (and Rosie and Craig and their wonderful washing machine) and scoring some free cheese, and Lucinda for the romantic weekend in Paris. Thanks to Pam, John, Richard, Jenny and Elaine for looking after the love of my life so well while I was away – sorry, as always, for any Outrages, and I hope Philip the Pheasant gets over it in time. Thanks to Caroline Stafford and Caroline Craig for lighting and then stoking the fire of my cycling obsession.

Lastly, thanks to my fabulous peloton: Matt, Tess, Tor, Lucy, Ned, Ali, Bea, Martha, Caroline, Harry, Jay and Gemma, who is not my wife, but probably ought to be for being such a good sport. I really couldn't have done it without you lot. Thanks for keeping me cheerful, feeding me wine and when all else failed, sending me videos of people slipping over on ice.